Love You
to Pieces

Love You to Pieces

Creative Writers on Raising
a Child with Special Needs

Edited by Suzanne Kamata

Beacon Press, Boston

Beacon Press
25 Beacon Street
Boston, Massachusetts 02108–2892
www.beacon.org

Beacon Press books
are published under the auspices of
the Unitarian Universalist Association of Congregations.

11 10 09 08   8 7 6 5 4 3 2 1

This book is printed on acid-free paper that meets the uncoated
paper ANSI/NISO specifications for permanence as revised in 1992.

Text design by Tag Savage at
Wilsted & Taylor Publishing Services

Library of Congress Cataloging-in-Publication Data

Love you to pieces : creative writers on raising a child with
special needs / edited by Suzanne Kamata.
    p. cm.
  Essays, poems, and short stories on parenting disabled children.
  ISBN 978-0-8070-0030-4 (acid-free paper) 1. Children
with disabilities—Literary collections. 2. Parents of children with
disabilities—Literary collections. 3. Parent and child—Literary
collections. I. Kamata, Suzanne

  PS509.C52L68 2008
  810.8'03527—dc22   2007038366

For Lilia,

the one who opened my heart

Contents

Introduction

I'm the kind of person who looks to literature to make sense of life, so when I learned that my daughter was deaf and had cerebral palsy, I sobbed for a while and then logged onto Amazon .com. I was looking for deep and sustaining stories to guide me on the long path ahead, and while I found many cheery volumes offering hope and inspiration, that wasn't exactly what I wanted. I needed to know that others had felt the same kind of pain, fear, and anger that I was feeling, and I wanted a better idea of how my daughter's disability would affect my marriage, my son, my work, and other aspects of our lives. The best novels, short stories, and memoirs can pull us into the lives of their characters and provide a deeper understanding of others, while poetry can distill and illuminate moments that longer essays gloss over.

I didn't find as many books as I'd hoped, and I wondered why. According to the March of Dimes Global Report on Birth Defects, every year 8 million babies worldwide are born with genetic birth defects. Hundreds of thousands more are born with serious birth defects of postconception origin. Although 3.2 million of these children don't make it past their fifth year, more than 4 million do, and the majority grow up with some kind of disability. So where were all the novels about parenting a child with cerebral palsy? Or a deaf child? Or one with muscular dystrophy or Down syndrome? Could it be that those in the trenches were too busy to write? After all, as any reader of these stories, poems, and essays will see, parenting a child with disabilities takes a lot of time—a lifetime. Some of us have to help our children move from room to room, from wheelchair to toilet, from house to hospital or therapy center. Some of our children cannot be left alone, and cannot live unsupervised even as adults.

Not so long ago it was common, even recommended, to institutionalize such children. In 1950, Nobel laureate Pearl Buck published *The Child Who Never Grew*, one of the first memoirs on parenting a developmentally disabled child. Her daughter Carol had been born nearly thirty years before, but Buck had kept Carol a secret. This groundbreaking work encouraged others, such as Madame Charles de Gaulle and Rose Kennedy, to speak out about their retarded children for the first time, but it is important to note that Carol spent her life in a nursing home. More recent stories, including Bernard Malamud's "Idiots First" (1961) and Ann Tyler's "Average Waves in Unprotected Water" (1977), are about sending disabled children away. Many of these children were hidden behind walls as the shame and burden of society, and perhaps silenced with drugs. Who knows what kind of lives they—and their caregivers—led?

In the past, moreover, children with disabilities didn't live as long as they do now. Twenty years ago, Vicki Forman's son Evan ("Coming to Samsara"), who was born at twenty-three weeks' gestation, weighing one pound and three ounces, probably wouldn't have survived much beyond his first days. The shunt for hydrocephalus was not developed until the 1970s; Marcy Sheiner's son ("A Homecoming") was one of the first to undergo such an operation. Thanks to antibiotics, children born with weak respiratory systems can now survive pneumonias that were previously fatal.

*

The essays, poems, and short stories collected here came to me in various ways. I read Catherine Brady's story "The Lives of the Saints" long before I became the mother of a disabled child, yet it has stayed with me over the years. I discovered other pieces through my avid reading of magazines, literary journals, and online publications. Finally, I put out a call for manuscripts, which brought in more inspiring, heartbreaking, and sometimes amusing writing. I have arranged the writings more or less by the children's ages and stages, from premature birth to adulthood. By reading from beginning to end, we are reminded that raising a child with special needs is a lifelong journey that confronts parents of disabled children with issues faced by all parents: school performance, rebelliousness, a child's sexual awakening, first employment, independent living, and other milestones.

This book is about those who engage in the day-to-day care of disabled children. It is important to note, however, that while we might admire these mothers, fathers, and other caregivers—such as the sister who bakes a blue cake for her disabled and orphaned brother in Jayne Anne Phillip's "Termite's Birthday, 1959"—they are ordinary people, not saints. In "Magic Affinities," a frustrated mother bangs her autistic daughter's head against the wall, reminding us that disabled children are three to ten times more likely than other children to suffer abuse. In "Moonrise," a mother writes of her anger when her son, who has muscular dystrophy, falls in a parking lot: "Such terrible impatience rises in me now. Am I really such a witch, such a bad mother, that when I'm loading groceries and my son falls, I don't have the time or patience to cope?" When you open this book, expect gut-level honesty.

These writings also offer moments of triumph and joy—a developmentally disabled girl tossing a basketball into the air (*Jewel*), a boy with Down syndrome astounding his academic parents by memorizing the Beatles' oeuvre ("Great Expectations"), a brain-injured boy walking onstage to play the violin ("The Concert"), and the beauty of the bubbles that a mother blows for her autistic child, "a strand of hand-blown beads / to grace the throat of a lawn" ("Form and Void"). A disproportionate number of the selections concern autism; the relatively vast amount of writing on parenting children diagnosed in the autism spectrum reflects what *Newsweek* has called the "epidemic" of autistic disorders. Conversely, little has been written about the rarer diseases covered here, such as Angelman's syndrome and fibrodysplasia ossificans progressiva (FOP). I suspect that Carol Whelan-Zapata's story "Ordinary Time" is the only piece of fiction in print that takes FOP as its subject.

Regardless of the disability involved, some common themes run through this book. One is the difficulty of communication. In some cases, mothers and fathers of disabled children have to learn a new language in order to talk to them or interpret their signals. For example, my native tongue is English, while my daughter's first language is Japanese Sign Language. The mother in Maggie Kast's "Joyful Noise" is probably the only one who understands what her autistic son is talking about when he says, "Liptauer." Sometimes the parent is just guessing, like the poet Rebecca Balcárcel, a "frantic driver / in the race for meaning" when her son tries to make his needs known ("Severe Language Delay: In the Kitchen with My Three-Year-Old").

Grief is another connecting thread. Experts argue that parents of disabled children pass through the stages of grief as outlined by Elizabeth Kübler-Ross. In his classic manual *Baby and Child Care*, Dr. Benjamin Spock writes, "You must work through the stages of grieving: shock, denial, sadness, anger, and finally accommodation. You'll notice that I don't use the word 'acceptance' because I'm not certain that most parents ever really accept this blow from fate." Indeed, every developmental milestone that is missed—or skipped—can bring on the process anew. In Margaret Mantle's "Victoria's Wedding," grief is awakened by the dream of an event that a mother knows can never take place.

Some parents explore spirituality as a path to accommodation. After wishing that her premature son would die, Forman begins to understand the nature of suffering thanks to a Buddhist book. While Penny Wolfson mourns her fifteen-year-old son's diminishing physical strength, she assumes he takes comfort from his belief in God. In Catherine Brady's "The Lives of the Saints," the mother of a child with spina bifida comes to believe that her suffering over her son's disability brings her closer to God.

As I write, newspaper headlines blare the latest in stem cell research and suggest a future eradicated of imperfect children. Deaf activists warn that cochlear implants in children, chosen by hearing parents, pose a threat to deaf culture. In the Netherlands, lawmakers have approved child euthanasia for those deemed terminally ill and in great pain. In 2007, the American College of Obstetricians and Gynecologists recommended that all pregnant women, not just those over thirty-five, be offered screening to determine whether their child has Down syndrome, a practice that implicitly encourages the abortion of fetuses who test positive. It is unlikely that any of these issues will be resolved quickly and cleanly; there will always be a need for more information, thought, and discussion. In the meantime, literature eases loneliness and helps us understand and empathize with those unlike ourselves. It is my hope that this book will serve as a kind of support group for parents (like me) in far-flung places, and, in the midst of a heated public discourse, lead both to conversation and to quiet contemplation.

Suzanne Kamata
Aizumi, Japan

Coming to Samsara

Vicki Forman

The day I give birth is hot, a Sunday. The heat's been rising since Friday, the same day my pains started. My husband has picked this day to visit a friend in from out of town but at the last minute I have to tell him no. "You can't go, I'm not feeling well." Only then do I tell him about the cramps, the dull pains in my belly. "They're not contractions," I say. "It's something different." When, at one in the afternoon, I start to bleed, there is no way to deny it: time to get help.

Even as I call the doctor I tell my husband I feel certain everything is fine, that I'm simply having more trouble from some early complications, those that had cleared up in the past few weeks. I am only six months pregnant. I can't possibly be in labor.

The OB on call tells me to check in to Labor and Delivery. "Things can happen fast with twins," he says. I walk into L&D at three in the afternoon and am hooked up to a monitor that reveals that I am having contractions every two minutes.

When I finally connect the contractions with the pain in my belly—or the monitor makes the connection for me—I am stunned, silenced. OK, I think, I'm having preterm labor. No need to panic here, there's a lot they can do. In my mind I'm still going home in time for dinner. I wait for the doctor to examine me. The nurse has a glance and says, "Oh my, you are bleeding." The doctor's glove comes out red. The nurse now has a flashlight beamed on me below. "Oh god," she moans, and her expression—a quick glance, a cringe, a look away—tells me everything I need to know.

"Is your husband here?" the doctor asks. "Who's here with you?"

My husband appears from around the corner—he had simply gone to park the car, my daughter is with him still, this was not meant to be a long visit by any means. I am six to seven centimeters dilated, the doctor announces, much too far gone to stop the labor. I am six months pregnant; my twins are no larger than my hand; I am having my babies today.

*

One of life's great illusions is the notion that we can want—and get—things on our own terms, no matter what. It's human nature to seek pleasure and avoid suffering, but what happens when suffering finds you? My husband and I had tried for two long years to conceive these twins, had lived through miscarriages and fertility treatments to bear them. But when I learned they were coming so early and so fragile, I had only one wish: to let them go. I begged and pleaded with the army of doctors and nurses who came around in the hours between three and seven. I told them I knew about morbidity and mortality, I knew the babies could not possibly survive or be normal if they did.

But they didn't allow me to let my babies go that hot summer night. Instead they wheeled me into an operating room and prepared for a C-section if the delivery didn't go well. "These babies will be born with signs of life," the OB told us. "The laws of the state of California require us to save them." With that, he put on his gloves, covered his face with a mask, and went to work.

At 7:45 they broke my water. Evan slipped out a moment later. It was an easy birth. I did not watch but heard his frail, kittenish cry. I forced myself to look then—he was alive—and my frightened glance showed me his flattened body, surprisingly large head and fragile limbs. Five hundred and forty grams was his weight. Later I learned just how small this was: one pound, three ounces. Not two weeks earlier a national magazine had featured a baby this small on its cover, a baby attached to tubes and lines, being kept alive with a respirator and all else. "Small Miracles," the headline read. At the time, I'd shivered at the sight. There was no connection between this gruesome sight, this "baby" the size of a human palm, and the babies growing inside me. I had my own tiny version now, a boy from whom most would turn away and think: that's not a baby, there's nothing here that resembles a baby.

Eleanor was born a full twenty minutes after her brother. At first, the doctor couldn't detect a heartbeat. The team surged forward and soon a ruddy, mammalian form was presented to me. "Your daughter," the doctor said, pushing her forehead to my face. "Give her a kiss."

My daughter? My daughter was a blooming toddler at home with friends. This was my daughter? Nothing resembled the human. I could see her tendons and muscles. Only the palest sheen of skin hid this blatant shape. But it was her color that shocked me most: rusty, raw, more skinned animal than human being.

In the aftermath of the delivery, the room fell quiet. The team, and the babies, vanished. Only my husband, the doctor, and a nurse remained. Like the scene of an accident in the last moments of cleanup, all was silent, businesslike. Machines were removed, the nurses took off their gowns. An ennui descended, and as they wheeled me out of the room I visited the clock. Eight-thirty. Not even six hours from start to finish; the sun would be down, my daughter in bed.

At times, in the minutes and hours and days that followed, I could nearly forget what had happened. The babies would die, I told myself, this would all be a terrible memory. I could get pregnant again, carry to term. I wanted another child, not two twenty-three-week fetuses fighting for their lives. We watched the clock and waited for someone to come and report on their status. My brother arrived. I bled a little, was moved to a room in Maternity. In the hall, babies cried, balloons arrived. My husband returned home to the comfort of our daughter and I spent the night alone, waiting for someone to deliver the news about my babies and their fate.

But no one came, and in the morning, after my doctors arrived with their pronouncements—"the uterus can only handle so much volume," one told me, and "I think we can all agree that it couldn't have gone any differently," said the other—I got dressed and mustered the strength to see my babies, Forman Twin A and Forman Twin B in the NICU, where they clung to their fragile lives.

I have a picture taken of Evan at three weeks of age. Even then his inchwide ventilator tube was bigger around than his leg. That first morning he lay in a bed by the door, the bandages, cotton, and dressings glowing larger than his body. Bilirubin lights hovered over his incubator and the heat and the brightness were intense. He was at his Hollywood premiere, this baby, on display for all to see.

I soaked it all in—the tubes, the lines, the IVs. Small breaths were puffed into his chest fifty times a minute, courtesy of a ventilator. His skin was dark, furry. When I was ready to see Ellie, the nurse who escorted me to her bed tried to tell me things, facts and figures about Evan's status, preparing me for his sister. Evan was saturating well, he was receiving 80 percent oxygen, he had had insulin and Phenobarbital and some Ativan to keep him quiet. His head ultrasound had been normal. Later, I would learn his odds of surviving these first few hours, let alone the first few days: 40 percent, at best.

Did the babies have a name, she asked? They wanted to make signs, wanted to call them something other than Twin A and Twin B.

I answered the nurse and tried to incorporate. I was a mother. I had had my babies. They were here now, no longer inside me. I could pump my milk and they would store it. Visiting hours were unlimited. The nurses and doctors were there to answer any and all questions. Support groups met, chaplains visited. You had to scrub in the hall outside each time and scrub inside between babies. No jewelry, no cell phones. I don't know why it took so long, but when I got to Ellie, my stomach finally heaved. Here was the same bruised and ruddy thing I'd seen at birth, twitching and shivering now. My baby, my daughter. Nothing could protect her, nothing could change what had occurred. I began to cry. A nurse offered me a chair. I refused, stumbled my way back into the hall, got lost, then finally found my room. On the way past the nurses' station a young woman handed me forms to fill out for birth certificates. "Congratulations!" she trilled. I crawled back into bed.

In the days that followed we moved haltingly, never sure where to put our feet. Eleanor developed bleeding in her brain; Evan's eyes stayed fused shut; my parents arrived from out of town—"To see them before they die," my mother said. I wore a T-shirt for days that read ZOMBIE. A Polaroid from these collapsed moments shows me staring downward, at nothing, eyes glazed. Friends called, messages stacked up. We had the first of many conferences about the twins, their future, and their prognosis. Blindness, delays, cerebral palsy, mental retardation. The same team that had labored long and hard to resuscitate the twins no matter what were now delivering, finally, all the bad news.

Four days after she was born, we removed Ellie from life support. The bleed on her brain foretold an outcome even the doctors could not sugarcoat: she'd be vegetative, in a wheelchair with no knowledge of who we were or where she was. They took her off the vent and let us hold her until she died.

In this time, and for months afterward, I could read only one book, a Buddhist book. *When Things Fall Apart*, it was called, and it spoke of essential Buddhist concepts: suffering, compassion, loving-kindness. We cremated Ellie and kept her ashes at home—no cemetery seemed quite right just yet—and I went to the hospital every day, this book in hand. While I read I sat by Evan's incubator, listening to the beeps and wheezes of his ventilator. I read about fear and came to understand how this one-pound baby needed me in a way I had never conceived before. I read about compassion and saw that over my reluctance to have him live and my fear of what his life might be, his needs began to triumph. I read about suffering and came to understand that if I didn't sit there, learn how to change his three inch square diaper, wait for the moment he would open his eyes for the first time and question the doctors about their every move, who would? I was suffering? I had not gotten what I'd wanted? What of Evan?

For the Buddhists, I read, the material world hinges on a continuous cycle of life and death, birth and rebirth, and, along with it all, impermanence and suffering. Buddhists call this cycle samsara and describe life as a process of trying to avoid and conquer its dimensions while getting caught on it all the while. We think we can escape samsara when our needs are met; we think when desire is fulfilled the suffering won't come back. We think we are immune from the cycle of life and death and that we can hold impermanence at bay. If my journey with Evan and Ellie has taught me anything, it is that desires cannot stay fulfilled for long—"the wave crashes," my friends and I like to say—and that longing always comes back. We get, we want. Nothing lasts, nothing is known except birth and death—and the endurance of the human spirit, of course. If I were a true Buddhist I might say our overpowering desire for another child brought us Evan, and I'd call it karma. But I'm as much a Springsteen fan as a Buddhist, and in the face of my experience I often find myself recalling his plaintive words of rebirth and renewal, his plea for the small hopes that emerge through the grief of longing and death: "Well now everything dies baby that's a fact / But maybe everything that dies someday comes back."

No account of this journey to samsara would be complete

without a description of Evan, the agent of this change. Our boy survived five surgeries and is legally blind. He can't drink from a bottle—something's wrong with his swallow, probably the result of being on a ventilator for so long—but he's slowly learning to chew and muster baby food. The rest he takes through a feeding tube permanently inserted into his stomach. A few months after he was home, when we thought we were settling in with a blind child on a feeding tube and oxygen, he developed a seizure disorder and turned catatonic. Now he takes three medications a day for his epilepsy, along with a drug for his heart and the occasional homeopathic remedy.

Because of Evan, we live in the world of special needs and therapy visits, state programs and doctors appointments and insurance forms. It's not a world our old friends can understand but we have found new friends who also inhabit this divide. There are other people, we've discovered, who get something very different from what they want. Because of Evan, my father, a retired child psychiatrist specializing in children with developmental delays, now has a firsthand experience most of his colleagues will never know. And my mother has started watching gory medical programs, searching, I am convinced, for the episode in which I am allowed to let my twins expire.

Early on in Evan's life, I had no idea how to stop wanting. If he were to die, I thought, I would be happy. No, not die, but live. Not live but be healthy. Get off the vent. Breathe on his own. Survive his surgeries. Be able to see. Learn how to eat. Not need a feeding tube. Go home without oxygen. Be cured of his heart ailment. On some days, I thought, "I will be happy if he can simply keep his eyes open for more than an hour and not be so knocked out from the medication." This wanting became a distillation of all the wanting I'd ever done in my whole life, it seemed, the fervor was that intense. But one by one he did those things and still I wasn't happy and I thought, *Darn, samsara again.* Even now, each doctor's appointment can be a struggle between wanting and getting—wanting to hear good news, sometimes having to hear bad. I steel myself for the worst and remind myself that no matter what news I receive, it doesn't change who Evan is or what he might do. Getting what you want doesn't make you happy, I remind myself. There's always more longing behind fulfillment.

Once a month we visit the grave where Ellie is buried, the one that took us a year to find. There's an opening to the sky in the nook where her ashes are placed, and graves of other children, too. We didn't notice these early deaths when we picked the spot, but it's comforting to see the other parents and remember we're not the only ones with grief and loss. My daughter likes that the rain falls down into the space and that Ellie can see the sky. Sometimes Josie talks to her sister out her bedroom window, as if the same sky that Ellie can see also transports her words. We made the mistake of telling Josie about the concepts of reincarnation and rebirth and every so often we have to correct her assumption that Ellie is coming back as Ellie, that she'll get to meet this baby sister she never saw and never knew. "It's taking so long for Ellie to get here," she said just the other day.

But if everything that dies someday comes back, then we have also learned the joy of rebirth. Three long years ago, all I wanted was another baby. Today, I try to hold fast, to wait and see what happens if I don't want anything at all—for Evan, for me, or for us.

Without Strings

Hannah Holborn

One a.m. Too late for coffee, yet my mother's long coral nails tapped to the music of Dolly Parton as she sipped a cup of sugared Nescafe. Her body vibrated with guitar twang and dehydration. Footsteps in the hallway sent a violent message; Vance, my mother's dimwit lover, hated that I was there.

As did I.

The lights flickered off, then on. The toilet flushed, gurgled, flushed again. "Bet that's a load off his mind," I said. My mother's face remained a practiced blank. She had lost boyfriends because of my playful teasing, more boyfriends than she could count.

I was trapped in her kitchen. Trapped by rain—had arrived on foot without coat or umbrella—and by a return of childhood inertia. I needed someone to jerk my strings and make me move, but the puppet master, my father, was six feet under on the outskirts of town. Because of my father, my mother had never developed the knack.

"Spill," she said.

Five blocks away, my husband and "the beans" slept, unaware that one-third of them was missing. She would wake soon, my young daughter.

Gloria never slept long.

The day before, at the end of the world, we had been informed that sleep disturbance was part and parcel—also absence of speech, facial abnormalities, jerky gait, protruding tongue—not yet, but one day—a fascination with plastic and water, hand-flapping, frequent laughter, a permanent smile. We had mortgaged a new house in a single-family neighborhood with good schools for a Happy Puppet Child.

"We met with a geneticist today," I said as I shifted the green lace tablecloth toward my lap. I squeezed the fabric's nub between my wooden fingers. "It's not good."

My mother, ever patient, waited.

"He said Glory's genetic gift means she might never potty train and she won't ever talk. Sound familiar?"

"Well, good," my mother said. "I suspected Angelman's. Now you can help that little darling instead of pretending everything is hunky-dory. Now you can figure out the upside."

"Pardon?"

"When your father passed, you said it was a relief we were finally out of his misery. That was the upside."

"That was the only side, Ma. Glory being like my cousin Gerald isn't like Dad dying."

Vance shuffled into view. His house-coated barrel of a body blocked the only exit from the kitchen. "The offer stands," he said. Earlier on he'd volunteered to rearrange my face.

"My price has risen," I said. "Two hundred bucks up front and now you have to wear a rubber."

"To the moon, Alice." When Vance jostled my shoulder his housecoat flapped open. Unwashed trucker scented the air. He opened the refrigerator, rooted around, and came up empty.

I glugged down the last quarter of the last can of Labatt's. "Ah!" I said. "That hits the spot." When I slammed down the can it made a wet ring on my mother's green tablecloth.

"You little shit. That's my beer." Vance raised a meaty fist.

"She's upset, honey," my mother said.

"Well, boo-hoo. It's always something with Alice, ain't it?"

"It's news about the tyke," my mother said.

"What's wrong with my girl?"

Gloria was not the foul man's girl. My taunting grew barbs.

"Go back to bed . . . Tony." Tony, my mother's other lover, didn't drive long-distance.

My mother patted Vance's butt, drew him close, and whispered something into his cauliflower ear. With a final glare for me, he trotted off to bed like a frisky spring lamb.

She struggled to her feet. "One day, Alice," she said, "you're going to see me lonely." Her head wobbled as she made her way to the stove and a lemon-shaped timer. She wound the timer and then placed it on the table between us. I had two minutes to unload my grief. She tipped a Virginia Slim out of its package. Her thin lips wrinkled when they held the tip.

"OK. You want to know the upside? Easy. They can do antidrool surgery on Glory when she's older."

"I didn't raise you to be snide."

I took in the bottle depot of a kitchen—empty beer cases stacked high, rinsed shot glasses upside down on the green rubber mat by the sink—and wondered what she did raise me to be. Last year's calendar still hung on the wall. *Dance at the Legion* and *Art's funeral* were marked in red. Death and debauch were my mother's red-letter days.

"Then how about this; she won't need much to be happy. I mean, if happiness is one of the symptoms, it figures." The timer's shrill made me jump. "Right?"

"Glory's got one up on the rest of us then."

"I guess she does."

My mother tamped out her cigarette. She stood and then glided past me smelling of carcinogens and rose perfume. The familiar combination provided strange comfort. Her hand swept my head, sparked me to life. She had the knack after all, only her knack didn't hurt. Tears of self-pity formed in my eyes. "I just wanted her to be normal, Ma."

"Bulltwitty. You and Andy never wanted that."

Andy and Alice, the perfect yuppie couple, wanted more. My mother was right, but still I was stunned that she had perceived the truth.

My mother bid me goodnight before disappearing into the cavern of her bedroom. Vance's baritone rumbled. Bedsprings gave way. My mother laughed. I hated that she was chipper when she should have been crushed by my news.

I parted the curtains to press my face against the cold. The rain had stopped. "Hey, Tony," I called as I left. "See if you can find the upside. You've got thirty minutes." I wound the lemon timer, set it down outside the bedroom door, and then let myself out of the house.

At night our old neighborhood looked unchanged from the time of my childhood. One working-class family per dwelling, painted porches, hardy rose shrubs, nothing extravagant. Daylight revealed gardens gone to weed, porches that hoarded litter, and too many cars in front of each house. My father had raged when I left home to marry Andy. To his mind I had sold out my working-class roots for a pretty college boy. But if leaving cost me my soul, returning, I suspected, would cost even more.

I jogged the six blocks to my new and exclusive neighborhood. There the houses were tall replication Victorians. Front porches sported hanging moss baskets filled with designer annuals and swings that might never be used. Small yards shared a thin strip of green space. To make room for this, a developer disbanded a mobile court of retirees, many of whom were my parents' friends. The developer paid residents to disperse without a fight and most embraced the windfall. The few who went public said they feared the loneliness of dislocation. Their story didn't make the front page.

On my street, I walked past three FOR SALE signs. Dislocation still ran like sewage under our postcard-pretty setting. Transfers, bankruptcy, and divorce: these things took their toll. Even so, my neighbors slept with confidence inside their heavily mortgaged homes knowing that their children would be icons of socially conscious fashion, win athletic awards, read before kindergarten, earn honors, be beautiful or handsome or both. When grown they would graduate with multiple degrees and then move to the United States because the wages are higher. They would marry well and buy nicer homes than these. They would make their parents proud.

They would avoid my daughter like the plague.

The sting would be mine and Andy's, not Gloria's. Like my cousin, she would laugh and grin and be a whirlwind of misdirected activity. She would flap her hands for fun and offer stiff hugs and wet kisses to whoever would receive them. She would still swim with a lifejacket in her twenties. She would never marry, never give us grandchildren.

But, if we let her, she would be happy.

Inappropriate joy scudded through me like the clouds beneath the smiling face of the moon. A breeze scoured my already spotless street. It felt fresh and good. I hurried, eager to be home before the clouds regrouped.

In my house, lights were on, lights and the usual doleful music. I opened the door on a disgruntled husband and a Happy Puppet Child. Andy swiped at a puddle of Gloria's drool that marred the perfection of his silk pajamas. "It's past one, Alice. Some people might live lives of leisure, but I have to get up for work in the morning. Where the hell were you?"

His relief as he relinquished our daughter betrayed the false bottom of his anger. The taint of Angelman's Syndrome was in my blood, not his. Sooner rather than later, he would leave us and try again with someone better. I could read in his face that his future plans included such consolation.

I carried Glory into the formal living room. "Home," I said.

He slapped an ivory wall to avoid slapping me. "If you consider your mother's hovel home, you should have stayed."

Glory felt soft and pliant against my body. I bent with her to play an old vinyl album, one from my childhood, Handel's *Royal Fireworks*.

Andy ran his fingers through his perfect hair. "For your information, you're not the only one in this house who's suffering."

I twirled around the living room to make my tiny daughter laugh. "That's right," I said. "You are."

The horn section signaled the triumphal entry.

We danced without strings.

SMA Baby

Ellen Bihler

Jesus himself
appears eleven times in this room.
The saints, taped and tacked
to headboard, walls, ceiling,
watch over the infant.
Mother Teresa ministers to the poverty
of barren nerve endings.
St. Anthony of Padua holds
a small boy under Ian's window,
where street noise wades in
like a message in a bottle.
St. Jude has seen worse.

Spinal Muscular Atrophy Type 1 is an inherited neuromuscular disorder characterized by degeneration of the anterior horn cells of the spinal cord and motor nuclei, causing severe muscle weakness. Death usually occurs before age two. Cognitive ability is not affected.

Ian floats on blankets, adrift
on uncharted waters,
a small boat unaware
of its precious cargo.
Fetal stem cells navigate
around blocked neural pathways,
bail the deep waters of damage.

*At twelve weeks posttransplant, the rats partially recover control of
their hind legs.*

> Annemarie celebrates the side to side
> motion of his left arm,
> as righteous as blood flowing miraculous
> from the palm of St. Catherine.
> The rotation of elbow and forearm
> brings applause.
> Mother and child beam
> at each other like lighthouses.
> The remainder of his hand
> lies still like a beached fish.

*Only about four human stem cells per rat become motor neurons that
actually extend out of the spinal cord and into muscle, potentially cre-
ating a circuit that could control movement.*

> Brendan, patron saint of sailors,
> is the rope that ties Annemarie
> to her son. She must will his arms to rise,
> his legs to kick
> free of gravity like a dolphin leaping.

At six months posttransplant, the window of regeneration closes.

> Ian's brother and sisters are seagulls
> that swoop in and out, squawking optimism
> carrying bits of news in their beaks.
> Only Annemarie stays on, his anchor,
> measuring hours
> by the distance she has still to fall.

A Homecoming

Marcy Sheiner

I was on my hands and knees scrubbing the bathroom tiles when
Bob walked in on me.

"What the hell are you doing?" he asked, taking his penis
out to pee.

"Cleaning."

"You're scrubbing the tiles with a toothbrush. What's gotten
into you?"

"Don't you remember? Angie's coming over today."

Bob grunted. He had never liked Angie. For a long time I'd
thought his animosity derived from her rejection of him when
he'd made a pass at her back in high school; she'd gone out with
his best friend instead. Later on I realized he was jealous of our
closeness; when she'd gone to Japan to get married I'd sobbed
inconsolably, but when he went off to the National Guard I'd
barely shed a tear.

"Will you be home in time to see her?" I asked, hoping the
answer would be no.

"I don't think so," he said gruffly, buckling his belt and tucking in his crisp work shirt. "I have a couple of appointments
tonight."

"Well, OK, I'll tell her you said hello."

He left the bathroom and I continued scrubbing. Luckily,
I'd cleaned the rest of the house the day before, and had made
tuna fish salad for lunch. Most of my morning would be devoted
to making myself look as much like my old self as possible.

I opened the door, feeling a mixture of caution and anticipation. Before me stood the girl who'd been my closest friend throughout high school, holding a dimpled cherub of ten months on one small hip. We laughed simultaneously, then moved into an awkward embrace, baby Darlene giggling and pulling on my hair.

"Hello there!" I exclaimed, appraising the baby, who gurgled. "She's adorable," I said. "Come in, come in."

I led her into the kitchen, where Daryl sat in his carriage infant seat, playing with Quacksie. "Who's this?" Angie gushed, placing Darlene on the floor by her feet. The child immediately pulled herself onto all fours. She resembled, I thought, a tadpole, as she slid across the checkered linoleum. Angie tickled Daryl's neck. "I'm your Aunt Angie," she told him.

"An-gie!" he said, smiling and waving his arms around excitedly.

"I don't believe it! He said my name already! Darlene only knows how to say Mama."

Darlene had made her way over to the cabinets and was tugging on a knob. The door opened.

"You don't have locks on your cabinets?" Angie asked incredulously.

"I haven't needed them yet," I said, my face flushing.

"I'll have to watch her every second," Angie moaned. "She gets into everything. Get over here," she said brusquely, swooping Darlene into her arms. The child fought to be let down, but Angie held fast. "She drives me crazy, she's into everything in the house," Angie said.

I tried to appear sympathetic and understanding, but, given that Daryl couldn't crawl, I hadn't experienced this phase of motherhood yet—and fervently wished I had.

Angie had brought an infant seat, which she put Darlene in for lunch. We fed the babies, making small talk. Never had Angie and I been so distant, talking about the weather, my apartment, old friends she wanted to visit. Always, we had cut right to the chase, confiding intimate details of our lives. After the kids were fed and we placed them in the playpen in front of the television, we sat face-to-face at my kitchen table. There were no more distractions. I wished there were.

"Do you want to tell me about it?" she asked, lighting a cigarette and holding my eyes with hers. I stared into those same green pools that I knew as well as my own face, thinking how beautiful she was, those big eyes lighting up the olive skin around them, her lush berry red lips now in repose, not smiling or chortling to the babies. I had never ceased to be almost hypnotized by the beauty of that face.

"About what?" I asked, looking away.

"About what! Daryl. The operations. The hydroencephitlus."

"Hydrocephalus," I corrected automatically.

"Whatever. I know you been hurtin'."

I stood and walked to the sink, stalling, filling a glass with water. "Do you want anything to drink?"

"Marcy, get your ass into that chair and talk to me."

I sat down, defeated. "Well, there's not so much to tell. He had his last operation a few months ago and he seems to be doing OK. With any luck he's going to live a normal life."

"But tell me what it's been *like*," she prodded.

I opened my mouth, then shut it again. I looked down at my hands, traced a line of sugar on the cool Formica table.

"Come on, Marce. Barbara must have told you about my letters, what a hard time I had when Dar was born."

Barbara had told me: With barely disguised contempt she'd detailed Angie's sleepless nights with a colicky baby, her loneliness, her feelings of inadequacy. "I wish she'd stop being such a baby," Barbara had said. "She's a mother now, she needs to grow up."

These judgments had the effect of making me conceal my own ambivalence about motherhood from Barbara. I wondered, though, why Angie hadn't confessed all this in her letters to me. As if reading my mind now, she said, "I didn't complain so much to you—I figured you had it worse than me."

"You should have," I said, surprising myself. "I would have felt better knowing someone else wasn't a happy perfect mother."

At this she laughed, a sound without mirth, full of irony and bitterness. "You're right, I should have told you. I guess I just wanted to talk to you in person. You know I was in labor over twenty-six hours? When I called my mother and told her it hurt, she said, 'What'd you speck?'" Angie's perfect intonation of her mother's Italian accent brought to mind a vivid picture of the tiny silver-haired woman. "I mean, the woman had seven kids," Angie continued. For the next half hour she chain-smoked and talked, relating her labor in minute detail, her first night alone with the baby, and subsequent nights when she tried in vain to comfort a very unhappy Darlene. "I felt so alone, and so helpless," she said. "I'm glad to be home."

I sat mesmerized, as always, asking encouraging questions, nodding in agreement, laughing at her rueful stories. I was glad to be off the hot seat, not to have to tell her my story. She had always been able to captivate my interest, even when about the most mundane topics. It was partly her face, so beautiful and so changeable, that held me; it was also the way she spoke, straight from the heart, so different from the way that most people talked. That voice washed over me, bathing me in love and emotion, offering a space to reciprocate.

But I did not reciprocate. I simply could not begin to tell anyone, not even Angie, the painful truth about Daryl's infancy. On some level I was ashamed to introduce so much misery into a situation—motherhood—that was supposed to be glorious. It didn't matter that Angie didn't think it was all so glorious: I was hung up in my own self-judgment, afraid of receiving hers.

She was telling me about her flight from Japan when a loud

wail rose up from the living room, and we both stood automatically and ran inside. Darlene was standing up, holding the playpen netting, bouncing up and down on chubby legs. When she saw Angie, she lifted her arms and wailed louder to be let out. Angie sighed and reached for her. Daryl sat quietly, watching this mini-drama with interest.

I lifted him out of the playpen and strapped him into his carriage. Angie put Darlene on the floor. She immediately scampered on all fours toward the bathroom. "Damn, now we can't talk," Angie said, following the baby's trail.

I sat down on the sofa and gazed at Daryl, content to sit confined in his usual position. Waves of envy washed over me: I wished he could crawl around like Darlene.

"No!" I heard Angie shriek from inside. "Bad girl." I got up and went to see what was going on: Darlene had grabbed a can of Comet from the bathtub and was sprinkling it liberally around the floor and herself. Angie dove down to take it away from her. I laughed. "She's so cute," I said jealously.

"Cute, huh? You're lucky you don't have to deal with this."

I turned quickly and headed back to the living room, stung to the core. Lucky? How could she be so insensitive? I wrapped my pain around me like a protective shawl; so, Angie was just like everyone else—totally unaware of what I was going through. Never mind that I'd refused to tell her: she should have guessed. "Fuck 'em all," I muttered to myself, then went over and squeezed Quacksie.

"What wuzzat?" Daryl giggled just as Angie came into the room, swiping at Darlene's face with a wash cloth. She smiled. "He's really smart, isn't he?" she said.

*

A few days later Angie called and asked me to go with her to visit Kathy.

"I don't know, Ange," I said evasively. "I don't think we have anything in common anymore." I'd meant to say that I didn't have anything in common with Kathy, but it came out as if I meant both of them.

"What do you mean?" Angie was understandably insulted. "We're all mothers. And we've been friends for years. Isn't that enough?"

I didn't tell her about the time I'd had Kathy and her husband George over for dinner. Daryl had been particularly trying that day, throwing up and crying, while I attempted to cook a gourmet meal. Kathy, pregnant with twins at the time, expressed wonder at my perfect table setting, my elegant stuffed shrimp, the homemade dessert. Daryl was fussing, and I rocked him as I talked to her. "It wouldn't have been hard," I blurted out unthinkingly, "if it wasn't for *him*."

Kathy's jaw dropped. "Well, isn't that just too bad," she said in a scolding voice.

"Come on, we'll have fun," Angie insisted. "She wants to see you. And you need to get out of the house."

*

Since marriage and motherhood, Kathy had gained a good fifty pounds. She greeted us in a flowered housedress. "It's about time!" she boomed, taking Darlene from Angie's arms. She held her up and studied her little face. "And who are you, pretty girl? You can't possibly belong to this old woman, you're too gorgeous."

Angie laughed good-naturedly, while I inwardly noted that Kathy had never held Daryl.

Kathy's year-old twin girls sat on a blanket on the living room carpet. After much fussing and gushing over the babies, we spent a good half-hour setting them up with an assortment of toys. Kathy turned the television to cartoons. Hesitantly, I placed Daryl on the floor in his infant seat; I felt uneasy leaving him in such a vulnerable position with the other babies, but admonished myself to relax and let him be a "normal" child. This is the first time I remember feeling utterly confused about how to treat Daryl, torn between wanting to keep him safe and wanting to treat him "normal." It was certainly not the last.

We retired to the kitchen to begin an endless stream of coffee and cigarettes. Kathy and Angie, who'd both been Navy wives until recently, compared notes—mostly a litany of complaints.

"The air in Japan was disgusting," Angie said. "When I hung my sheets to dry they ended up black from all the soot. I had to hang them in the bathroom. You wouldn't believe what a filthy country it is—men pissed in the street like it was a public toilet."

"I hated San Diego," Kathy chimed in. "I was so happy to come home. I can't imagine being in a foreign country, you poor kid."

"Did you see the Pacific Ocean?" I asked her.

Kathy shrugged. "You've seen one ocean, you've seen them all."

Leave it to fate, I thought, to let these two ingrates travel the world while I'd remained stuck on Long Island.

"Those Navy doctors," Angie said, forcefully stubbing out a cigarette. "I swear they didn't know the first thing about delivering babies. I was in labor for twenty-six hours with no painkillers or anything."

"You poor thing," Kathy said in mock sympathy. "Try having twins. Try a C-section."

I wanted to speak, to say something about my particular horrific birth experience, but the words stuck like glue in my throat. If Kathy had no sympathy for Angie, why would she have any to spare for me? Also, it felt too much like we were competing for who'd had the hardest time—a competition that I felt, by almost any standard, I had won hands down without saying a word.

Suddenly a loud crash sounded from the living room, followed by a scream and a wail. I was on my feet instantly, Angie right behind, Kathy lumbering after us. Daryl lay on his side strapped into the plastic seat. His forehead bore a red mark, obviously from some thrown object. Darlene stood in front of him, looking puzzled. One of the twins was whimpering; the other watched in wide-eyed curiosity.

My heart dropped to my stomach, and my stomach felt like it had fallen out through my vagina. Quickly I righted the infant seat, undid the straps and took Daryl out. In a few seconds he stopped crying; but for the fading mark on his forehead, he seemed unharmed.

Angie swooped down on Darlene, slapping her on the hand. "Bad girl." Darlene let out a shriek that spiraled into wild sobbing.

"It's OK, Angie, he's fine," I assured her, devastated that she'd hit Darlene.

Kathy turned to the startled twins, frowning. "What are you two looking at?"

"She has to learn not to hit other kids," Angie insisted. "Come on, you're going down for a nap."

"Oh, leave her," Kathy said. "Here, we'll put the girls in the playpen." She dragged a folded playpen from the hall and Angie helped her set it up. The twins were plopped inside without much ado, but Darlene cried and pulled at the sides.

"No," Angie insisted. "You're staying in there now." Kathy distributed cookies, and soon everyone quieted down. I took Daryl into the kitchen, setting him in his seat on the floor, inwardly admonishing myself for having left him open to the attack.

Kathy had looked at him warily. "Can something like that hurt his, uh, his head?"

"The doctor says it's not that easy to damage the shunt."

"Is that what that scar is?" Angie asked.

"Yeah. It drains the fluid."

In silence we stirred sugar into fresh cups of coffee. I wondered what they were thinking, and hoped they wouldn't ask me more questions about Daryl's condition.

Finally Angie said, "It's a bitch, isn't it? I mean, nobody told us how hard this would be."

"You got that right," Kathy said.

"Yeah," I sighed, feeling connected to them at last.

"You hungry?" Kathy asked after another short silence.

"Yeah. What's for lunch?"

Kathy heaved herself out of her chair and opened a cabinet to reveal row upon row of small colored jars. "Strained carrots, rice pudding, beef, apricots ..."

"God, I hate that shit!" I said.

"Then help me make tuna fish."

"That is so like you, Kathy," I complained. "You don't see me for six months and when I do come visit you I have to make my own lunch." My mood was lightening up; I was beginning to remember why I loved these two women.

Angie giggled. "Now," she said, tears forming in her eyes. "Now I feel like I'm finally home."

"Severe Language Delay": In the Kitchen with My Three-Year-Old

Rebecca Balcárcel

He cries, "uh-bee"
"uh-bee"

and I am frantic driver
in the race for meaning
careening past furniture, basketed fruit,
contents of drawers and the refrigerator
revving around the circle of possible answers
to our interactive multiple-choice

between shouts,
my words lost in the linoleum pattern.

I pound a wedge of quiet
between uh and bee,
sort cubes with painted letters, grabbing "T"
for
tu-bby a-beet bu-tty
"N"
nu-bby a-bean bu-nny

Here the rosed wreath:
"Yeah, uh-bee," his calmer voice,
bunny rescued from couch cushions
and me gulping
second after second of silence.

Magic Affinities

Evelyn Sharenov

In the fourth month of a blessedly uneventful pregnancy, she dreams she is being wheeled into the delivery room. The swinging doors close behind the gurney in a mad hollow flapping that signals something oddly final. Jason is shut off from her on the other side.

The antiseptic room is filled with steel equipment that makes unearthly whirring noises; green blips move silently across black monitor screens in an even rhythm. The combined smells of ether and sweat are nauseating. People mill around, waiting for her to finish. They urge her on. She screams and pushes. A thin thread of pain that connects her to life breaks. Then, either the pain is gone or she is gone—she is not sure which, so distant is she from this event. Jason appears then, his head in a halo of bright light; he is clapping. She can neither see his face nor hear the applause.

The obstetrician holds the baby up; the tiny blood-smeared body is a black silhouette against the great white domes of the OR. It opens its mouth, its face creased with effort, prepared to utter its first wail of protest. No sound comes out. The doctor presses his lips to hers; it is a perfectly healthy baby, he reassures her, pushing the words into her mouth. She is trying to speak, but too weakly to be heard. It has no voice, she is trying to say. Is she the only one who cannot hear her child?

She wakes herself, sitting straight up in bed, throwing off the nightmare with the blankets. Jason sleeps peacefully next to her, in blissful ignorance of the horror she has lived through and survived. She does not know whether to hate him or love him at that moment.

In her universe, love wins out. She takes comfort from his warm presence. He is tethered in bedrock. She can hold on to him. She prods him gently until he rolls on his side, one eye open a crack. Only then does she permit herself great sobs. She is wracked by fear.

Jason shimmies sleepily over to her side of the bed and puts his arms around her. She cries pathetically into his naked shoulder. "There, there now," he croons softly, rocking her. "What's the matter?"

She recounts her dream in detail, stuttering, as if it is unspeakable.

"It's a bad dream," he soothes. "Nothing more. Just a bad dream." He murmurs incantations in her ear, her hair, against her neck, mantras of well-being.

But mothers have premonitions about their children; it's instinctual, she insists, weakly, as she feels the power seeping from her dream, drained by Jason like poison sucked from a viper's bite. She sleeps in his arms all night, reassured. Peace is restored in their bedroom. The quiet air, heavy and warm around them, is scented with their easy inhalations and exhalations. Their bodies, curled into each other, form parallel lines down the sheet, like a curved road traveled at night.

In her fifth month she undergoes amniocentesis. She is thirty-five that year. Even if her obstetrician had not suggested it, she would have insisted. For three weeks, she does not leave the house, awaiting the results. During this time the baby begins to walk around in her belly, like a hamster on a treadmill.

"You're not a worrier," Jason tells her, "but I'm afraid having this baby is going to kill you."

"This is my reign of terror," she tells him.

It is no longer a simple matter to be pregnant.

When the test results come back negative, they celebrate. It is a normal little girl she carries, not something monstrous. The world seems a less dangerous place. She exercises, eats well, takes vitamins and a small glass of sherry now and then. She rubs cream into her taut skin and preens, content. In August she suns herself, lying naked in the soft grass in their backyard. She is sleepy. The sun presses her into the earth; she is heavy and slow. Jason comes home from work early.

She lets go of her dream. Dreams don't foretell. She does not have precognition. She is consoled and able to go on. The world is filled with hope.

In the sixth month, defiantly pregnant, she accepts a dinner invitation in the city.

"I haven't seen the girls in a while. They feel abandoned because of the baby," she tells Jason. He does not feel particularly close to her friends, although she has taken great pains not to shut him out. He does not share their college memories with them.

"You mean the girls with the old faces," he teases.

The truth is that Emma needs to talk about her pregnancy, to anyone who will listen and even to those who won't.

"They haven't exactly been encouraging," Jason says.

When Emma first told them, her friends said she was making a mistake. That it would ruin her figure and her marriage and the rest of her life.

"There are two kinds of marriages," Grace said. She has never been married. Her certainties rule her life. "There are child-oriented marriages and sex-oriented marriages. You can't have it both ways. Which one do you want?"

Surely she contains enough love for both, Emma thinks; she had an abortion, many years earlier when Jason was in medical school and they could not afford a child. She never told Jason and she never made that mistake again.

She has made her decision. She is pregnant, radiant, and they go to the party. She wears a white knit dress. Her dark hair is pulled sleekly back. She has never felt better.

All the way from Glen Cove to New York, Jason regales her.

"Grace will get drunk and forget she's middle-aged," Jason says. "She will show off her little middle-aged titties. Alice is married for the fourth time and smug. She will be there with her latest husband and will talk about her latest abortion. She prides herself on her fertility, but doesn't have the guts to finish what she starts. She is a perpetual option holder. Zach is a failed poet and he will patronize his wife. Who does he think he is? I mean, he teaches at Bronx Community, not at Columbia."

Emma smiles, beginning to think she has made a mistake accepting this invitation.

Jason begins to whistle. Driving through the night on the long dark stretches of highway, Jason is relaxed and whistling. Emma recognizes the "Poet and Peasant Overture."

"Poet and Pedant Overture," Jason says and grins.

"Very amusing."

"See what I mean? That's just what Zach will do. He'll grade my humor. He won't laugh at it."

"I didn't realize you hated these people so much."

"I don't hate these people, Emma. I hate what they do to you. Sometimes I'm afraid you envy their uncommitted lives. Sometimes when we're with them, I don't recognize you."

Emma is crying, carefully, into a tissue, aware of her makeup. Her feelings are easily hurt. Jason apologizes and she feels better.

"You'll get a chance to meet John, Alice's new husband," Emma says. "He's a lawyer. Maybe you'll like him. You can talk malpractice." Jason laughs. By the time they arrive they are in the same good spirits as when they left their house.

The evening goes pretty much as Jason predicts. But Emma still feels she has had a chance to show herself off as they make their excuses at midnight. And Jason, low-key and substantial, seems to enjoy John. In spite of himself, he speaks at length and enthusiastically about Emma's pregnancy; he is excited by the coming birth of their daughter.

He has good instincts, Emma thinks on the ride home. They

make love on the living room floor. They are high and in too much of a hurry to get out of their clothes and into bed. Then they laugh for several hours, going over what everyone said.

"I don't envy them," she tells him. "They don't have you." She is certain of this now.

*

"I guess there's something to be said for meaningless ritual," Jason says after Isabel is born. He is referring to the rampant superstition that has pervaded Emma's maternity and that has brought forth a perfect child.

Jason comes in the morning before rounds; his stethoscope dangles from his neck and he looks clean and professional. He comes after evening rounds, tired and stubbled. He visits with Emma for hours, sitting at her bedside.

Emma and Jason grin at each other, proud of themselves. Emma now permits her mother to purchase a crib, a highchair, a bathinette, a carriage, a layette, a bird mobile to hang over the crib. It is bad luck to buy these things beforehand.

The child is named after a dead grandparent on Emma's side of the family. To an Ashkenazi Jew, it is bad luck to name the newborn after a living relative.

When Emma's mother looks at the newborn for the first time, she pronounces a *kinahurra* over it to ward off the evil eye.

Emma's mother insists on keeping an eye on Jason while Emma is in the hospital.

Although she trusts him, it cannot hurt to be watchful, she tells Emma in a conspiratorial tone. Indeed Emma's mother was vigilant of her father up until the day he died.

Jason calls her Tyrannosaurus mother. Emma loses patience with her entirely now that Isabel is born and healthy. All the compassion she denies her mother, she lavishes on her daughter.

Her hospital room is like an untended garden. It is filled with flowers, which she gives away to patients who are less fortunate. The room is painted a sunny yellow; although it is November, it is warm and safe. There are no shadows in it.

She keeps the tea roses Jason brings. The gift card reads: She is the best thing we've done.

Jason sits next to Emma on her last night in the hospital. He holds her in one arm and cradles the infant in the other. They are without breach. The moment of strangeness passes, the knowledge that when they go home the next day, they will be three. Jason touches the infant's fingers and toes, lightly strokes the silky fontanel in her skull. He takes pleasure in the feminine smells that surround him, the powdery baby, his musky wife. The baby falls asleep in his arms.

"I'm having impure thoughts," Jason whispers.

"Soon," Emma sighs. She kisses him, her lips remain on his. She is happy to feel physical desire, like a light tickle, in her thighs.

They sit together for a while.

No one, not even Emma, understands why she is relieved to hear the baby cry.

Emma's friends visit frequently that first year. They bring expensive gifts for Isabel, tiny blue velvet smocks and lace-trimmed blouses. They dress her up and play with her, as if she were a doll. She is a bright child, good-natured and anxious to please her mother and her Aunt Grace and Aunt Alice. She develops quickly. Her eyes focus, change from blue to brown. She grasps their fingers, leads them to her mouth. Soon she sports one, then two milk teeth that look silly in her otherwise empty gums. She rolls over in her crib, sits, half crawls, half walks—like a crustacean, Emma thinks. Isabel pulls herself up, stands, lets go and stumbles.

Jason and Emma sit on the floor with their arms outstretched to catch her. Isabel's arms are wide open to balance her first halting steps toward them. "She walks like she's straddling a horse," Emma says.

Isabel falls into Emma's lap. She seems about to cry, changes her mind. They all laugh instead. She rises, tumbles, does it again. This time she heads for Jason. "Daddy's girl," Jason says.

She will be tall and slim, like Emma, but her easy temperament is Jason's.

When Emma and Jason make love, he does not seem to mind that part of Emma is listening for the child's cries, that their bed is not the moist secret refuge it once was. He believes Emma when she speaks of maternal telepathy. Her breaths are Isabel's breaths. She anticipates Isabel's fevers, Isabel's hunger, her nightmares, her sorrow. Jason watches Emma flinch, her empathy so powerful that she feels when the child cannot have or do something it wants to have or do. Emma shares the frustration, the joy, the sadness that Isabel experiences in her young life.

When Isabel is one, they take her with them when Jason goes horseback riding. It has been years since Jason has ridden, since before his marriage to Emma, in fact. Isabel and Emma watch from the grass outside the corral.

It is summer. Jason is shirtless and tan, astride a chestnut mare that belongs to a friend. Jason has not forgotten his command over the giant beast. "It's like riding a motorcycle," he calls to his family, but his voice is lost in a hot dry breeze. He gallops fiercely through the field. Emma is stunned by the sight of her husband, so pagan and glorious above her, the sun behind him. He is suddenly a stranger and she does not belong. She is frightened by this dangerous masculine adventure. She would rather be at home, with Isabel, in her garden.

That summer she cultivates morning glories and snapdragons, marigolds and pansies, anything that is colorful, splendid to the eye. Honeysuckle grows wild in the yard. It is a disordered profusion of scent and color. She begins a vegetable garden which yields, surprisingly, tomatoes, lettuce, zucchini, radishes, carrots, and of which she is very proud.

The baby rides her hip while she works. It seems that her

hips have been made wide to accommodate her child. They fit together perfectly, a blend of form and function.

In the privacy of their yard, she nurses the baby, lifting her embroidered blouse and tucking the baby's head under it, leading Isabel's mouth to her nipple. She watches Isabel suckling, smoothes the fine wisps of hair from the baby's damp forehead. Later she places the baby on a receiving blanket in the grass and stretches out next to her. The baby holds a bottle of Jell-O water from which she sucks contentedly while she watches her mother.

The afternoon passes too swiftly for Emma. She makes dinner for Jason. She eats with the baby. Copper pots line the walls, in need of polish. She is growing sweet red peppers and basil in window pots, and the kitchen is warmed by the slow movement of summer drafts.

Jason eats in silence, reads a novel later in the evening. The house is hot with the buildup of days of sun and humidity. They don't talk much; the summer heat is bleeding them.

"We have to put in air-conditioning," Jason mentions.

"At least it's still cool in the bedroom," Emma comments.

In bed they hold each other before they become too sticky. They fall asleep on separate sides of the bed.

*

When Isabel is two, they take her to Montauk Point. It is midwinter and dreary in Glen Cove. Gray slush lines the streets. The neighborhood trees are bleak; the park is colorless. It seems that everything has been washed away by the season. So they go to the sea.

Jason is more handsome this year than last. He has grown a beard and put on ten pounds. Middle age becomes him. Emma is lovely. She is at her most beautiful that year, Jason tells her. They read Isabel fairy tales and believe in them. When Emma thinks of motherhood, she imagines herself as the warm center of her family. She is the hearth. Jason and Isabel gravitate to her. She loves them both with what is best in herself.

They stop at a diner for breakfast before continuing on to Montauk. Once there, they park the car and clamber down muddy paths, over rocks, across a field of rotted timber that has washed up from the sea, perhaps from a sunken galleon, Emma thinks.

And then they are on the beach, looking out at an ocean, tossed, whitecapped, ominous, unsafe. There is no more land. It is just the three of them, alone, stranded in time and place, on this last stronghold of humanity. They are content, isolated on this devastated landscape.

They find unusual shells; Emma picks them up, gently dusts the sand from their delicate pink interiors—baby's ears, she calls them—and places them in a string bag she carries. Seaweed has washed up onto the clean white sand. It smells like spoiled fish. Isabel is fascinated by the plants. She jumps on them, popping the bubbles in their stems. She laughs gleefully at the gurgling noise this makes, the plop, squish. She is easy to please, indeed prefers such pastimes to other more expensive and complicated toys.

Jason points out the tide pools. They squat beside one and look for the beginnings of life somewhere in the murky water. "These are your humble origins," Jason says.

"Yuck," Emma says. "Is there no poetry in you?"

They look at each other over Isabel's head and laugh.

"Swing me, swing me," Isabel pipes up. Jason and Emma hold her hands and lift her between them, swinging her over the tide pool, over puddles, curbs, any and all obstacles that stand in Isabel's way.

"Wheee..." she screams, delighted and frightened at the same time.

"Over she goes..." Emma and Jason call out.

When Isabel tires of swinging down the beach, she sits in the sand and digs. She is bundled up in a snowsuit, a bulky little fig-

ure with a red nose and chin exposed to the cold. She is absorbed by the deepening hole, the discovery of layers of damp
sand, like layers of a dead civilization unearthed. She jabbers to
herself incessantly.

"I'm going around the Point," Jason announces. He kisses
Emma on the lips briefly, and Isabel on the cheek. The baby
pays no attention.

"Be careful," she says, more to herself than to Jason. She
wanders up and down this side of the island. She is reluctant to
approach the Point. The tide will rise in an hour, she calculates,
followed by an early dusk. It will be difficult to get back over the
rocks and driftwood when the water begins to wash up. As soon
as he disappears around the Point, she begins a nervous wait for
Jason's return. A quarter of an hour passes, then a half hour. Isabel continues to dig. Emma wanders over to her protectively.
"You'll be in China soon," she says.

"China, China, China, China," Isabel jabbers.

Three-quarters of an hour go by. The water is beginning to
inch closer to Isabel's foot, up the beach. Mist clings to the sea.
The last of the winter sun sails behind a cloud. The sky is a
bleached diffused white, darkening toward the horizon where
the sea and sky mix. There is no line to mark where one ends
and the other begins. It is the end of the earth and Emma is
frightened that she will fall off into nothingness. She goes to Isabel and lifts her up. She starts to carry her back to the car,
thinking she will call the Coast Guard and get help if Jason does
not return before the tide comes up. She looks toward the
Point; beyond it there is a wall of gray impenetrable mist. Far
out at sea, a storm is navigating its way to shore. Emma cannot
hear even the muffled undertones of a foghorn or the clanging
of marker buoys.

Emma is running now; the baby is bouncing and heavy, at
first laughing at this adventure and then silent. Emma does not
feel Isabel's weight. She is panting and sweating. Sunset and the
tide overtake her. Jason does not reappear. Emma imagines that

he has been swept out to sea. Her fear is vivid and bright. She is convinced he is gone forever.

She places Isabel on a rock and begins to maneuver around it. Then she turns and looks behind her. The low flat sky presses darkness to the Point; a shadowy figure, tall, lumbering, is coming around it, emerging from the mists like a creature out of legend. It is covered in kelp; its arms, kelp-draped, are extended out in front of it. Emma begins to scream. She cannot stop. Isabel is crying, grabbing for her mother's neck. Emma stands in front of her, placing her body as a shield. The sea bubbles up to her ankles and recedes, sucks at her feet.

When Jason catches up to them, he is laughing.

"That's not funny," Emma yells at him. Then her voice cracks and she is crying. "Thank God you're alive," she whispers.

Jason holds her and Isabel to his chest. He cannot understand what he has done to cause his wife to be this upset.

He helps her over the rocks, carrying Isabel in one arm; he retrieves a piece of driftwood for Emma because she likes to collect things. This goes in the trunk of the car.

Driving home, calm at last restored, Emma finally laughs at her foolishness. She removes her wet sneakers and socks. Isabel is quiet, sleeping in the back seat. Emma reaches over and covers her with a plaid wool throw. It begins to rain.

Nearing home, the red street lights are smeared by the rhythmic swing of the windshield wipers. Emma is lulled by the sound. Their shadowed faces are illuminated, rain-dappled, at each intersection, and are washed clean by the wipers. In the darkness of the car, these faces are composed, sleepy, satisfied. Emma is huddled into her parka. Jason drives with his hand on her thigh.

*

Emma's friends phone infrequently. Up until recently, Emma would recount Isabel's latest exploits, how intelligent and becoming the child was, how her teachers at school thought she had great potential. Now nothing is mentioned. She knows what they are thinking in that flat silence. They never ask, "How is Isabel?" and Emma does not volunteer any information. In some ways, she is grateful that they do not pursue it so she does not have to answer any painful questions.

When they invite her and Jason to dinner parties, she knows, without it being specified, that children are not welcome. Emma understands, but is reluctant to leave Isabel with a sitter, or even with her own mother.

Isabel is indeed a beautiful child. Her hair is thick, dark, glossy. She is slim, without the usual trace of pudginess common to children, and which Emma has always found unattractive. Isabel's fingers and toes are long, slender, white, tapered, like Jason's hands. They are graceful, giving Emma hope of musical aptitude, although Isabel has given Emma no sign of interest in either the records Emma plays for her or the songs she sings herself. Isabel's eyes are the focal point of her face, of her entire being. They are wide, sloe, black. They dominate her face, staring as they do into the middle distance. They are without expectation. She is five years old and quiet.

At home, Isabel stares out the window for long periods of time. Emma wants to shake her awake, but stops herself. She does not want to disturb her as she dreams her way to adulthood. When Emma takes Isabel on an outing, she is always on the lookout for what will bring those eyes into focus, arouse a spark of interest.

*

Emma does not tell Jason that she has taken Isabel to a reader-adviser in Harlem. She knows what he will say—or will not say, but will think.

When Emma was four years old, her mother took her to a gypsy who had a storefront practice in their neighborhood. Emma was fascinated by the apothecary jars filled with exotic herbs, the incense burning in a small bowl on the gypsy's table, the darkened room, the Persian rugs and wall hangings. Surprisingly, she was unafraid of the gypsy herself.

"See for yourself," Emma's mother told the gypsy. Emma's mother removed Emma's bonnet. "She's four years old and she's still bald. The kids in the park want to know why I dress such a cute little boy in dresses. Can you do something?"

Emma recalls the episode vividly, although she had no concept at the time that the hairless state was something to be concerned about. The woman smelled of rancid cooking grease. Her face was seamed by wrinkles that held it together. Her hands were coarse and ropy over Emma's own little fair ones. The gypsy was the color of clay—sienna. She instructed her mother to cut Emma's hair at six p.m. under the light of the next full moon. Her mother was reluctant to cut what little dark fuzz Emma had on her head, but the gypsy reassured her that if she did as instructed, Emma would grow a luxuriant mass of hair within a half year. Emma's mother followed the gypsy's prescription and Emma grew a mass of rich brown curls that was the envy of the block. She was the only girl in the neighborhood who did not require the permanent wave that was so fashionable that year.

The reader-adviser looks into Isabel's eyes, hold the child's cool hands. This woman also smells of rancid cooking grease. She has the same teas, crystal ball, tarot cards as that other gypsy. The woman then turns her attention to Emma. Isabel is a special child, she says hypnotically. Her future should be carefully guided; she must be watched over, because she is special. Emma listens carefully. The air is still and dreamlike, smoky. Emma gladly pays fifty dollars for her time.

Jason eats dinner in silence. In the family room Isabel has started rocking herself. The house is silent.

"Would you please put on the stereo?" Jason says.

"What would you like to hear?"

"Anything. I don't care."

Emma says, "I think she's doing better."

Jason does not answer.

Later that night, Jason covers her body with his. It is dark. They make love only in darkness, never in daylight, nor as when they were first married, with small red votives burning on the nightstand. They touch without seeing, groping in the dead of night. He is particularly rough with her, almost violent when he comes.

When Emma makes occasional advances, tentatively reaching for him in a restaurant or at the movies or while he is reading, he gently removes her hand.

He becomes rigid about birth control. He withdraws before he comes. Over coffee one morning, Emma looks at him and knows he will falter.

Things do not fall away singly, sensibly, one at a time, but in multiples.

*

There are times that spring when Emma prays for the silence of the past winter, the dreary freighted overcast days of November and January, when there was no sun, when life was a simple succession of centerless hours.

Emma's mother has had a stroke. Although it is mild and she recovers, there is damage—the kind you cannot see. It is not measurable, but something is gone. The woman does not want to hear anything terrible about the world, about Emma and Jason and Isabel. She wants to die knowing that everything is all right, settled, safe. She has taught Emma well. Emma cannot have an intelligent conversation with her.

Jason has moved out of their bedroom. The agreement is mutual and wordless. He is having an affair. Emma does not know the girl, nor does she care to. He wears a new spicy cologne. She will not let him touch her. She hates him, but she also understands. He still lives there; he eats and sleeps in the house.

After Jason goes to his room, Emma stays awake and takes Isabel into her lap. She puts her head near Isabel's and listens. She listens with an intensity, a hope that, if such things were possible, would raise the dead. At that time of night what she hears is silence and despair, that same silence that has haunted all her seasons for the last three years. As Isabel has grown in size, she has withdrawn to a place where it is not possible to reach her; her retreat is complete and irrevocable.

When Isabel was an infant and Emma held her this way, she could listen in on her thoughts, her infant's universe of hunger, wet, fear, pleasure. A mother knows when her child is in trouble. There is a magic affinity that binds them. Emma realizes that if Isabel were sitting in the yard and wandered off, tempted away by a stranger, in trouble, perhaps abused, Emma would not know.

She holds her close, presses the child to her, trying to show the measure, the strength of her allegiance, but it is as if all sound and feeling are drowned out by the rush of common blood in their veins.

Emma asks so little of the world, perhaps not enough. She wants her daughter's life to be easy. She wants her daughter's life restored.

In early April the silence that has seemed so firmly ensconced in their home ends. After the first assault on it, Emma knows that that silence was as fragile, as tender as the linings of the shells she once collected at Montauk Point. In early April Isabel begins banging her head into the walls and screeching. She growls and rolls across the floor toward Emma. Emma backs away in fear; her heart is pounding during the first episode; she is summoned from sleep to behold Isabel's madness. Isabel's long silence is ended. That is when Emma begins praying for the silence of winter.

She travels to the city, making the long drive without complaint, to escape the watchful eyes of the suburban neighborhood, to escape the tended for the less tended, the city, the zoo, a place where animals prowl.

Isabel has some relatively calm days, when the demons that beset her abate. Emma takes her in the car, where she stares placidly from the car window. Emma holds her hand as they wander through the Bronx Zoo. New generations are emerging from their snowsuits. The sky over the Bronx is a clear expanse of unstained blue. People appear out of nowhere, like migrating birds. A gorilla scratches and spits, peels a banana, opens an Oreo and licks the cream center before eating the cookie, things that delighted Emma when she was a child and still do. There is always a crowd around the monkey house. Emma walks on, pulling Isabel along. Families picnic or row, traveling together like ducks paddling on a lake.

Isabel's grip on Emma's hand is tight and strong, as if she senses her mother's thoughts. They stop at a cage in which a wolf is circling. Isabel stares at the empty white eyes of the pacing male. It stops and stares back at her.

It is Emma's nature to try to find something poetic in everything. She sees Isabel as a feral child, daughter of a wild beast. Isabel's madness exists only in a human universe. This other world, this is where Isabel belongs, among the killers, the wolves, the lions, the bears, the wild dogs, the inhospitable elements. It is not a comforting thought, but she wants to leave the child here, in the zoo, and walk away free.

Emma shakes herself awake from the dream. Isabel comes home with her.

She takes Isabel to Montauk Point. Perhaps the child will remember some past happiness. But in returning here, it is Emma who recollects a better time. Emma hopes, in a dark moment, that the child will be carried off to sea, swept away, as all sadness runs off into the sea.

She cries as she drives home—for Jason, for Isabel, mainly for herself, for a life that is not her own. Isabel seems unconcerned that her mother is upset. Emma denies the child. She resents its being a girl. This is Emma's daughter. Not Jason's son.

Late that night when the house is quiet, Jason appears. His hair is disheveled from sleep when he comes out of his room. He finds Emma on a stool at the breakfast bar, drinking a cup of cocoa. Isabel is asleep, curled in her lap. He stands there watching them.

Emma is conscious of her nightgown, of how she looks. The nightgown is freshly laundered, white, trimmed with lace. Her hair is combed, her face is composed and unmade-up. The kitchen is neat, things in place, copper pots glowing from their hooks, dishes glued together after Isabel breaks them, plants watered. The house has always been gracious, although there were days when it seemed warmer. Still, Emma is grateful for small things.

Jason's face wavers, the assurance gone from it.

"You can't go on like this," he says. "You can't follow her into madness—no more than you can follow her into death."

Emma looks at him. The shadow that crossed his eyes is gone.

"Good night, Emma." He ruffles her hair, turns and leaves the room.

She listens for him from her bed that night. He is right, she thinks; madness is, of necessity, a very private place. She hears him get up, go to the bathroom. It is three in the morning. In that moment, she hopes he will come to bed.

*

Emma's life, which has been drifting and disembodied, is sharply focused and shattered one morning that spring.

Isabel is screaming and banging her head into the window wall of the family room. The room shakes from the pounding and Emma is certain the windows will shatter. In a single moment, Emma is transformed. She holds Isabel's head in her bloodless fingers. They are cold but resolute, the circulation gone from them, as if they disavow what she is about to do.

"You want to bang your head? Well, here, let me help you." Emma grabs the girl's head and slams it into the wall, hard. The wall resounds with the blow, empty and hollow. Emma pushes her head once, twice, a third time. "You want more?" She thrusts the child's head into closet doors. Cracks appear in the plaster. She throws her into walls, onto the floor. The child screams; she struggles against her mother's grip. She tears at the grasping fingers but cannot dislodge them, untangle them from her hair. Her head is cut and bleeding, her forehead bruised and lumpy. She tries to bite her mother with swollen cracked lips, then kicks at her, shrieking, in pain, indignation . . . Emma could not begin to know or understand. She cannot hear her child.

Emma stops herself. It is an act of will. Otherwise, she is afraid she will kill the child. She looks at the child's face. Isabel's eyes are startled. It is a sign, the first in years, and Emma dares to feel hope in the midst of her desperation. The blank wall is gone, if only for a moment. Then Emma is crying. She pays no more attention to Isabel that day.

Instead she works in her garden all afternoon. She needs the certainty of planting a strawberry and harvesting a strawberry. The sun is gathering strength. It beats into her back and hair. Her skin grows warm; her face is ruddy and intense with the season's burgeoning life. There are tiny buds on all the trees in the yard. She is surrounded by delicate colors and scents. There is an urgency to her movements. She gets a lot done.

When Jason comes home for dinner that night, earlier than usual, she tells him what has happened that day. He nods. She does not need forgiveness for her act of violence and Jason does not offer any.

After dinner he sits with her in the kitchen.

"If you want to work with her, I'll help you in any way I can. If you want to have her put away, I'll arrange for it."

"Thank you." Emma is grateful enough to love him again.

"She's like a terminal illness. Life without hope isn't possible. So we can't admit there isn't any."

"Don't say that. Don't say there's no hope. We can try. If it doesn't work out, we'll discuss the other possibility."

Jason agrees.

The next day Emma buys a puppy for Isabel. Perhaps there will be that telepathy between them that Emma used to share with her. The puppy sniffs suspiciously at Isabel and shies away; it does not recognize a playmate in her. Instead, it follows Emma around the house all day and at night it jumps into Jason's lap and falls asleep.

The puppy loves the garden. Whenever Emma works out back during the summer, he is beside her. When he ventures a few feet away, it is to romp in dirt and leaves and flower beds, wreaking havoc. He runs small fierce circles. Emma can only laugh. She sits on the lawn and plays with him. The air is hot and thick; pollen rides the damp breezes. Her limbs are leaden. By the end of summer, she is very brown and the puppy is too large to curl up in Jason's lap, although he continues to try.

Emma works with Isabel all summer. She does not think beyond that. She is healing from the wounds of beating her child. The days take their shape from how well her work with Isabel goes. On good days Emma congratulates herself. She is excited and sleepless. On bad days she thinks of having another baby.

Some spell has been lifted from their house. It is no longer still but seems to rise from the earth, growing like her garden, elemental, filled with life. Emma's laughter, quiet at first, becomes more powerful and certain, as if it is a skill she must relearn. Plates clatter when she sets the table for dinner. She prepares a new dish; Jason compliments her cooking.

Jason takes out their old grill, cleans it, barbecues salmon steaks and new potatoes during a blazing August afternoon. They eat outside, on a blanket in the grass, grateful for a cool dusk.

Emma imagines Jason with his girlfriend, visualizing them together. She is glad of the darkness, her eyes overcast. She turns her head away from their picnic and swipes at her eyes, pretends she has hay fever.

She looks forward to autumn and its rituals, the shorter days, raking the yard, the Jewish holidays, the new year, the colors of change. They have new neighbors; she invites them to dinner. She has her hair cut. She still does not need a permanent wave, but she has it dyed to cover the strands of gray that have begun to sprout like weeds in a garden. She continues to work with Isabel. During the broader days of summer she had more hope than in the narrower days of fall. Still, she goes on.

She has lunch in the city with Grace and Alice. They laugh a lot, get drunk, forget to eat their food. Grace is quiet and settled with her life. Alice is still married to John. She is forty years old and visibly pregnant. Her father and mother have died in the past year; she feels exposed; she wants this baby.

Emma feels festive and young with her friends.

She races her car when she hits the highway. The suburbs flash by. She raises the sunroof and wind rushes through her hair, between her fingers, up her skirt. At home, she sits on the porch and waits for Jason to come home. Isabel is at a special school. Emma has her afternoons to herself.

Jason takes her out to dinner at a local Italian restaurant. It is a restful meal. Although she drinks several glasses of wine, she is sober by the time coffee is served. Jason drives home slowly. They are quiet. When he stops for a red light, Emma asks him to pull over. He does as she says. They are parked on a dark, tree-lined street in an old established neighborhood.

"What?" Jason asks.

Emma does not answer for some time.

"What is it?"

"Jason, do you want a divorce?"

Now Jason is silent.

"No," he says finally.

"But you've thought about it?"

"Haven't you?"

"Are you still fucking her?" Her tone is more accusatory and bitter than she would have liked. She feels small and mean.

"No. Not for a long time."

"Do you want to move back to the bedroom?"

"Yes. I'd like that."

For months she will not be able to accept more than his physical presence in bed. He is careful. He does not touch her. For the moment, nearness is enough.

He does not tell her that in her sleep she holds to him. She presses her fingernails into his flesh. He lies there silently, the flash of pain a relief.

Little Locomotive

Gina Forberg

Every morning around 6,
each evening at the hour of 6,
all the time in between,
my son runs circles around
our dining room table.
We used to think of it as a game,
a chase, our own intimate Olympic event.
Ten laps became twenty, fifty, one hundred
Raymond was intense, intent on getting
his morning, afternoon and evening exercise.
"Sensory motor issues" were the words
the occupational therapist used. Bring on
the physioball, weighted vest, bucket full
of glossy, black beans. Apply pressure
to shoulders hourly; soft brush him
in a downward motion. Our marathon runner,
little locomotive became subject to the habits
of a dog. Daily we groomed him, waited for some
type of bone-biting response. We bathed him in lavender,
chamomile; massaged downward, stroked the crux
of his back, quieted any remaining nerve.
Today, after we brushed him, he rolled over,
put a fist in his mouth, spit it out, barked
at the sight of our hands.

Normal

Marie Myung-Ok Lee

On Saturdays I drive to another state to take J, my three-year-old, postcancer, autistic son, to the Happy Trails Stables, a facility for hippotherapy for mentally and physically disabled children.

I found out about Happy Trails back in another life—before I had J. As a child, I'd made a promise to myself that I would always try to do some kind of volunteer work. When a friend with a child who has cerebral palsy mentioned the stable, I thought, *Aha!* The perfect volunteer job. I had shown quarter horses as a child, and my skills could help severely disabled children. Noble and yet secretly indulgent of my addiction to the smell of horse manure.

The idea simmered on the back burner for years, but I never got around to actually calling Happy Trails. Miscarriages, pregnancy, an on-again, off-again writing career, my father's suicide, and a few other things got in the way—and now my son is one of those riding children whom I once envisioned with a mixture of pity and compassion. And I'm no brave horse-wrangler—I'm just a mom, planting my boot on the side rails, watching the parade of children go by.

Happy Trails is the Platonic ideal of a stable. You enter it via a winding drive that passes woods and rolling sedge fields. There is a barn, an arena, and an outdoor riding ring surrounded by a weathered whitewashed fence—it can't get any more quaint. Happy Trails even has its own art gallery displaying oil-painted renditions of its bucolic splendor.

What is different from your average stable is a long wooden ramp leading up to what looks like a stage set up in the arena, so that children of varying abilities can mount their horses. Wheelchairs can be pushed up the ramp. The tack room has a neat row of bridles with the horses' names—Kimmie, Paint, Thor, Gus—but also a row of pediatric helmets hanging next to thick web belts with handles, as well as an assortment of textured rubber balls and other tools used for physical therapy. On a table sits an issue of *Equine* magazine next to a splayed catalog of "mobility tools" for the differently abled: foam blocks, chew-toys, full-body wheelchairs, and an assortment of braces—unsettling in their scope and variety—to buttress hypotonic (low-muscle) children into a semblance of sitting or standing upright.

When J and I arrive, I put J's helmet and belt on him. Part of J's disability involves his extreme dislike of doing anything anyone wants him to do, and so the next phase involves me and his therapist dragging forty pounds of kicking, biting, and screaming J up the ramp and onto the back of his horse, Kimmie, who, amazingly, ignores the commotion.

The smallest children, like three-year-old J, do not use saddles but instead hang on to a metal steering wheel attached to what looks like a giant canvas luggage strap circling the horse's middle. The children wear web belts around their middles so that the "side walkers"—an adult volunteer and the therapist—can hold the kid on the horse, while a third volunteer holds the horse's lead.

Kimmie is a placid gelding the gray-white color of old underwear. In all my years of being a serious rider, I have never seen such unbeautiful horses as I have here: swaybacked, knock-kneed, strange mixtures of breeds, like the stumpy pony who looks unmistakably part draft horse. These mounts have no wild oats to sow; they are all at least fifteen years old. Gus, the one who is so swaybacked that he looks like some kind of camel, is purportedly fifty years old, which would translate to about 130 years in human age.

They come to Happy Trails in a variety of ways: most are donated or plucked from the dog food factory line to retire to a nice life of working a few hours a day and then spending the rest lazing in pasture. The horses must have an even, plodding gait and unflappable personalities. As a test, a trainer gets on their backs, screams, flails, falls off—does everything short of shooting a gun. The horses that remain unmoved are accepted.

I think J secretly loves riding, but he is big on what the therapists call "counter-control." For example, during his Skinner-based therapy, when we reward him with edible treats, he often hands the treats back—after spitting on them—to show us he can't be bought.

So no matter how much he really enjoys riding, the fact that we are making him do it has to be acknowledged first. As he tantrums up the ramp, J tries to pull off his helmet, kicks at me and the therapist, and reaches over and yanks patient Kimmie's mane. (Horses actually have no nerve endings in their hair's roots, but J doesn't need to know this). What the therapists have learned to do is to toss J on like a sack of potatoes and start running off the minute J's little butt hits Kimmie's back. J has no recourse but to hang on for dear life.

Kimmie trots off. J screams with rage, tiny hands clinging to the steering wheel. But there is a flash of happiness in his eyes. A moving roller coaster! He loves it, truly.

In the lingo of therapists, riding a horse challenges balance, bilateral movement, and cross-midline skills (e.g., moving your right arm to the left, which requires a surprisingly complex brain action), skills that the able-bodied take for granted. For children who have never walked unassisted, being atop a moving horse actually allows them to experience the rocking pelvis sensation of human walking.

J has motor delays, likely stemming from the trauma of his spinal cord cancer, and could use some of that cross-midlining. The therapists also assure us that hippotherapy will help him with his relationship skills, since many autistic children end up bonding with their mounts. And it has the further benefit of be-ing fiscally therapeutic for Mommy and Daddy: we spend more than twenty thousand dollars a year out of pocket on his various therapies, but our state Medicaid, though collapsing under the weight of drastic budget cuts, shells out the ten dollars a week for this.

During our first sessions, I was so consumed with getting J successfully atop his horse, and then bursting with pride to see my little guy bouncing atop Kimmie—what a good seat! just like his mommy!—that I was oblivious to my surroundings, the other children, the other parents. But then the therapists started taking J for little trail rides around the farm, leaving me behind with nothing to do but watch the other kids going round and round the indoor ring.

My initial impression was that the whole enterprise was a Flannery O'Connor story accompanied by Diane Arbus photos. The bucolic setting, the misfit horses, the impossibly deformed and damaged children. Some kids, like J, scream. Others jibber-jabber. There is also a silent rider, who is microcephalic, adult in size but still able to wear those tiny pediatric helmets.

There's the family whose daughter (seven? nine? twelve?) is in a full-body wheelchair, her limbs the texture of overcooked spaghetti. I always admire the aplomb with which the father or mother—they seemed to switch off—manages to get their daughter ensconced in the wheelchair, grab their Dunkin' Donuts coffee out of the van's cup holder, and wheel to the tack room. One day I saw that the mother had added a baby on her hip to the whole load, and I thought, *Wow, that's nice, at least they have a healthy daughter*. Then, when I came closer, I saw that the baby had floppy limbs encased in plastic braces, much like her sister's.

There is also a father and son who have the session right af-ter J's, so as we finish up, we often see them unloading. The boy, about twelve and quite large, has some kind of mobility prob-lem, but he doesn't use a wheelchair: his father hugs him around the armpits from behind and the two of them "walk." They do this every week, stubbornly, lovingly, insistently. I can't help wondering what will happen as the boy grows larger—he's bordering on the obese—and the father weaker. This center will not hold.

*

Unlike my friends, who spent their pregnancies cupping their hands on their bellies and smiling knowingly, I was tormented during my pregnancy by visions of deformity. The very opacity of my skin over my womb only added to my anxiety. Anything could be growing in there, I thought.

As a child, my physician father tried to get me interested in medicine by bringing home medical texts from the office. I became fascinated with one, *Gross Malformations of the Human Anatomy*. I could spend hours poring over the pages, cataloging the endless ways things could go haywire in the process of a sixteen-celled blastocyst actually growing, dividing into muscles, bones, organs, skin.

Being at Happy Trails was not unlike seeing the strange wanderings of my mind somehow realized in front of my face. The visual trauma was different from being in the oncology ward, where every child has a chemo stent in his neck, or at J's autism school, where every kid is staring off into space and making bizarre noises. Here on display is the full wild range of disability and damage: brain injury, malformed limbs, genetic deformities.

One day I spotted an older rider—she had some wrinkles along with obvious mental retardation—and I wondered what she was doing at Happy Trails. Then I saw a much older, much wrinklier couple—her parents—and realized that yes, she is someone's child, and yes, as these children grow, their deformities will grow along with them. I can't help being curious now when I see someone new at Happy Trails—what are these riders' disabilities, and are they physical, mental, or both?

It didn't take long to find out. Some of the parents look bored out of their skulls and seemed happy to converse with a scruffy Korean American woman who looks twelve years old. (I am often mistaken for J's babysitter.) They talked strangely freely of their children's disabilities and confirmed my suspicions that many of the physically handicapped children have mental problems as well. And here I thought we were such singular victims of bad luck, a child with cancer and autism.

I hesitated over revealing too much in return. There's a part of me that wants the world to know how much J has suffered—spinal-cord tumor at eighteen months, endless painful surgeries, full-body casts and wheelchairs, and now the pain of autism—so the world will be "nice" to him. But at the same time I have a fierce faith that he will recover, and so I don't want him to be burdened with the history of being the cancer kid, the autistic.

When the parents spoke of their children's disabilities, I was happy to listen. But when confronted directly with their offspring and their shocking deformities, I had to consciously force myself to act "normal"—i.e., making eye contact but not staring too little or too much, because I know too well how I feel when this is done to us.

But after a few weeks of putting on this careful act, a strange thing happens: I find something in my brain softening and shifting and I start seeing so-and-so's kid only as so-and-so's kid. Not to sound too Jerry Lewis, but I start seeing the child and not the disability.

It is the brain's instinct to normalize, basically. Good and bad things alike. My husband said that his high after being granted tenure at a great university lasted exactly three hours, and then it wasn't exciting anymore.

After hanging around Happy Trails long enough, the families become familiar as well. Coming from three different states, they are mostly upper middle class and educated, typical of people who have the time and skills to seek out such esoteric therapies, basically the same kind of folks I deal with every day in our college town. We talk about meaningless things, the weather—which is always changing, this being New England—as well as things that matter. How cuts in spending are affecting special education. About new medical procedures that our children have to undergo. Occasionally, of progress.

And it starts feeling good in its own odd way, this mundanity.

"You got enough room, Al?" one of the fathers calls as he moves his car, knowing that Al needs extra elbow room to haul out his enormous son. This casual consideration—not the condescending, you-poor-people, special-needsy politeness but just nice everyday politeness—is rewarding to us all. As Al parks and then struggles with uncorking his gigantic son from the car and then does their plodding tandem walk, a scene that would certainly draw popeyed stares anywhere else, the rest of us chitchat. For us, it's just another Saturday at Happy Trails.

*

I used to wonder how they convinced the people in *Gross Malformations* to submit themselves as models. The photos are uniformly stark, wholly unflattering black and whites. The subjects, when their faces are shown, stare off without a trace of emotion—no happiness, rage, shame, anger, or pride. They wear no clothes, no identifying markers except for their deformities. What would be in it for them? I wondered. I doubted they would go home and tell their friends, *Hey! I'm appearing in this book called* Gross Malformations!

But I remember when I started imagining the people—webbed hands, gaping cleft palate, an unclosed abdominal cavity through which small intestines poke out like Polish sausage—back in their lives, back at home with their "gross" malformations. There was probably an altruistic sense that they were helping the cause of medicine. But maybe there was also a sense of belonging—there's no reason to be embarrassed over being naked and showing off one's deformity when everyone else was naked and showing off, too. The more the merrier.

And we, too, welcome any and all to our select society. With our cups of coffee and cars with the handicapped placards hanging off the rearview mirrors instead of graduation tassels, there we stand with our jagged, battered hearts in the middle of life, our lives, lives about which the Buddhist in me says simply: They are what they are. And, just as I imagined the models for the *Gross Malformations* book did, after our sessions are over, we pack up our kids—wheelchairs, crutches, braces, damaged brains—and head back into the world with all its grimly fixed judgments, all the while contemplating, *What is normal, exactly?*

Form and Void

Barbara Crooker

The autistic boy is blowing bubbles
with his mother, shimmering orbs
that glitter and dance
on the face of the lawn.
He prances after them, staring
with the deep mirror of his eyes
as they pop and disappear.
Flapping his arms, he chases them
toward the garden cosmos,
their mauve & lilac gowns
of silk voile waltzing
in the breeze.
He orbits around his mother
as she dips in her wand,
produces these baubles
from breath and film.
The glassy bubbles rise in a swirl
of pink & blue, a moment's iridescence.
This is the only magic the mother can conjure:

she cannot help him talk or say his name
but they can do this together,
blow bubbles on a breezy afternoon,
make a strand of hand-blown beads
to grace the throat of the lawn.

Doing Jigsaw Puzzles

Barbara Crooker

For David, age four, who has autism. In *The Snow Queen,* by
Hans Christian Andersen, Kay, who has a splinter of glass from
a hobgoblin's shivered mirror in his eye and heart, must solve a
puzzle in order to win his freedom.

> My son David is working his puzzles,
> not wooden templates where the pieces
> click neatly in their slots,
> but ones of his own devising,
> shapes moved to fit some other pattern.
> If even a millimeter of space is off,
> he throws the blocks from the table.
> And Kay, in the Snow Queen's crystal palace,
> works his pieces, trying to solve
> the ice puzzles of reason,
> must make the letters spell ETERNITY
> to gain his freedom and a new pair of silver skates.
> He doesn't succeed. But he goes on
> and on, matching the borders
> with his sharp flat pieces of ice,
> fitting curve to curve,
> straight line to straight line.
> A silver splinter of ice
> has lodged in his heart;
> his blue fingers keep working the puzzle.
> Soon, Gerda is coming, lips red as summer's roses.

She will thaw his hands; her tears will wash
the splinter out.

But David still sits here, working his blocks.
His eyes glaze over, his gaze is far away.
An invisible icy membrane
is cast over him like a caul.
Nothing in the world can touch his heart.
And love's first kiss won't break this spell.

The Lives of the Saints

Catherine Brady

The Mysteries

Lying on the floor, Danny watches me lift his leg, massage the atrophied muscles in the circular motion that is supposed to enhance blood flow. I hum, the few lines I can remember from Bach's Double Concerto, because the music turns the narrow corridor of these repetitive, aching minutes into something as vaulted and buttressed as a cathedral. From the kitchen Ian and Fiona offer a counterpoint, the clink of a spoon in a cereal bowl, Ian urging Fiona to hurry. At five, Fiona isn't old enough to understand time, and she makes us late for school nearly every morning.

Danny already has a complex understanding of time. He loves the measured grace of Bach that tricks us both past the ache he feels in his hips when I work his lifeless legs. He watches me steadily, as steadily as I am hurting him.

Ian doesn't change Danny's catheter or work his atrophied muscles. This is my job, as it was my job to knit Danny whole when he was growing inside my body. He is still so small for his age, a bony bundle that I can easily lift from the van to the wheelchair. Ian and I have large wrists and knuckles, long legs, strong backs, ledged hips where Danny can still be propped like a baby, the least of weights, a tow-headed fairy, less dense than we are, more pure, so astonishing he makes me wonder at the mystery of his making.

Danny asks me if I know that spiders have knees. He coils

and uncoils his fingers delicately to illustrate the jointed working of a spider's legs.

"Do they move one leg at a time?" He'll know the answer; he pays attention to tiny things.

He nods. Then he asks me when we won't have to do this anymore.

He's full of questions about the obvious lately, busy reconstructing the world according to reason rather than wishes: Why do I need to sleep? Why is Fiona a girl and I'm a boy? I tell him that we'll always have to do his physical therapy.

"But when I walk," Danny says, "then I'll be an airplane pilot."

My fingers dig into the cup of Danny's heel. He can't feel it. We've all done such a good job of living around that basic fact, even Fiona, who fetches things for Danny with automatic willingness. But he has begun to compare himself to other kids for the first time. He boasts that he's the best reader in his second-grade class; he notices that he can't play baseball at recess. Ian went out and bought him a mitt, and now he plays catch with Danny in the backyard, where Danny's wishes collide with his newfound faith in practice every time he can't reach far enough for the ball.

"You know you can't walk, honey." I sit Danny up, ask him to tell me quick what he wants for breakfast.

Spina bifida means divided spine. That Danny could be born with his spinal cord exposed, an open wound on his back, seems as much a miracle to me as the perfect functioning of the secret coding that takes place in the womb, that forms the spinal cord from a trough and sheathes it with the vertebral column.

I pull up Danny's elastic-waisted pants, work to get his shoes over his limp feet. Fiona cries in the kitchen. I can just pick Danny up and put him where I want him, but she will plop down on the front steps to protest the pressure of the clock. When I wheel Danny into his classroom, late again, his teacher will be understanding. She's happy to have Danny in her class.

It's so good for the other children. They vie for the chance to stay inside with Danny instead of going out to the yard at recess. Next year, Danny will have to leave the school. The third-grade classrooms are on the second floor, and there's no elevator, and Danny will grow too big for me to throw on my hip and cart up the stairs.

Submission

Two days after he was born, after a surgeon had closed the wound on Danny's back, the wound became infected. The infection could have killed him. Ian and I stayed in the neonatal intensive care unit until the nurses sent us home at midnight to sleep. I was still grieving for the simple fact that I couldn't hold my baby, couldn't take him from the clear plastic incubator, could only reach through the armholes to stroke him. It seemed to me then that nothing would be wrong if I could have him in my arms, if Ian and I didn't have to climb in the car and go home where Danny's crib and the dressing table Ian made for him were waiting. But that's shock.

Somewhere on the way home in the dark, Ian pulled the car over to the side of the road and began to cry. To moan, to bring up air from deep within his chest. And I cried, "God, God, God," just that name. I wasn't asking for anything, just letting the rawness of that name push its way up my throat like a fist. I found God, in that growling right now, knew that I would never ask why, never ask for this to be fixed or undone. A God who could answer such prayers would be too cruel.

We've been lucky. Danny's wound was not high enough on his spine to cause hydrocephalus, though at first we had to make weekly visits to the pediatrician so she could wind a tape measure around Danny's skull to check for swelling. Danny can't walk, but he is otherwise perfect. Ian would be angry to hear me say that, *perfect*, but I don't talk to Ian about this if I can help it, just as I don't talk to him about God. For him, saying *God* is like saying *shit* or *damn*, a momentary bubble of rage or frustration. He thinks I've fallen back on the superstition of my Irish Catholic upbringing, or that it's guilt that makes me seek the comfort of a mere presence.

I got pregnant with Fiona when Danny was eighteen months old. Ian wasn't ready to go through another pregnancy. We'd been told the incidence of spina bifida births was higher among Irish women. He wanted the alpha-fetoprotein blood tests, the ultrasound, the amnio. I didn't want to know, to choose. I wanted to be left alone to be greedily pleased by the butterfly flutters of life in my belly. Ian badgered me with *what if* each time we waited for the test results. When Fiona was born, the doctor freed her shoulders from the birth canal and let me pull her the rest of the way out of my body myself, let me hold her slickness against my newly slack belly. A miracle again, her wholeness, her health. Ian and I both cried to see her.

Prayer

Ian and I are reading in bed when Fiona wakes up from a bad dream and calls for us. I go in to tuck her back into bed. When I kiss her, she sniffs at my breath and says, "I smell shocolate," and then she begins to weep and beg for some chocolate for herself. It isn't just greed that makes her cry, but hurt feelings that I would sneak this pleasure without including her. Finally, I cave in and feed her M&M's in bed.

When I come back to Ian, I dump his book on the floor and crawl into his arms. Ian kisses me and hisses between his teeth, "I smell shocolate," and we are turned aside from one pleasure to another, to the intimate indulgence in the charms of the child we made. She's been making odd little boxes out of the scraps in Ian's garage workshop, and all she'll say when Ian asks her what she's making is that it's an invention. We wonder how we'll make her understand about time, especially on school mornings, and Ian says I should just leave her home one day, let her learn from the consequences.

"I'm a bad mother," I murmur against his shoulder. "I can't resist the impulse to jump in and fix things for them."

"You're a good mother," he says.

"You're just saying that because you want me to service you," I say. I let my hand stroll down his furry chest.

"But you'd be a *great* mother," Ian says, "if you'd learn about F18s so Danny could talk to you about them."

Danny's decided that the F18, like baseball, is a male topic he has to reserve for discussion with his father. "I wish you would tell him that he can't be a pilot," I say.

Ian won't let Danny quit playing catch until he's caught three balls in a row, and sometimes when they're done, Danny's face is sheened with sweat. In the house, Ian insists that Danny stay in his chair, gets mad when he sees I've let Danny out to hitch himself around on the floor, but he won't build a ramp to the front door so Danny can get in and out under his own power. Beneath my fingers Ian's heart pulses like a steady motor to produce the calm of his warmth. I don't want to argue. I want to hunker down inside the holy skin of right now.

I reach to turn off the light, but Ian asks me to leave it on. He unbuttons my nightgown and helps me lift it off over my head. His hand curves around my breast, but then he stiffens. He reaches past me and pulls the lamp on the nightstand closer.

"You have another bruise," he says.

The bruise on my shoulder is already only a faded yellow, a pale smear he wouldn't have noticed if the light weren't on. "It's an old one," I say.

"No, it's not. Ricky hit you again."

I can lie by omission, but I cannot get away with a deliberate lie to Ian.

"Are you going to write him up?"

At the Youth Guidance Authority, even the volunteers are

required to write up the kids' offenses. If I write Ricky up, they'll probably cancel his tutoring sessions. I'm teaching him to read, and I think we are making progress. He no longer strikes out with his fists. The mark on my arm was left by the spine of a book that he meant only to slam through the air. It isn't really his fault that he is living in a thirteen-year-old body that has so far outgrown the five-year-old fury he needs a chance to feel.

"It was an accident this time," I say.

Ian rolls away from me. "I don't know why you volunteer for this. Why you have to take on the hopeless cases."

"I like teaching."

"You should have a real teaching job. Both the kids are in school now. They don't need you every minute."

"Don't nag," I say. I climb onto Ian and straddle him. I search in the froth of fur on his chest for the tiny knots of his nipples. He sighs. He gives in to persuasion.

Penance

Ian wants me to go back to work full-time, now that Fiona is in kindergarten. I don't see how I can. My tutoring hours are scheduled around the midday trip back to school to change Danny's urine bag so he won't have to have a stranger do it. After school I take the kids to art class or deliver Danny to physical therapy or pick up Fiona from soccer practice. This year I have to visit schools, find a good one that can accommodate Danny's wheelchair. Ian says I've done my penance, the spina bifida support group can survive without me to lick stamps and xerox pamphlets, Danny's entitled to an attendant in the classroom, Fiona has too many afterschool activities.

What I do not want to give up is the sweet slowness of motherhood. The way you have to flow like water around interruptions, sudden crises, the storming force of a five-year-old's wants. Yesterday Danny did his homework at the kitchen table while I made dinner. Fiona spread paper and crayons every-where, determined to do homework like Danny. At the stove I stirred oregano and cumin into black bean soup. At the table I leaned over Danny to check whether he was carrying over into the second column of numbers as he added, and turning back to the stove, I dripped syrupy liquid from the wooden spoon onto Fiona's mock homework. After we patted Fiona's paper dry, I washed lettuce, went back and forth from Danny's math to the sink to the stove, picked up a bowl of faded narcissus blooms to dump the spent bulbs in the garbage, and got stopped by Danny. He wanted to know what was inside a bulb, what it made the flowers from. He wants to learn every secret in the universe, every secret adults have been able to keep from him until now. I got a knife and we cut into the bulb together, with Fiona crawl-ing up onto the table, complaining we wouldn't let her see. We found out that a bulb is just an onion, concentric rings of wa-tery tissue. We were so satisfied: we knew something, but the mystery of the flowers remained intact.

Works

I come home to an empty house. Ian forgets about the kids' bedtime when he takes them down to his garage workshop. He loves everything about making furniture except the fact that only rich people can afford to buy his custom tables and side-boards. When I go downstairs to fetch the kids for bed, Danny is pulled up to the table helping Ian plane a plank of cherry, re-leasing the rich smell of the wood in the fresh shavings, and Fiona is on the floor hammering away at her invention.

Nobody's glad to see me. Fiona immediately starts to cry and beg for more time, and Danny pleads in his calmer way. Even Ian asks for five more minutes, so I pull up a stool and watch them. Sometimes I worry about how much time the kids spend in the workshop—though Ian takes each completed piece of furniture outside to hand oil the wood, the finished pieces are brought back in, where they weep their new coat of poison into the air.

Ian asks me how the visit went, and I tell him fine. When parents of newborns call the support group, someone always goes in person to bring them literature, to hold the baby and coo over it. I always bring photos, Danny the poster child at the beach with his sister or perched on a carousel horse, smiling.

Ian reaches up to the orderly tool rack above his worktable and pulls down safety glasses for himself and Danny. Then he lays the plank on a sawhorse, tightens the vise that holds it in place, and begins to saw its end, where he has traced in faint pencil the shape of the grooves he'll match to the tongues already cut into the table's base. With a steady hand, he cuts out the perfect ellipses of the grooves. I've never seen Ian damage wood. My father was a carpenter, in the trades, and he hauled off on two-by-four's all day and didn't worry about splinters. Ian was a philosophy major when we met in college, and he treats wood as if it would be a sacrilege to harm its integrity—cuts along the grain, accommodates knots and fractures, avoids using nails whenever he can. Now he sands the grooves to the smoothness of polished stone, and urges Danny to move his hands more gently as he helps to sand the wood.

Fiona elbows Danny and demands a turn with the sandpaper. He refuses her.

"Danny," Ian says, "you always share."

Danny tears off a stingy strip of sandpaper, and Fiona is so tired she just grips it and cries. I haul her into my lap. By the time Ian lays the plank of cherry on its base—it's the top of a console table—she is sucking her thumb. I remind Danny that he's late for bed and it's a school night.

"I'm not going to bed," Danny says.

Ian looks at him funny. "I'll glue this in place with you tomorrow," he says.

"I'm not going," Danny says.

"Sure you are." Ian swings Danny out of the chair and smacks him onto his hip.

Danny struggles in his father's arms and reaches for his chair.

"Danny," Ian says in surprise. We get this from Fiona, but from Danny, never.

I've abruptly forgotten all I know about tantrums, sit mired by the same confusion I feel when I visit the new parents, as if I can't begin to imagine what they must feel.

Danny howls, pounds away at Ian so that Ian flinches, jerks his head back. Ian spills him onto the floor, where Danny wriggles, coating himself in sawdust.

"Behave yourself!" Ian says.

On his back, Danny inches himself away from his father on his elbows, dragging the dead weight of his legs, screaming up at him that he won't go to bed, he won't go. Ian swallows hard, tells Danny to stop that.

Ian scoops Danny up again, quickly. He fits Danny's shoulders under his arm, so Danny can't get his arms free, can't twist his torso uselessly. Then he kicks Danny's chair out of the way and makes for the stairs.

Danny howls all the way up the stairs, howls when we take him to the bathroom to brush his teeth, howls when we give up on trying to get a toothbrush in his mouth and dump him in bed, howls when I try to read to him.

"You can't make me sleep," he screams at me. "You can't make me!"

I shut the book, and Ian moves for the door. When I reach for Danny to stroke his hair, he swings wildly at me, hands fisted. Ian tells Danny to calm down and tell us what the trouble is, but Danny howls louder to drown out his words.

"Let him cry it out," Ian says finally.

I don't want to leave Danny like this. I never left the kids to cry themselves to sleep, even when they were babies.

"Maybe he doesn't like us carting him around anymore," I say. "Maybe you should put in that ramp."

"Oh, Jesus," Ian says. "He's never minded it before. He's just being bad."

Danny's crying keeps Fiona awake for another hour. Finally, he stops. In the morning when I get up, I find him asleep on the floor in the hallway. I can imagine the work it took for him to lift his legs over the side of the bed with his hands, grip the edge of the bed and push off so he'd slump to the floor, haul himself to the door, pull himself up to turn the knob, so he could curl up out here. When I wake him, his first words are, "You can't make me sleep." He's limp with exhaustion when I carry him back to the bed, asleep again in spite of himself. I keep him home from school.

Mortification of the Flesh

Hunched over the picture book, glancing up at me now and then from beneath his heavy eyebrows, Ricky sounds out the words on the page, and the effort of his muscles, his tongue, produces a halting, crippled language of moaning vowels and spitting consonants. He's reading *Little Bear*, a favorite of Fiona's.

He pushes the book away from him. "I'm tired of this mess."

"We have twenty more minutes," I tell him. I slide the book back toward him, put my elbow on the table and rest my chin in my hand. "You're making good progress."

He works his shoulders, like a football player collecting his body in readiness, and his arm brushes mine as he bends his neck to the book again. Even this glancing touch of his has an aureole of hurt, of shame, that plucks at my nerves and makes me edge away from him.

"His mauth-er smill. Duh. Smiled. Lid-ul Bear was hap-pee." Ricky tosses the book and scrapes his chair back, seems to grow bigger as his body spills over from the tension of concentration, arms and legs tumbling free like clumsy clubs. I pick up the book, and he slaps at it lazily. His knuckle grazes my mouth, and for a moment we're both startled. How can the looseness of his limbs have such force?

I taste blood. Ricky mutters that he's sorry, but he watches me suck blood from my lip with a keenness that approaches hunger.

I'm not really religious. All that clings to me of my mother's faith, her special devotion to the Blessed Mother, the Hail Marys counted on the beads of the rosary, is the impulse to yield, to trust some looming vagueness that can descend like fierce beauty.

"What if I read to you for a while?" I say.

He shifts in his chair, but lets me get the book and begin where we left off the last time I was here. Ricky likes fairy tales, from the real Brothers Grimm, not the bowdlerized children's picture books. Ricky likes the fat book I open, likes to look over my shoulder at the tiny print, which satisfies him that we are not reading "no baby shit" like *Little Bear*. He's a little restless at the beginning, when the true mother lying on her death bed draws Cinderella to her and tells her to be good and pious, but he grins with pleasure when the stepmother moves in, "vile and black of heart."

When I get to the part in the story where the stepmother makes Cinderella pick lentils out of the ashes in the fireplace, Ricky nods. "That's how they do you here," he says. "They make it so you have to get written up. No way they gonna let you have all these privileges they tell you about."

Ricky interrupts me again when Cinderella succeeds at yet another impossible task set for her by her stepmother. "Now that bitch gonna find something else she have to do before she can go to the dance."

For a moment I wish I could pull him into my lap or curl up beside him in bed to read to him, so that we could hear the words of the story in the warmth of each other's body heat. I want to reroot his life in the pleasure my own children have had, pressing against me as I read to them, interrupting as Ricky does, to wonder or be satisfied, to be fed by the sound of my voice, the soft pulse of my breath on their scalps, the fit of their smallness against the rolling slopes of myself.

Cinderella goes to the grave of her dead mother and gets magical help so that she can go to the ball, and this pleases Ricky almost as much as the wickedness of the stepmother. He hasn't seen his own mother in over four years.

Ricky laughs when the prince comes to Cinderella's house, bearing the shoe, and the stepmother urges her eldest daughter to cut off her toes so that her foot will fit in the shoe. In this, the story's free province of anger, he roots himself. But he worries when the ruse succeeds and the prince takes the stepsister with him on his horse, exhales relief when the prince discovers the blood running from her shoe and returns the false bride to her mother. After Cinderella tries on the shoe, after she marries her prince, pigeons come to peck out the eyes of the wicked step-sisters, and Ricky claps his hands and says, "Oh, that's good."

I close the book and retrieve *Little Bear*. "A few more pages of this, OK?"

"You said if I do my work, I can play cards," Ricky says.

Sometimes we play poker. Ricky likes to play for money even though he doesn't get to keep it, so my purse is always weighted by a Baggie of pennies.

"Not today," I say. "You didn't work hard enough."

He swings his arm. "That's not fair. You said."

"No cards today."

He grabs my arms in both of his. "You said, you said," he pleads. I'm looking into the eyes of a child, and his fingers are grinding against my bones, and I have to grit my teeth to stand it, and I know that his fingers will leave marks again, that his pain will bloom and fade on my skin for days after this.

Renunciation

Ian and I arrive at the school at two-thirty and go to the principal's office. Danny's teacher, Louise, is there, waiting for us, with Sandra, the principal. Sandra offers us coffee, flutters over us till we settle into the two chairs pulled up before her desk. The teacher called at noon to ask us to come in today, and I'm nervous.

"What's wrong?" I say. "Did something happen to Danny?"

"Danny's all right," Louise says. She bites her lip, looks at the principal, and then goes on. "It was James's turn to stay in with Danny at recess this morning, and when we came back in, I caught them lighting matches."

James, hell on wheels, is Danny's favorite in the class. This morning Danny asked me if James would be at his new school with him next year.

"Not Danny," I say. "Danny wouldn't do that."

"Danny had the matches," Louise says. She won't look at me.

"OK," Ian says. "Boys will be boys. Is that why you called us in? Is that all?"

"They were burning paper," Louise says. "I had to open all the windows to air out the room. They could have started a fire."

"How did Danny get ahold of matches?" I say.

"We'll talk to Danny," Ian says. "And whatever the punishment is, Danny will have to live with the consequences."

Sandra clears her throat. "The ultimate consequence for starting a fire is typically that the child is expelled."

Ian stares at her. His voice is scratchy when he speaks. "It's kid stuff," he says.

Sandra says, "Given the age of the children, we'd be reluctant to take the step of expelling them. There are other measures that seem more appropriate."

Louise takes a deep breath. "I'm concerned about Danny.

He's been—difficult these past few weeks. He won't cooperate in group projects. He wrote on his desk."

"Oh, come on," Ian says. "How many kids write on their desks when the teacher isn't looking? You're making a mountain out of a molehill."

I think of Louise interrupting class to greet Danny when we arrive late, always taking the time to settle him in. She's had plenty of chances to act worried. "Why didn't you tell me Danny was having problems?"

"I guess it's like your husband says," Louise says. "You take any one of these things by itself, it doesn't seem like much. But now I think Danny's feeling left out. All the other boys are on the soccer team together. He can't join the kids at recess."

"Goddamn it," Ian says. "You were so happy to have us enroll Danny here. It would be no problem to accommodate his chair. You can't even figure out a way for him to get out to the play yard, and you want that to be his fault."

I put a hand on Ian's arm, but he shakes it off.

Louise opens her mouth to speak, stops, and looks at Sandra.

"It might be time to consider therapy," Sandra says. "Nobody wants to blow things out of proportion, but maybe it's better to be on the safe side."

Ian gets to his feet. I can feel Louise and Sandra shrink back from the sheer fact of his size as he stands over them.

"You're a bunch of prissy hens," he says. "What we ought to do is sue you for not putting in an elevator so Danny can move to the upstairs classroom next year."

Ian turns and walks out of the room, yanking the door open and slamming it behind him. Sandra and Louise look at me, and I look back at them. They are poised to flinch or to leap from their chairs.

"I'm sorry," I say. "I hope you can understand. Ian and I will talk about this. We both want to do what's best for Danny."

It goes away, the tension of whatever they were waiting for.

"Teresa, I'm sorry," Sandra says. "I'm so sorry."

"You're not going to expel the boys?" I say.

"No. A two-day suspension, out of school."

"That makes sense," I say. "What they did was dangerous."

A buzzer sounds to mark the end of the school day, and noise erupts in the hall as kids pour out of their classrooms to collect their backpacks and jackets from their lockers. In a few moments, Danny and Fiona will be waiting for me at the front door.

I feel as if I have to collect many things, piles of packages, parts of myself, in order to get up out of this chair. I thank Sandra and Louise for their concern, and then I go to meet Danny and Fiona.

Fiona rushes me when she sees me, hangs on my arm as I move to Danny in his chair, tells me she has to bring in an egg carton for art tomorrow.

Danny looks up at me warily. "Am I in trouble?"

"Big trouble," I say. "We're going to have a serious talk when we get home."

"We didn't mean it," Danny says.

I wonder where Ian is. I look at the long line of cars pulled up before the school, and I'm relieved to see the van near the tail end of the line.

"I don't want Dad to be mad at me," Danny says.

There's a tightness in his face that reminds me of Ricky's face as Ricky struggles with the humiliation of printed words. Now I can see James and Danny dropping burning paper as it curls and blackens in their fingers. I feel sick, so sick that I want to scoop Danny in my arms to hide this from him.

I can't allow myself that impulse. I crouch beside his chair so that our eyes are level. "I think *you* must be mad."

Softness briefly resurfaces on his face. I brush his hair back from his forehead to get a last glimpse of that angel's face before it sinks and disappears.

When Ian pulls up to the curb, he gets out of the van to lift

Danny into the backseat. I fold the chair and put it in the van, buckle in the kids before I climb in the front beside Ian.

I don't trust myself to look at Ian. A thrumming rises from him, frantic as a pounding fist, and it's all I can do to keep my body from answering it, from moving into step with Ian's the way it always has, so many times, to find such pleasure. At the first stoplight we come to, Ian puts an arm over the back of the seat and glances back at Danny. He says, "No TV for two weeks, young man."

Signs

After we get home, Ian whisks Danny up the stairs and I follow with Fiona, the kids' backpacks, and the wheelchair. When I unfold the wheelchair for Danny, Ian drops him in and says he has to go back to the workshop, make up for the time he lost this afternoon. He's out the door before Fiona starts to beg for a snack.

In the kitchen I toast bagels and slather them with cream cheese, cut apple slices, and pour juice for the kids. They sit together at the table. Danny complains that Fiona is chewing with her mouth open, and Fiona hotly denies it.

She starts to cry. "Make him say I'm not."

"You're a pig," Danny says.

Fiona hits him, and when Danny swats back, she easily snakes out of his reach.

"I hate you," Danny says. "I hate you."

I pull his chair back from the table. "Danny! Don't talk to your sister like that."

"I hate you," Danny says. "I hate everyone."

I look down at his stony little face, the stubborn set of his jaw that is so unfamiliar, so new. I pull up a chair beside him and reach for him. "Come here, honey."

He crosses his arms and shakes his head. "I'm not a baby."

I pry his arms loose and lift them from the chair to my lap.

He struggles at first, the way he struggled with Ian the other night, and then he folds his arms again in tense resistance. I stroke his hair, I hum for him the music that he likes.

"You're my baby, even though you're big," I say.

He turns his face sharply, butting against my collarbone. Suddenly he's weeping, not making noise like a little kid does, but hacking at air. He clings to me. The marks Ricky left on my arms ache a little under the pressure of Danny's hands, each oval, each imprint of Ricky's fingers a distinct tiny echo of the pain that made it. There is no renouncing this, my beautiful boy crying in my arms.

Fiona goes away and comes back with a Lego truck. "You can have it, Danny," she says. She tries to press it into his hands, but he won't take it, and the truck drops to the floor and snaps into pieces.

Fiona plops down to put it back together, forgets about us as she goes about her task. She can't figure out how to reattach the bumper, keeps breaking off more bits of the truck.

"Gimme," Danny says with sleepy interest. He squirms in my arms, and I set him down on the floor so he can work beside Fiona to put the truck back together.

I tell the kids I have to go talk to Daddy and I'll be right back.

I carefully step over the profuse mess of Fiona's invention when I enter the workshop. Ian has left the sliding glass door open. He's outside on the patio, oiling a display cabinet, and the radio on his worktable is turned up full blast. He's not wearing the face mask like he should be. I turn off the radio. The smooth circling motion of his arm stops a moment, then continues. For a moment I feel so sorry for him.

The cabinet he's working on matches two that are already complete, waiting in the workshop to be delivered. Each cabinet has doors made from leaded stained glass that Ian salvaged and reframed. I can't resist the impulse to touch the smooth top of the cabinet nearest me, and the wood slips gloatingly under my hand.

Ian's back is to me. He still won't come in. He's left a saw lying on his worktable, a sloppiness that is unlike him. I raise the saw like a hammer and bring it down on the unmarred wood of the cabinet. On impact, the saw recoils like a spring, its shudder echoing in my arms. Raw bite marks stipple the dark finish of the wood. I bring the saw down again, slashing this time so that I make one smooth long scar, one searing consequence. I move to the next cabinet and the saw sings in the air as I bring it down with all my force. The wood splinters beneath this blow.

Ian comes inside now. He yanks the saw from my hand. He throws it away from us. He steps back from me, leans against his worktable. He's breathing hard.

I reach for him. He catches my wrists and traps them in one fist, his elbow locked to keep me at a distance.

"Ian, please."

"You're sick," he says. "You need help. Look what you let that boy do to you."

With his free hand, he pushes up my sleeves to expose the bruises above my elbows, the tawny scatter of spots on a fawn's back.

I try to raise my hands, but I can't get past the barrier of his stiff arm, the handcuff of his fist.

"Don't you touch me," he says.

I walk at him, into him, into the brace his arms make, move through them somehow to press myself against his body, the big awning of his shoulders, the twin solid knobs of his hips. I lean into him, keep pushing. This first, and then I will comfort him. Then I will tell him that suffering brings us closer to God.

Living with Lilia

Suzanne Kamata

Eighteen years ago, I came to this country to teach English. I fell in love with and married a Japanese man who, before meeting me, had never been out of the country. As a person who enjoys solitude, I thought I was well suited to a Japanese marriage. My husband, Yoshi, worked seven days a week, up to twelve hours a day, teaching high school and coaching baseball. His job involved many evenings of eating and drinking without me. In the early years of our marriage, when he was off with the teachers in his department or parents of his baseball players or other coaches, I had the evening to myself—time to write, or read, or to go for long, contemplative walks. Although we took trips together, I was free to take off to Europe to participate in a writing workshop for a couple of weeks or to visit friends across the United States, on my own. I'd always liked having autonomy in our marriage, even though I sometimes regretted not being able to entertain or attend social gatherings as a couple. Then we decided to start a family.

I knew that having children would be difficult in Japan. My sister-in-law, whose children were six and eight, told me that she'd never had a babysitter, and that the only time she was ever apart from her daughters was when she went to get a haircut. Most nights, her husband played mahjong after work and didn't get home until after his family was asleep. I found this hard to believe, and I vowed that things would be different after my husband and I had kids. I would have a life of my own. Yoshi and I would go out on dates. I would find a baby-sitter.

The premature birth of our twins, at twenty-six weeks, changed all that. For one, it immediately set us apart as a family in a very literal way. For the first four months of their existence, we were fractured. Our babies struggled along in their Plexiglas Isolettes in the NICU at Tokushima University Hospital, where the doctors and nurses did most of the feeding (intravenously, and later, through gastric tubes) and changing of diapers. Only parents were allowed in that chamber of bright lights and beeping monitors. We had to have permission from the doctors and nurses to hold the babies. My mother-in-law wasn't allowed to see them at all.

When Jio and Lilia were both finally released from the hospital, our family went into isolation. The doctor warned us that a simple cold could turn into a life-threatening respiratory infection. He suggested the possibility of heart failure. It would take at least two years, he said, for their lungs to fully develop. In the meantime, we would need to avoid crowded places—supermarkets, restaurants, nursery schools, libraries, playgroups, birthday parties—all the venues where new mothers converge to share wisdom and reduce stress. Walks around the neighborhood were risky because there'd always be some bent-backed granny wanting to poke her finger into their plush pink cheeks. The world was suddenly teeming with germs.

*

My parents and other relatives were fourteen time zones away, but my Japanese mother-in-law came over to help several times a week, resulting in the usual generational and cultural disputes. For instance, she wanted the babies to be swathed with blankets in the middle of summer, while I wanted them to be comfortable; she wanted to give them homemade carrot juice with honey, while I raged about the possibility of botulism. Still, I needed her help. I also called upon a battalion of older Japanese housewife friends, mostly women who'd faithfully attended the English classes I'd taught at the town hall, women interested in foreign cultures.

In some ways, I remember those days as idyllic. Jio and Lilia slept through the night from the time they came home from the hospital. They took long naps, sometimes simultaneously, and I had all those helping hands, allowing me to go for walks or write. But still, I longed for my peers—other mommies navigating the same terrain, with children who might become friends with mine.

For a long time, I figured that this intense period of isolation would be followed by a more or less normal experience of motherhood. I believed that once my twins caught up, once their lungs had developed fully, they would have a typical childhood—one comparable to that of the many children I'd taught at public schools in Japan. Of course, they'd have their differences. My children would speak both Japanese and English. Instead of going up to Kamiyama Shinrin Park or even Tokyo Disneyland during summer vacations, they'd jet off to America. And I was looking forward to seeing how that twin thing would develop. My grandmother, who was a twin, often spoke about the special bond she'd shared with her sister. My sister-in-law spoke to her identical twin on the phone several times a day. Would my kids develop a secret twin language? Would they bond most intensely with each other, like the books said, making me the third wheel? Being twins, I thought, automatically gave each of them an ally. Sure, they might be bullied a bit in Japanese public schools, where everyone is supposed to look and behave in the same way, but they'd have each other.

I didn't know then that Lilia was deaf and that her brain had been injured. I didn't know that, because of her, our home would become a house of Babel, where we would use Japanese, English, and Japanese Sign Language in various degrees of proficiency, sometimes translating for one another. Jio and Lilia would not be able to go to school together, and would develop separate cultures. One would start to walk and then run and then climb trees, while the other would drag herself along the floor with one arm until finally, years later, she learned to crawl. And instead of surrounding myself with older, supportive Japanese women interested in foreign cultures, I would soon be spending a lot of time with Japanese mothers of deaf children who viewed me as profoundly "other." Now, no one ever asked for my autograph or invited me to appear on TV or threw parties in my honor. At the deaf school, I was simply the gaijin who had a hard time learning to finger-spell in Japanese, the klutz who didn't know how to make tea. And I understood. These mothers didn't have time to think about foreign cultures. They had problems of their own.

One mother worried that her youngest daughter's deafness would affect her hearing eight-year-old daughter's marriage prospects. Other mothers lamented the fact that their children were not welcome in public schools. Although Japanese law requires disabled children to be educated, they are mostly limited to schools for the disabled, unless their mothers are willing to spend months or even years lobbying for a spot in a public school.

It's always the mothers. In Japan, child-rearing is shared by the mother and grandparents. The father's job is to make money. The fathers are working until 11:00 p.m., or abroad on business trips for multinational corporations, or off playing pachinko or drinking with coworkers. The teachers at the deaf school say that it's harder for Japanese fathers to accept their children's disabilities. Maybe that's because they are so removed from the daily lives of their families. The mothers I've met at the deaf school clearly love their children and constantly advocate for them. But most of the fathers can't even be bothered to learn sign language.

According to Japanese tradition, my husband, as the eldest (and only) son, is responsible for taking care of his mother in her old age. Yoshi assured me when he asked me to marry him that his parents didn't expect us to move in with them, but when we decided to buy a house, his mother confessed that she'd been hoping we'd all live together. I thought of my grandmother, who'd blamed her divorce in part on her live-in German mother-in-law. I couldn't imagine sharing a kitchen—a life— with my conservative Japanese mother-in-law.

However, a month after we signed the deal for our new house, my father-in-law was diagnosed with lung cancer. Another month later, he was dead, leaving my mother-in-law all alone in her large house. Yoshi's Confucian ethics kicked in. From then on, he lobbied for us to move in with her. For ten years, my response was, "Hell, no!"

When I tried to teach her a few signs, she seemed unwilling to learn, but Lilia adored her. I gradually came to realize that Grandma's reluctance to learn sign language might be a good thing. We were living in Japan, but I made many mistakes in speaking Japanese, and I can read and write at only a very basic level. With my husband gone all the time, there was no one around to model Japanese for Lilia. If we lived with her grandmother, whom she adored, Lilia would have incentive to learn the language. I'd also have a little help around the house.

For a while, I tried to be independent, taking my daughter to the deaf school and to her various therapies, doing research on the Internet, talking to other moms. But after five years of spending almost every waking moment devoted to my children with no real end in sight, I was ready for some respite. My daughter still couldn't walk, and although she'd had an operation for a cochlear implant, she couldn't talk. She would obviously need me for a long time. At least my mother-in-law would be able to look after the kids for a small part of the day, long enough for me to make a run to the grocery store. And she'd be able to help with Japanese homework and occasionally baby-sit when Yoshi and I could arrange a date night. So, after ten years of "no," I finally said "yes" to living with my mother-in-law.

Yoshi's idea was that we would sell our house and renovate his mother's larger house, adding a small annex for her, where she would be assured a bit of privacy. Our new dwelling would be accessible and healthy—a haven for our disabled daughter. There would be a ramp for her wheelchair. The doors would slide open easily. The wallpaper would be resistant to bacteria and mold. The floors, where Lilia tended to crawl, would be heated in winter, and there would be bars on the walls that she could grab onto when she tried to walk. After his mother died, Yoshi said, Lilia could live in the annex, where there was a small kitchen and a bath.

I had been led to believe that my mother-in-law wanted us to live together more than anything, but she balked at first. She said that the neighbors would talk about Lilia. *What would they say*, I wondered. That she couldn't walk? That she was deaf? That she couldn't talk? All of these things were true, so why bother hiding them? I'd read that, according to traditional Japanese belief, a child's disability was deemed to be due to the sins of the mother. Was it possible that my mother-in-law's neighbors would think that we were tainted somehow? Could they be that superstitious at the dawning of the twenty-first century? If so, I figured they were due for some enlightenment.

We moved in at the beginning of summer. Not long after that, I saw a girl wandering in the street by herself. She was wearing a red helmet, the kind worn by disabled children who are apt to fall down. I was stunned. Why hadn't my mother-in-law mentioned this child? Did she even know that there was another disabled child living just a couple houses away?

Several months later, I set out on foot for the grocery store. I had gone just a few yards when I heard a familiar voice. I turned to see two little girls, siblings, who attend the School for the Deaf, my daughter's school. They were visiting relatives —the people who live in the house across the street. Once again, I wondered why this coincidence had never come up in conversation. How lonely it must be always to be hiding one's differences.

Pushing my daughter in her wheelchair to the grocery store sometimes feels like a political act. *Here, look at her*, I want to say. I refuse to hide this kid. She is beautiful and smart and friendly. If you look at her enough, you will get used to the legs that don't work, the magnet sticking to her head, the hearing aid nestled in her ear. Lilia demands attention. She smiles at everyone we pass, and, usually, they smile and wave back. I wouldn't be able to hide her away even if I tried; she wants to be out in the world.

I like to think that we are promoting tolerance and social justice in this farming community, but sometimes I dream about bringing her back to the states where I believe we wouldn't have to fight so hard. At the same time, I know that my daughter loves and needs her father and grandmother, and that she is a part of this culture. Lilia, who bows without thinking, who is endlessly folding paper into origami shapes, who adores kimono, is more a part of this country than I can ever hope to be.

This is not the family I imagined back in Michigan when I was playing with my dolls, back in the days when my dad came home at 5:30 every evening and was home every weekend, and my grandparents lived in other cities. Our family life is sometimes messy and complicated, but it is rich. Living this way has opened my eyes to the possibilities of family. I once believed that my children would grow up and leave, but now I expect that we will be responsible for each other in one way or another until we die. And although my husband and mother-in-law may still be thinking that Lilia will be dependent on us for her entire life, I am imagining the ways in which she might be independent. Perhaps one day she will have a family of her own— a husband and children, or a group of caring friends who live together. Maybe they will be Japanese, maybe many different nationalities. Maybe they will be disabled, maybe not.

In the meantime, we continue to learn by living with Lilia. So far, she has taught us never to take anything about the body for granted, including the ability to breathe; that there is always something to laugh about; that there are worse things than being noticed by the neighbors; that you don't have to be able to walk in order to dance; and that there is no such thing as a normal family.

Termite's Birthday, 1959

Jayne Anne Phillips

Nonie hates the idea of blue cake, she says it looks like something old and spoiled, too old to eat, though it's light and delicate and flavored with anise. But Termite likes it, and he likes pink cake that tastes of almond, and mostly he likes me putting the batter in different bowls, holding them in the crook of his arm while I bend over him, stirring. I tell him how fast a few drops of color land dense as tinted black and turn the mix pastel. I make three thin layers, pale blue and pink and yellow, and I put three pans in to bake, shut the door of the oven fast to pretend I'm not making everything still hotter.

"Hot as Hades today," I tell Termite, and I move his chair so he gets the hint of breath from the window. The radio cord still reaches and he turns the knob with his wrist, slow or fast, like a safe-cracker, like there's some sense to the sounds, the static and the interrupted news.

"Don't try talking to me in radio," I tell him, but he does anyway. As long as he holds it, he'll be trying to make it talk. I take the radio out of his lap and put it back on the counter, and I hold a bowl of icing down low. I hold the little bottle of blue, no bigger than a doll bottle, in Termite's hand, and we let just three drops fall. Divinity icing makes peaks and gets a sweet crust like meringue. Mine is like sugared air that disappears in your mouth. Nonie says I'm a fabulous cook. I could cook for a living, she says, but not at Charlie's, where she works, or anything like it. The egg whites can go bad fast in hot weather but I turn up the fridge to keep the icing cool on the lowest shelf, and we'll eat it today, this birthday. Nick Tucci will take some home to his kids. Nobody makes those boys cakes. Rat boys, Nonie calls Nick's kids, like she's disappointed in them. Delinquents like cake too, I tell her. You be sure cake is all you're making them, Nonie says. Then she'll say she wasn't born yesterday, like anyone ever bothers me. I tell her no one does. They only look. Looking never bothered anybody.

It's true. It's like I've got a beam out my eyes that backs people off. Now that I'm seventeen and graduated high school, I've got a clear space around me I didn't have before. I wonder it that's like a future, or a place where a future will be.

I remember when Termite came. Nonie is our guardian and our aunt but I'm Termite's sister. In a way he's more mine than anyone else's. He'll be mine for longer, is what Nonie says. Nonie isn't old but she always says to me about when she's gone. She looks so strong, like a block or a rectangle, strong in her shoulders and her back and her wide hips, even in her legs and their blue veins that she covers up with her stockings. Your mother didn't bring him, is what Nonie told me, someone brought him for her. Not his father. Nonie says Termite's father was only married to my mother for a year. He was a baby, Nonie says, twenty-three when my mother was thirty-five, and those bastards left him over there in Korea. No one even got his body back and they had to have the service around a flag that was folded up. Nonie says it was wrong and it will never be right. But I don't know how Termite got here because Nonie sent me away that week to church camp. He was nearly a year old but he couldn't sit up by himself, and Nonie had him a baby bed and clothes and a high chair with cushions and straps, and she had papers that were signed. She never got a birth certificate though, so we count the day he came his birthday, but I make him a birthday when it suits me.

Pale-blue divinity sounds like a dress or a planet. Blue icing does look strange, like Martian food, unless I trim it, so I saved out some white for a lattice over the top, or garlands and flowers. A decorated cake looks like a toy, and people do want it. I'm putting the icings away to keep them cold and I've got my whole face in the fridge, near the steaming icebox at the top. The sweat across my upper lip dries in a sudden tingle and then I hear someone at the door. The bell rings, and it rings in a way I can tell is new.

Good thing or bad thing, I think.

Termite gets quiet.

"Who can that be?" I say out loud, like a charm. Like we're in a TV show about a charming mother and her kid. But we don't have a TV. Termite doesn't like those sounds. Joey always had the TV on at Tucci's, and Termite wouldn't even go inside. Back then, all those summers. He liked to be moving, or by the river, in the tunnel under the cool of the bridge. There's two bridges in town, both spanning the river: the spiny one for cars, all metal ribs and rattles, and the concrete one for trains, wide enough for four lines of track. Once they used all the tracks, Nonie says. Now just two are kept repaired, but the arches of the bridge are just as wide and the tunnel below as long and shady and deep. Termite likes it best. The echoes.

The doorbell rings again, twice. Somebody won't give up.

I push Termite's chair out past the dinette into the living room. I leave him sitting by the piano and through the window in the door I can see somebody. Brown suit-coat and trousers, in this heat. Tie and button-down shirt. Glasses. I open the door and there's a man standing there with his briefcase in his arms, like he's about to hand it over to me. Not a real old man. Thick lenses in the glasses, so his eyes look magnified. Owl eyes. White-blond hair parted to the side under his hat. Fedora, like a banker's.

"Hello there," he says. "Hope it's not too early to stop by. I was hoping I could speak to—" He looks down at the papers he's got on top of the briefcase.

"My mother's not here," I say.

"—your aunt. It says here your aunt. You must be Lark."

"You're from Social Services," I say.

"Yes. I'm the new caseworker assigned to your family. Actually, I live two streets over, moved in a week ago. I was on my way to work, so I thought I'd stop." He smiles in a nervous way. "That's the good thing about these small towns," he says. "You can walk to work. Anyway, I can. I suppose you can walk to the high school."

"I'm not at the high school. I take a secretarial course." I've got my hand on the door and I push it shut just a little.

He steps up closer and looks over my shoulder at Termite in his chair. "This is your brother? Termite. A nickname, I'd guess. What's his real name?"

"Terence," I lie. I always seem to start lying to these people real quick. Even if I don't have to.

"By the way, my name is Robert Stamble." He sticks his hand out at me from under the briefcase.

Stumble, Stamble, I think. And from then on he's stumble, stammer, tumble, someone tripping in my head. Right away, I think he'd better leave. He thinks he means well and he doesn't know anything. I can smell it on him like a hint, like the Old Spice smell of his aftershave. I hate that smell. Dads wear it in Dadville. I look at him closer and see that he doesn't even look old enough to be much of a dad. He's pale pink as the rims of a rabbit's eyes, and blue-eyed behind his thick glasses. Hiding in his suit.

"Nonie's not here," I say, "and she says the check we get from Social Services is not enough to be harangued or bothered about. If you want to make a home visit, you should arrange it with her."

"You know," he says, "we're very much in favor of in-home care whenever possible, and we want to support you. There may be ways we can help. Physical therapy. Equipment. A wheelchair."

"He's got a wheelchair," I say, "a big heavy one. We keep it in the closet. He doesn't like it, but we use it for his medical appointments."

He fumbles around, opens the briefcase, shuffles papers. "Oh. Yes, of course, says so here in the file." He looks up at me. "One of the chairs Alderson passed on to the county."

Alderson is the state hospital that closed last year, one town over. They shipped the craziest loonies somewhere else and let go the ones that were only taking up space.

Stamble persists. "Still, don't you find it easier than—"

I get it. He's seen me pull Termite in the wagon. I do most every day. The wagon is deep and safe, with high wooden slats for sides, and long enough Termite can stretch his legs out. It's like the old wagons they used to haul ice or coal. It was in the basement of this house when Nonie moved in, she says it's probably older than she is. "Termite doesn't like the wheelchair," I repeat.

Stamble nods. "He's a child. He should have a smaller chair, one his size. Something portable would be easier for you."

I think about that. Portable. Coming into port, like on a boat. Termite, bobbing on the waves. I'm watching him through a round window small as a plate. A porthole. We're coming up on a pretty little town by the sea, and Stamble blink, blink, blinks. For a minute I think he's fooling with me, then I realize he's nervous. Where did they get him?

He goes at me. "The newer chairs are lightweight. Easy to fold and unfold, take in and out of an automobile, whatever."

"We don't have an automobile," I tell Stamble, "and I've never seen a chair like that around here." I step back. "Anyway, he doesn't like the chair he already has."

"Maybe he needs a chance to get used to it, gradually of course. Does he mind the medical appointments?"

"No, not really. I wouldn't say he minds."

"Because if he associates a wheelchair only with something

he doesn't like, you could maybe change that by taking him to do something he really does like ... in the wheelchair."

I shift my weight and stand so he can't see behind me. Termite stays real quiet. If he knows when to be quiet, I don't know how they can say he doesn't know anything. "Maybe so," I tell Stamble. "I've got to go now. I've got a cake baking." I'm easing the door closed.

"Hot day for baking," he says. "Someone's birthday?"

I nod and smile through the narrow space that's left. "You can call Noreen," I say. "If there's anything." And the door is shut. I feel the knob turn in my hand and I hear the click.

"Very good to meet you," I hear Stamble say from outside. "I'll see what I can do about a more suitable chair." Then I hear his footsteps going away. Termite has his head turned, his ear tilted toward me, and he doesn't move. I walk across the room to turn his chair back toward the kitchen and then I smell the cake, a sugary, toasted smell with a brown edge. "Oh, no," I say, and move him back just enough to get the oven open, grab the layer pans with the hot pads. The cakes are a little too brown on top, but not bad. I show him one. "It's fine," I tell him. "A tiny bit burnt, not so you'd taste." *Tiny bit,* Termite says back to me in sounds like my words. *Tiny bit.*

"Don't you worry," I tell him.

*

I decorate the cake in three pale colors and keep it in the fridge all day so the icing sets up just right. After supper Nonie tells me to take the plastic stacking chairs out of the shed where they stay clean and I put them beside Termite's chair. I have a little round plastic table I put there too, for the drinks. Nick has mowed the alley. He takes off his work shirt and washes like always at our outside spigot.

"Cocktail hour at last," he says. He puts the shirt back on and his wet skin soaks it through in spots, but he buttons it up like he's in a formal situation and combs his thick dark hair straight back with his hands. Water drips on to his collar in rivulets.

"Take a load off, Nick. You want some ice tea?" Nonie comes outside in her housedress. She takes off her apron and folds it in pieces, smaller and smaller, like her own flag, her own little ceremony.

"Jesus, is that all you're serving tonight?" Nick Tucci says. "I work like a dog on the pasture here and you give me some tea?"

"I made a cake," I tell him. "A birthday cake. I'll get it in just a minute."

"Another birthday? Lucky fellow." He puts the flat of his palm on Termite's head. "How you doing, Junior?"

Termite never answers Nick Tucci, he just gets quiet and holds still, like he thinks Nick is part of the mower or he carries the sound of the mower inside him. Maybe the sound is in Nick's hand, like a vibration, and Termite hears it. Maybe the vibration is there.

"Junior ought to take up for me," Nick Tucci says. "We men got to stick together."

Nick won't call Termite by his name. He says that it's the name of an insect, a bug, not a kid, a boy, but he's the one who never waits for Termite to talk back. He fixed Termite's chair, though. There was this upholstered chair with arms Termite liked to sit in like a nest, and Nick turned it over one day so its bottom showed all strange and naked. He took off the flimsy wooden stumps it had for legs and screwed on silver wheels he said were strong enough for carts that move pianos and refrigerators. He said they were sure strong enough for this dinky kid, and the chair was narrow enough to fit through the kitchen door, all the doors. Nonie says Nick is handy. Charlie, now, he can't fix a sink or a lamp cord. Nonie does all that at the restaurant, but Nick helps her here. Nick fastened a handle on to the back of Termite's chair so we could steer it, and he put a wooden ramp stapled with stair treads leading out the back door, over the stoop, and the one step.

Termite was smaller then; he was so small when he started liking that chair that his feet didn't reach to the end of the seat cushion. His legs were always curved like they are, but we used to keep them out in front of him. It was later that he would whine and make noises until we tucked them under, like he didn't want to see them any more after he knew what they were.

Nick sits down in his own chair now, and Nonie sits just opposite, and he fixes her with a look. "Noreen," he says, "I'm forty-two years old."

Nonie has the blue Fiestaware pitcher that's squat and fat and sweats on its cold round sides, and she pours us three glasses of tea. "You're a spring chicken," she tells Nick. "Good God, you can't complain until you're fifty, like me, and if you're a man, you can't complain then."

"I got this passel of wild teenagers running around. They got three junkers between them now and I never know where they are."

"Who says you need to know? You ran around plenty, Nick. You might not remember, but everyone else does."

"Yeah," he says. "I'm still running. All day I feed the wrapper, and every night that beer gets colder."

I think about Nick and the wrapper, how he stands between the belts and lifts the bales from one to the other. The plant makes business forms and the wrapper is the big machine that thuds a few thousand pages into a batch, wraps and seals them in plastic for shipping. Bale in and bale out, Nick Tucci says, his calling in life.

"I could near dive into that beer," he goes on. "I get too thirsty to live."

"You don't want to get that thirsty," Nonie says.

Termite says exactly what she does, without the words being in it, and he starts moving.

"What is it he wants?" Nonie says. "Lark, get him a plastic

glass and his straw, and get him that little doodad he likes. I swear, he's crazy about that thing."

"I'll get the cake too," I tell them.

While I'm in the kitchen I can see them through the window, and I can hear them, but they are talking like I can't, like they think they sent me to another country.

"What are you going to do about her, Noreen?" Nick Tucci says.

"What do you mean? She's finished her first year down at the secretarial school. That will give her something, a lot more than her diploma from that high school Zeke doesn't show up to half the time. She's got some financial assistance, for the good grades she always had. Barker girls can even be legal secretaries, if they go all three years. The last year is work-study. Maybe she can get a job with one of the lawyers in town."

"She just going to sit here for three years, taking care of Junior in the day, and typing at night?"

"What would you like her to do, Nick?" I hear Nonie say. "Run around with one of your boys, maybe?"

I'm looking for Termite's doodad, the little pitcher he likes. Where had that old thing got to? It's small, pale-yellow porcelain, doll size, easy to lose in a sinkful of dishes. He doesn't like me to wash it at all or take it from him, but he holds it so often I want it to be clean. The fat moon face on the front is winking and smiling, maybe that's why Termite likes the feel of it.

"Jesus, Noreen," Nick says. "Someone, sometime, is gonna drive up here by the alley and open the door for her to jump in. Don't you know that?"

I have to move all the dishes that are drying before I find the pitcher in the sink; it's so small it falls through the skinny rubber rungs of the drainer to underneath. I've got it in my hand, washing and drying the face. I can hear them outside, I can hear them perfectly well.

"Uh-huh," I hear Nonie answer. "And you think she's just going to ride off and leave Termite sitting here." There's a beat of quiet like a pause in a song. "You remember their mother, and I do," Nonie says, "but Lark is nothing like her."

Nick doesn't say anything then, and Termite doesn't say anything either. It's no wonder I think he does understand some of what people say. I hear the bell on his chair. He rings it, just a small, glancing sound, once, twice, and three times.

Be right there, I tell him, but I say it in my head. I catch myself doing that, when there are people around, like I think he can hear me. Here's his plastic cup and straw, and the handle of the moon pitcher fits around my smallest finger, like a ring. I put the silver-plate pie server in my pocket, the one I found last week in the basement, in the boxes Nonie keeps down there.

The tray with the rim around it is good for carrying things. Plates slide and they don't fall off, but the edge is low enough that the cake still looks pretty, sitting in the middle with dishes and spoons beside. People ought to see something pretty moving toward them. That way they get time to want what they really can have. I like coming out the door with something on a tray. Nonie looks over, and Nick does, and Termite turns too, like he can feel them looking even if he can't see what they see, and then Nick is up and coming over to hold the door. He winks at me, pleased and jaunty. For a minute I see how he looks like his boys, young in his eyes like them, and how his boys might look when they're older, big-chested like Nick, and working at the plant. If they broaden out like him. I guess it takes a man built like Nick to run the wrapper. There's a lever a man has to swing timed just so, and Nick can fix the wrapper too, keep it running. It's as big as a couple of cars parked close, side to side; he says it makes a noise like a jet engine pausing to yell *Wham!* every thirty seconds. A man has to be big to throw that lever and stand in that noise, move the bales on time like he's part of a machine. Nick's boys are all long and thin, and they move fluid as dogs; they have taut ropes of muscle in their necks, like they're always tense or ready, and swells of hard crescent under their nipples. Come spring, Joey and Solly and Zeke work on their cars in Nick's yard. They go without their shirts and their pants ride low on their hips. You can see the perfect run of their spines as they bend over, lean and white, lost to the chest in their engines. They were always hard and skinny, when they were little kids, when we were all little kids. I can't see Nick's boys ever being big and broad as Nick, like a wrestler or moving so heavy, like he moves now, coming toward me. I can feel his footfalls on the stone walk through my bare feet. Then he's here, making a mock bow before he reaches to take the tray. I'm taller than Nonie now and Nick's dark eyes are level with mine. His forearms are furred with dark, curly hair. I look away when Nick gets too close, when he's a blur at the limit my eyes can see.

"Lark, you're too much," he says.

"It's just a cake," I say.

"Yes, it's a cake," Nonie says. She shakes her head at Nick.

"But look at it, Noreen. Little white garlands in the icing, and the garlands are braided. How does she do that?" He nods over at Termite. "You were here, Junior. How does she do it?"

"An icing bag with special attachments," I say. "Gourmet baking set. I got it for my birthday."

"My point exactly," Nick says. "For your birthday you want some fancy cooking gadget so you can make exotic creations. My thugs want new carburetors, so they can drive even faster and end up in the pokey in the next county, and their old man can come bail them out." He's carrying the tray in front of me and I follow the hulk of his back. "Joey's latest thought is to join the Marines. Driving delivery for the plant's not good enough, he wants to see the world. Zeke can't pass tenth grade but he's got him a car put together. And Saul. Now he wants a motorcycle."

"He want you to buy it?" Nonie asks.

Saul is the middle one, the one most like a wolf, with his green eyes and his thick fair hair, and that dark skin, like Nick's. Solly has been in school with me since first grade over on Lumber Street. They put him back a grade, though, for skipping school so much when he was nine or ten. He ended up a grade behind me, even though he's a year older. Their mother had left before school even happened, when Zeke was barely walking. Nick Tucci bought the groceries. Nonie took care of those boys and fed us all supper at night, then sent us all over to Nick's when he pulled in from work. She used his car to go off to Charlie's for the dinner shift, then closed up and got home around eleven, carried me down the alley from Nick's to my own bed. She says I never stirred, but I remember the leaves on the trees moving, blowing above me at night. There used to be trees all along the alley. That was a long time ago. After Termite came, Nonie's friend Elise stayed with him and me at night, and after Nick's kids would go home, Nonie went to work and Solly would come back over. Guess you think we're better than TV over here, Elise would tell him, better than Jack Benny. If we weren't doing homework she'd have us "helping out," running the sweeper, folding laundry, entertaining Termite. Elise brought over a clock radio she got with S&H Green Stamps, and she taught us card games so she'd have someone to play with. Solly played rummy with her while I read to Termite, or Elise would bring over whatever she wanted to hear. *Gone with the Wind. Little Dorrit. Ladies' Home Journal* magazine: "Can This Marriage Be Saved?" Elise said I was better than the radio, better than *Playhouse 90*.

When I was eleven Elise started running the minimart across from Charlie's. After that I took care of Termite myself. He was little. I could do it as well as anyone. Solly still came by. I know Solly like I know the shelves in my room, and the turn of the walls. There's always been a wild quiet about Solly. It stays in the air near him like a scent.

"Solly doesn't need me to buy him anything," Nick says now. We've reached our little enclave and he puts the cake on the round table. "He's been pumping gas and fixing cars down at the Amoco all year. Somebody pulled in with this thing on a flatbed and now Solly thinks he's got to have it."

"Well, he doesn't," Nonie says. "He lives with you and you're his father and you can tell him he can't have it."

"Sure," Nick says, "and I'll see his back real quick. The kid managed to get through high school not half trying. I want him to work this summer, save money, maybe go to college next year."

"But his grades weren't bad," I say. "Solly's smart. He should go to college. Couldn't he play football somewhere?"

"You tell him." Nick turns and looks at me. "I'm serious."

"That's not her job," Nonie answers him. Then, "She's the one should be going to college."

There's no college near enough, though. Nowhere I could take classes at night. "Sit down, Nick." I'm moving the plates, handing out napkins. I put Termite's moon into his palm. He holds it in his lap, rubs the flat of his wrist across its grimace of a face that's all wrinkles and bulging cheeks, like no face, even a porcelain face, is too small to wink or sigh. Termite moves his wrist across and across like he didn't have hold of it just this morning. I have the cake server, a shiny wedge shape with a carved handle and serrated edge, Lenox on the back in tiny script. It has its own velvety envelope to keep off tarnish; there's just a shadow of dark along the blade. I touch the shadow with my thumb. If these are my mother's things, why are they here? I always thought of her walking, moving, some landscape streaming away behind her. Now that I've actually taken something from her secrets, I think of a green lawn holding her, or a coastline where she disappeared, even an alleyway where it happened. A dark bitter alley, cinders and trash. No. Make it an alley like ours, grass, white gravel, summer dusk. I see Nonie recognize the cake server in my hand, but she doesn't say anything. "I'll cut the cake," I tell them, "if everyone will kindly take a seat."

Termite gives me his little half smile and starts talking. *Take a seat. Take a seat.*

"He sounds like a bird sometimes," Nick says.

Take a seat is what I say to him when we're in the basement, cooling off, sitting in the old couch that has its springs out right through to the cold cement floor. It's the couch Charlie used for years in the office of the restaurant, a narrow room behind the kitchen where Nonie did the accounts and bills. It's a big couch, long and broad enough for one person on top of another. This summer I realized the use they must have put it to those nights when I was a child, and slept at Nick's on a love seat by the living room door so Nonie could retrieve me without disturbing anyone. Or no one but Solly, who was likely curled up next to me. It was this summer too that I started looking through Nonie's boxes. Pretending is a lie I'm tired of telling her by now. Down there with Termite one of the hot afternoons, sitting at the workbench so he could use the big crayons he can hold, I saw how the boxes were stacked, balanced and squared, like they'd been there a long time. Termite holds the crayon tight. Once I get him started, he moves his arm up and down, back and forth, long arcs in one color across unfolded newspaper, while I draw in my notebook. He doesn't look at what he makes but I watch his colors get darker. Most of the time, I draw him. Standing in space. No chair, no alley. That day I turned the radio loud the way Termite likes it. "Heartbreak Hotel" was on and I looked over at the boxes. *Well since your baby left you. You've got a tale to tell.* The boxes had always been in that corner, sometimes covered with other stuff. They were big and they were all the same size, plain, like from a moving company, a solid dusty wall stacked four across and four deep. I went over and touched them, careful, like they were sleeping. The song went on about Lonely Street while I wiped off the dust. The boxes were solid and full and hard to rock, taped shut and never opened, addressed to Nonie in somebody's handwriting. I saw where they were mailed from and I decided to go slowly. I know the stuff in the two boxes I've gone through was never Nonie's. No pictures, though, no documents, no papers to tell me more than I already know.

Termite is still saying a one-note tone. *Seat, seat, seat.*

"Kind of musical," Nick says. "A bird making its own sense."

"Or not," Nonie says.

"Termite can imitate almost anything," I say. "Things just sound more like music in his version, since there are sounds instead of words."

Nonie leans forward to help Termite with his cake. He can hold bigger things than spoons—his pitcher, fat crayons. He holds his strips of blue because we wrap them around his wrist. But spoons and forks are too thin and hard. We know exactly how to feed him. Touch, touch, each side of his mouth, neat and fast. Nonie's looking at him and I wonder what she sees. "You never make things up, though, do you, Termite?"

"No," I say, "he doesn't."

It's a fact. Termite can only tell the truth. I know she means she wishes, she wishes he could say something more than the sound of what he's just heard. I pretend he knows more, backward and forward for miles.

"Good cake," Nick says. "And this cold tea is mighty nice, evening like this. The air is goddamn still, heavy as lead. That storm coming in. Tomorrow, or the next day. Rain all week, they say. Maybe it'll clean up the river a little. I don't like such a brown muck of a river."

"Lord, Nick," Nonie laughs. "That river was always brown."

"Not so, Noreen. The river was cleaner years ago. You could see into it. In the dark it was olive green. I remember."

"In the days it was—" She goes on at him, making fun now.

"Sapphire," I chime in. "It was sapphire. Bright, stone blue."

Nick Tucci gives me a look, then he nods. "Knocked your eyes out," he says. "Standing there under the rail bridge, watching the water. Oh, that blue river."

We're laughing, and Termite hunches his shoulders, throws his head back to look up into the plum-colored sky, like the river is up there somewhere. *That blue river.* He says it in high and low sounds, and the sky over us could be a river, bruised and deep as it looks. I reach over and tilt his chin down. His head is heavy and his neck muscles are not so strong. He throws his head back again, right away.

"He's got his opinions, has Junior," says Nick Tucci. "You tell them, Junior."

"Leave him be, Lark." Nonie's eyes get wet when she laughs hard. "He's taking a sounding. My god, that sky does look like it could fall. Should be a full moon tonight, but we won't see anything behind clouds like those."

I can see Termite's nostrils move, a vibration so slight, like the gill of a fish moving when it breathes, and I hear him smell the air like he's drinking it. I wonder, *Does he see the clouds at all, does he feel the color instead, or does he think a river is like a sky, so he looks up? Why would he do that?* Because it's true, he could think the sky is like a river that doesn't stop. Nonie would say he just reacts to us, our laughing, our shouting, whatever. She'd say I give him things to know, even if I don't know what those things are.

Then I think of the candles. "Not much of a birthday, is it, Termite? I forgot about candles."

"You don't need candles every time, Lark." Nonie feels the pockets of the apron she took off. They're all blue aprons. She wears them at work.

"I kind of promised him," I say. "Too late now." But Termite tilts his head back down, gives me his sideways look.

He can hold his head up now except for when he's tired. From the time I was a kid I thought his head was heavy because there was so much in it he couldn't tell or say. That everything had stayed in him, whether he recognized the pictures or not. That he'd kept all the words I couldn't call up, our mother's words and words about her. Words from before we were born, what I heard until I was three and forgot. Words about what house, what road or street, who was there, how she looked and talked, and why she sent us to Nonie. It's hard taking care of

Termite but she kept him for a year, she tried. Why did she try or stop trying? And I was a normal kid she didn't keep, except I'm not normal because I don't remember her. I've got my own big blank but no one can see it in the shape of my head, in how I speak or don't speak or don't move. It's like by the time he was born there was too much to know. It filled his head too full, then wiped it blank. If I said this to Nonie she'd say I like my own stories. There are birth defects, she'd tell me. No one knows why or what.

"Not too late," Nonie says. "We have most of a cake here, and a few leftover candles. Somebody celebrated at the restaurant today, with a piece of Charlie's lemon pie." Nonie has a partly crushed box of those little skinny candles they give away free at bakeries.

"Pie is all wrong with candles," Nick Tucci says. There are only three candles, but he's leaning forward, putting them on the cake. "Should be nine, right? Each one of these counts for three years, Junior, so the flames gotta be extra high." He lights them with his cigarette lighter, then he stands and picks up the plate and holds it just in front of Termite. Nonie and I get up and stand beside him, our faces either side of his, so close we touch, and we let the candles burn, then we blow, really slow, with Termite. The little flames flutter perfectly and go out just right, all at once.

I lean down close to him and whisper, in the powdery smell of his hair, "Your birthday, Termite, every day."

Every day, he says back to me, *every day, every day.*

Petit Mal

Michele Battiste

I don't believe much in luck unless it's bad and self-generated
Cameron has a horseshoe cut into his head, an oxbow
river carving a path around cowlicks
I learned a lot about topography in 9th grade, and I can guess
small sections of the earth's fate from a low-flying airplane
In 9th grade it was funny—What do you do when an epileptic
falls into a swimming pool? Throw in a load of laundry.

Seizure boy, surgery boy, retard
Cameron knows the names, thinks he earned them
The box in his chest sends a shock to his brain every 13 minutes
Seizures used to be a sign of witchcraft, but now I swipe
a card across his heart to charge him up
Magnetics, I suppose, or benediction
The shocks make him thirsty
Meds make him quiet, enough tranquilizers to down
a small poker club
I used to gamble but I had no luck with cards

He's twelve and rides the short bus, has trouble
expressing complex emotions
Autism can arrest communication skills
Sympathetic acquaintances say he was dealt a bad hand
Cameron traces his hand again and again until I run
out of paper
You are here, I tell him. I am here, too

He can spell a few names, writes them down and carries
them with him
The smallest seizures carry him away for a minute or two
He comes back like a lecturing professor who lost
his thought mid-sentence
I'm sad to be poor and living in Kansas
Cameron is learning to write my name

Great Expectations

Michael Bérubé

1. Was I Ever Wrong

In 1991, my wife Janet Lyon and I had our second child, Jamie. Jamie has Down syndrome, and I've been chronicling his adventures off and on, formally and informally, ever since he got through his first precarious year of life, when he was hospitalized for three weeks in the neonatal intensive care unit and then came home to nasal gavage feedings (administered by his anxious parents), supplemental oxygen, and an apnea monitor. In 1995, I started writing a book about him and our life together; it's titled *Life As We Know It*, and in the opening pages of the book I wrote that most of my time with Jamie—that is, when I'm actually with him, doing stuff—is lived pretty much moment by moment. But lately I've had reason to return ruefully to this passage:

> Occasionally it will occur to Janet or to me that Jamie will always be "disabled," that his adult and adolescent years will undoubtedly be more difficult emotionally—for him and for us —than his early childhood, that we will never not worry about his future, his quality of life, whether we're doing enough for him. But usually these moments occur in the relative comfort of abstraction, when Janet and I are lying in bed at night and wondering what will become of us all. When I'm with Jamie, by contrast, I'm almost always fully occupied by taking care of his present needs rather than by worrying about his future.

When he asks to hear the Beatles because he loves their cover of Little Richard's "Long Tall Sally," I just play the song, sing along, and watch him dance with delight; I do not concern myself with extraneous questions, such as whether he'll ever distinguish early Beatles from late Beatles, Paul's songs from John's, originals from covers. These questions are now central to Nick's enjoyment of the Beatles, but that's Nick for you. Jamie is entirely sui generis, and as long as I'm with him I can't think of him as anything but Jamie.

The clear implication here—and you don't have to be a literature Ph.D. to see it—is that a child with Down syndrome will never have the intellectual capacity to understand the Beatles' oeuvre, or even to understand that some songs preceded others, were written by different band members, and so forth.

Well, this is long, long overdue, but I owe Jamie one enormous apology: I couldn't have been more wrong. Over the years, Jamie has become so fascinated with the Beatles that he's memorized almost the entire songbook. He still has trouble identifying late Harrisonian ephemera like "The Inner Light," "Old Brown Shoe," and "Only a Northern Song" (all of which suck, anyway), and he's not crazy about the second half of the first side, and some of the first half of the second side of *Abbey Road* (with good reason). But in every other respect, his knowledge of Beatles music verges on the preternatural.

It started a couple of years ago, when he was fascinated with "Being for the Benefit of Mr. Kite" and "Come Together" (he still gets a kick out of "juju eyeball"), whereupon I explained to him that John had written those songs and that John liked to play games with words. Well, Jamie was so thrilled with this news that he demanded to know what else John had written. So I went back over the corpus, so to speak, and found to my surprise that John had written almost three-quarters of the originals on the Beatles' first four records. (My tally is twenty-five Lennons, ten McCartneys—though I'm counting "Hard Day's

Night" under John, even though Paul wrote the middle eight. I attribute "I Wanna Be Your Man" to both of them. As for songs after 1964, I attribute "We Can Work It Out" to Paul, even though John wrote the middle eight. If anyone knows which of them wrote "Tell Me What You See," let me know—I'm inclined to Paul, because it sounds to me like a rewrite of "Things We Said Today," but I'm not sure.) I revisited a mess of other things about John's early work as well, like his fondness for melisma (as in the final verse of "Not a Second Time," which gets positively silly in this respect) and his felicity with pop musical genres we ordinarily associate more with Paul (not only the remarkable "This Boy" and "Yes It Is," but the relatively obscure "Ask Me Why," which is way too complicated for its own good, but a hell of an effort nonetheless).

Before I knew it, Jamie had memorized "the Johns," as he puts it, and proceeded to master the other three as well (for Ringo, we go by the songs he sang, not just the two he wrote). Then Jamie wanted to know who wrote "Bad Boy" or "Roll Over Beethoven" or "Anna." Then he began to understand (as we made him presents of each CD) which records contained which songs. Then, as he began to ask which came first, I bought him one of my favorite extended pieces of rock criticism, Roy Carr and Tony Tyler's *The Beatles: An Illustrated Record*. By now, Jamie had a sense of the year-by-year, record-by-record trajectory, and an astonishing memory for other things as well.

"Remember when the Beatles were in the Bahamas?" he asked one day.

"Uh," I said, trying to think of the Beatles' world tours, "I don't think they ever played in the Bahamas."

"No, in *Help!*" he insisted, and proceeded to show me one of the pictures in yet another Beatles coffee-table book we'd gotten him. Yep, there were the Beatles in the Bahamas. Score one for Jamie. Now Jamie has a whole quiver of such questions. Remember when the Beatles had a pillow fight? Remember when

John disappeared in the bathtub? Remember when Ringo was combing his hair?

So when he's bored, or when we're trying to kill time in long lines or on long trips, Jamie will now ask me to "do all Pauls," or whomever, and I will proceed to pick random tunes from here, there, and everywhere. I'll sing about two bars—"Close your eyes, and..." and Jamie will immediately jump in and say, "*With the Beatles*. 1963. Next!" And I'll say, "let me think," and he will mock me, and I'll sing "Martha, my dear..." and he'll say, "*White Beatles*. 1968. Next!"—and this can go on, as you might imagine, for some time, until my own memory is exhausted. When we came back from a trip to Houston in March 2005, and waited fifteen minutes by the baggage carousel, we got through about sixty or seventy of these, much to the amusement and/or annoyance of our fellow travelers, one of whom asked, "Did you already do 'Norwegian Wood'?"

*

What makes this especially curious, to me, is that Jamie isn't just cataloging information and spewing it back; he's got everything cross-referenced somehow, and he never fails to name songs I've forgotten. For example, by the time we'd gotten on the shuttle bus to Extremely Remote Parking at the Baltimore/ Washington International Airport, Jamie was chortling in the back seat at the fact that I'd forgotten "Rain," "Any Time at All," and even "Don't Let Me Down" from the list of Johns. I never, never manage to remember the whole damn song list, and I always forget different songs each time (though for some reason I have particular trouble with "Paperback Writer" and "Drive My Car" among the Pauls). And Jamie never fails to catch the omissions. It's astonishing.

Equally astonishing is his ability to remember where we'd left off three or four days ago, and to pick up from there. "More Johns," he said one day last summer as we were tooling around

Paris; "If I fell in love with you…" I replied, only to be met with, "We did that already. Next?"

But even more astonishing is his ability to associate specific words with specific songs. One night we were doing the words on his spelling list, and when he came to "through," he sang, "Through thick and thin she will always be my friend." The word "you're" was met with "you're gonna lose that girl"; "picture" with "picture yourself in a boat on a river." On certain days he has to use his spelling words in complete sentences, and we've told him that he can't always just place them in Beatles songs, that he has to think up his own sentences. But if you'd asked me ten years ago whether I imagined that I would ever have to issue Jamie an injunction like *that—stop quoting Beatles lyrics in your spelling-word sentences*—I probably would have given you a very dirty look.

And so, Jamie, I admit it. Even when I was trying to represent you to the best of my ability ten years ago, I underestimated you. I was wrong, and I apologize. And through thick and thin, I will always be your friend.

2. Babe and BBQ

Before Jamie and I went golfing one fine day in 2006, we had a serious talk. It wasn't on the agenda; it just happened.

We were dining at one of our favorite lunch stops, Fat Jack's Barbeque. Suffice it to say that we don't go there for the decor or the ambiance. We go there to chow down on some serious meat (he takes the pulled pork, I do the brisket) doused with Mississippi Mud barbecue sauce. This time, Jamie brought along the quite wonderful animal encyclopedia he bought last year at the AAUW book sale (he went with Janet and picked it out himself). It consists of a loose-leaf binder full of information about various animals—their habitats, their diets, their mating practices, and so forth. While we waited for our animals to arrive on plates, Jamie asked me to go over some of the animals in his book, and I insisted on reading some of the fine print of the entries. Jamie usually resists this, but I managed to convince him that some of the fun facts on display were really kind of fun: who knew, for example, that the nine-banded armadillo is the only species of armadillo that can swim? Or that they always have babies in litters of four? Jamie understands the difference between animals that lay eggs and animals that have live babies, and knows that it marks the distinction between most mammals and most reptiles/birds. He also knows the difference between animals that have litters and animals that usually give birth to babies one at a time.

But after we'd discussed the Bengal tiger, the gorilla, the African elephant, and the nine-banded armadillo, it was the vampire bat that really got things going. I explained what the book meant by saying that the vampire bat is a "threat to cattle" because it can "infect them with the deadly disease of rabies." Jamie has heard of rabies before, and because we fought to have him included in regular seventh-grade science class last year (and because his science teacher was so receptive, and so inventive in finding ways to adapt his tests to his skill level, so that, for example, he was responsible for knowing only about half the components of a plant cell), he knows what a virus is. So he understood when I told him that rabies is a dangerous virus that can make an animal go crazy and die, and that you can treat it if you catch it early (or vaccinate against it) but that there is no cure once it reaches an advanced stage. And that's why we take dogs to the veterinarian, to make sure they have their rabies shots. Why, I said, even Lucy the dog has had a rabies shot.

"Like in *Babe*," Jamie said.

"*Babe?*" I replied. "I don't think there's any rabies in *Babe*."

"No, the doctor says, 'it can't be rabies.' He says to Mr. Hoggett."

"Oh! You mean when Rex bites Mr. Hoggett!"

"Right, exactly."

Right, exactly: in *Babe*, Rex the sheepdog has become increasingly furious with his partner, Fly, whom he sees as complicit in Hoggett's heretical scheme to train Babe to become a sheep-herding pig. Finally, when Fly approaches Rex to try to convince him that there's no need for all this trouble just because Babe is helping the boss, Rex calls her a "traitorous wretch" and attacks her. When Hoggett runs out to break up the fighting dogs, Rex bites him on the hand.

"No, not the hand," Jamie corrected me. "On the wrist."

Right, on the wrist. So, then. Why would Rex bite Mr. Hoggett when he knows perfectly well that the dogs are never, ever allowed to bite Mr. and Mrs. Hoggett?

"Why?" Jamie asked. "You tell."

"Well," I said. "You know he is very angry at Babe, and very angry at Fly for helping Babe."

"Why?"

"Because Rex thinks that only dogs should herd the sheep. He thinks it is wrong for a pig to do the job, and he thinks—as Fly says to her puppies at the beginning of the movie—that pigs are definitely stupid. He doesn't want Babe to do the job that he, Rex, is supposed to do."

Jamie and I have been over this ground before, usually when he asks, "What does Ferdinand say about Rosanna?" For when he asks what Ferdinand says about Rosanna, he's referring to the scene in which the farm animals watch the Hoggett family as they carve up a duck for Christmas holiday dinner. When Ferdinand joins the onlookers, the cow remarks, "If you're out here, then who's that in there?" to which Ferdinand replies, "her name is Rosanna. She had such a beautiful nature."

About the eating of Rosanna, our routine goes like this: Jamie asks me what Ferdinand is feeling, and we take turns enumerating the emotions. Angry. Confused. Sad. Frustrated. Worried. Ferdinand is consumed (you might say) by the belief that he will not be eaten if he simply demonstrates that he is "indispensable," as he mistakenly explains to Babe upon enlisting

Babe in the project of stealing the Hoggetts' alarm clock so that Ferdinand can go back to crowing at the dawn—one of the two activities, besides having sex with chickens, that keep roosters from being eaten. Or so Ferdinand thinks. "I tried it with the hens, it didn't work," he sighs. "But I begin to crow, and I discover my gift!" Upon witnessing the family dig into Rosanna, however, Ferdinand is beside himself. "It's too much for a duck," he cries. "It eats away at the soul!" "The only way you'll find happiness," replies the cow, languidly, "is to accept that the way things are is the way things are." "Well, the way things are stinks!" snaps Ferdinand, and he vows to run away. Which he does, leaving Babe to overturn the way things are by demonstrating that a clever and compassionate animal need not succumb to the forces of animal destiny.

So Jamie and I have had numerous discussions about the eating of animals. (We've also had a talk or two about whether animals can think, as well.) We acknowledge that poor Ferdinand is driven to distraction by the realization that humans eat ducks, and we admit that it is unjust for poor Rosanna, who had such a beautiful nature, to become Christmas holiday dinner. "But Jamie," I point out, "you love to eat ham and pork chops and sausages and bacon, and all of that comes from pigs." And hamburgers and steak that come from cows," he remarks. "Right," I say. "And chicken," he adds, conscientiously. "Right, chicken too. So you know there are some people who think it is wrong to eat any animal, and they eat only vegetables and fruits. Some eat fish and some don't. Some people won't eat milk or cheese, either." "From cows and goats," Jamie says. We have reached a tentative conclusion about this: we will continue to be omnivores. But we would prefer that the animals we eat not spend their entire lives in factories being shot up with antibiotics (which is, you'll recall, precisely where *Babe* opens).

Anyway, this shouldn't be very surprising. Ten years ago, if memory serves, there were indeed reports that *Babe* had led some children to rethink their love of hot juicy strips of bacon.

Instead, what was notable about Jamie's invocation of *Babe* this time was that he'd remembered—with that amazing memory of his—the film's one mention of rabies.

Now, back to Rex. It just so happens that one of the reasons Rex hates sheep is that they are the cause of his disability, and his disability, in turn, has prevented him from becoming a champion sheepdog. You see (as Fly explains to Babe), one night during a terrible storm, Rex tried to save a bunch of sheep from a flood, but the sheep were "too stupid" to follow his directions. The sheep perished, but Rex, faithful hound, stayed with them all night—and became terribly ill as a result, permanently losing much of his hearing. (Narrative twists like this are what make me argue that disability is ubiquitous in film, even if only as plot device, as in the premise of Garden State. Really. Go check: why does Zach Braff's character return home in the first place?) Jamie and I have discussed Rex's deafness as well as his anger at Babe, and the deft way these come together at the end of the film, when Rex decides to help Babe by asking the Hoggett sheep for the secret sheep password "baa-ram-ewe"— a scene in which he not only has to speak nicely to sheep for the first time in his life, but also has to admit to them that he's "a little deaf." All so that Babe can speak to the foreign sheep, guide them through the sheepdog trials, and take Rex's rightful place as a champion sheepdogpig.

So after Rex bites Hoggett, the vet rules out rabies. "Hormones," Jamie says. "What?" I ask. "Mrs. Hoggett says 'hormones,'" Jamie replies. Ah, right, exactly. Again with the memory! I ask Jamie if he remembers about hormones from seventh grade, when we talked about his pituitary gland and how hormones work in the body. "And remember when the doctor says, 'I could always snip, snip'?" I ask. "Right," Jamie says. "And does Hoggett want to do that?" "No," Jamie says. "Because he says Rex is a breeding dog."

Well, I'll be damned. I knew that Jamie had seen the movie dozens of times, and has replayed scenes (especially the ones involving Ferdinand) hundreds of times, but I didn't realize how deeply he'd thought about things like this. "That's right, Jamie," I explained. "The doctor is wondering why Rex would be so mean and aggressive, and it can't be rabies, so maybe, he thinks, it is testosterone, and maybe he should snip, snip Rex's testes with surgery."

At this point the owner of Fat Jack's is giving us a puzzled look.

"But then Rex couldn't have any more babies, and you remember that Mr. Hoggett sold Fly's children—with that sign 'pups for sale, by Rex, out of Fly'—to people who wanted sheep-dog puppies. So Mr. Hoggett might want to sell more puppies, and keep Rex as a breeding dog." And yes, Jamie and I have already discussed the moment at which Babe, seeing how depressed Fly has become by the sale of those puppies, goes over to Fly and asks her if he can call her "Mom." Jamie knows that's one of the reasons Fly likes Babe so much—because he knows when and why other animals are sad, and he tries to help them. (See also the vastly underrated and widely misunderstood sequel, *Babe: Pig in the City*, especially the pivotal scene in which Babe saves the life of the pit bull who'd been trying to kill him. Back in 1998, this scene was the first thing in Jamie's life, to my knowledge, that led him to think about why we need to breathe to stay alive, and why it is good to save someone from dying— as Babe does later with the much less problematic goldfish whose bowl has been broken by careless animal-control police.)

"Sometimes doctors do surgery so that animals cannot have babies. Think of Lucy. Before we got her at the pound, doctors removed Lucy's ovaries, and that's why she cannot have babies—because the doctors were afraid that maybe she'd have babies and she would have no place to live and no place to take care of her puppies. But with Rex, the doctor thinks that maybe he has hormones that are making him too angry, that his testosterone made him bite Mr. Hoggett. They don't understand that

Rex is really angry at Fly and Babe because he doesn't want Babe to herd the sheep."

"Ohh," Jamie said. "That's why they give Rex a shot."

See, the thing about the classics—like *Babe*—is that you can go back to them time and again, and keep rereading them with fresh eyes, so to speak. You can look at Judith Halberstam's queer reading of Babe, in which Babe and Ferdinand demonstrate the fluidity of categories of identity, or you can listen in on me and Jamie as we discuss how Rex's deafness deepens his disdain for sheep and fuels one aspect of his opposition to Hoggett's training of Babe (only one aspect, because although he and Fly disagree about Babe as sheep-pig, they agree, on anti-Habermasian grounds, that dogs should not speak to sheep in a way that invites reciprocal recognition). Most of the time, when Jamie and I talk about Babe we talk about whether animals have feelings, and whether one animal can behave like another, and whether it's OK to eat some animals (and if so, which ones and why). But this time, the bit about the vampire bat had led us back to Babe to talk about rabies and Rex and deafness and hormones and "neutering."

What a great movie. What a rich text about what it means to be human. Jamie and I will talk about it for years to come, I'm sure.

And then our pulled pork and beef brisket arrived! It was delicious.

3. Making the Grade

When Jamie entered kindergarten in 1997, Janet and I worried that he wouldn't be ready. Our concerns were not unusual—but Jamie was: he would be the only child with Down syndrome in Westview Elementary. He was assigned a paraprofessional and "pullout" sessions for occupational and speech therapy: standard fare, these days, for "special needs" children of all kinds. But at the age of six, Jamie wasn't very verbal, and we had no idea how he'd adjust to a real classroom after four years of child care.

Imagine our relief, then, when we went to our first parent-teacher conference that October and were informed that Jamie was "advanced" academically but needed some work with his social skills. He knew the alphabet and lots of fun facts about animals; he had shown off his amazing memory. How, we were asked, had he managed to learn so much?

Our first meeting with Jamie's seventh-grade teachers was not nearly so cheering. Despite his math skills—he can do two-digit multiplication with ease—he was failing to grasp the concepts of area and perimeter. He wasn't paying attention in science class, where his paraprofessional was doing much of his work for him; and he didn't seem to get French at all.

We'd asked for Jamie to be included in those three "regular" classrooms, on the grounds that he's good at math, fascinated with the natural world, and exceptionally curious about languages. But when we discovered that the next item on the math agenda would be the area of irregular shapes, we agreed to bail out.

We pleaded for French and science, though. "I know he's not getting it all," Janet said to his science teacher. "But he truly loves learning about the world around him, and we don't want that world to close in on him... just yet." His French teacher, unsurprisingly, had never had a child with Down syndrome in her class; she assured us that Jamie did not speak when he was called on and did not understand how to write complete sentences in French. "He doesn't write complete sentences in English, either," I replied. "And he's shy about speaking up. But he already knows the days of the week and the months of the year, and he's beginning to understand about time. Now, we don't want him to slow down the rest of the class. So if it's possible for him to take the class pass/fail, we'll do everything we can to help him."

I turned out to be wrong about time: Jamie never did understand why the French perversely insist on calling 7:40 eight hours minus twenty, so I eventually agreed with him that *sept heures et quarante* would get the general idea across even if it was marked "wrong" on the test. And even though he learned what *voyager* means, he never remembered that *tu voyages* has an "s" even though *je voyage* and *il voyage* do not. But he negotiated the hyphens and apostrophes of *qu'est-ce que c'est* with élan, he mastered the form of *est-ce que tu?* and he turned out to be a whiz with adverbs—getting them right *quelquefois* at first, then *souvent*. (Though *quelquefois* remains his favorite.) His pronunciation got better and better, too—no small thing for a child who didn't learn to read fluently until he was eight. It was hard enough for him to master English vowels and silent letters the first time around, let alone foreign imponderables like *ils aiment* and *les yeux*.

One day when we were walking Lucy, our dog, I told him how proud I was of all his hard work in French. He was in no mood for kind words: "It's too hard," he grumbled. "I always fail." He'd said something similar about science as well, when he had trouble keeping track of all the parts of a cell and began to realize that he might not achieve his dream of becoming a marine biologist. (I told him he could still shoot for the position of marine biologist *helper.*) Jamie is fifteen years old; he knows he has a disability, he knows that it's called Down syndrome, and he's very well aware of how hard he struggles just to stay in the same room with "normal" kids a few years younger than he. He even had an odd moment of illumination in January of this year when the science class turned to the details of human reproduction, and he learned that most of us have 46 chromosomes but that people with Down syndrome have 47. "Wow, one more," he said, intrigued and a little bit impressed. I wonder if he thought to himself, *You know, that explains a lot*, and whether this was any comfort to him in those rare moments when he thinks of himself as someone who always fails.

But despite his moments of despair, he never failed to re-member that *étudier* and *décembre* take *accents aigus* and that *mère* and *père* take *accents graves*. When we asked him, *Parles-tu français?* he never failed to say, *Je parle français souvent* or *très bien*—even though those answers are not quite true. And al-though he failed his science test on rocks, he learned a great deal about living things—which is where his real interests lie, any-way. When, in response to his query about why one of his Chal-lenger League baseball teammates was bald, I tried to explain to him what cancer is, and how cells could be sick, he replied, "like the cell membrane and the cell nucleus." When we went through the digestive system on one long homework night, I said, "Let's skip the pancreas—I don't think you know that one," and he shot back, "Lucy had pancreatitis and cannot eat any spicy food."

At the end of the year, Jamie's teachers and caseworkers ad-vised us that eighth-grade science and French would definitely be too much for him. Perhaps they feared that Jamie's parents, the double-barreled Ph.D.'s, would push their disabled kid un-til he broke. "That's fine with us," we said, to their palpable re-lief. "We just wanted him to get a sense of it all, and to stay in some regular classes for as long as he could." From this point on, we figure, we'll hire tutors for him, and they can teach him at his own pace.

It's true, he failed *quelquefois*. But in eight years of inclusive education, he learned more about the world than we—or, pos-sibly, he—could have hoped for when he started kindergarten. Now that Jamie has finally left the "regular" classroom, all we can hope is that he taught his teachers and classmates a few valu-able things about people with 47 chromosomes. And that they'll remember.

From *Spells and Auguries*

John Morgan

In November 1993, without warning, our son Ben went into a coma. This sequence deals with his illness and its long-term consequences.

Punctuated Equilibrium

The pitcher you made in school, like some old
bottle melted and recast (a piece of
depression glass, cherished over decades, green
with tiny bubbles, scattered through),
brushed
by the clumsy tabby, tumbles from the shelf
and splashes on the floor with the clash
of an antique skull
pitched on a pile of bones.
Nature has it in for us, I sometimes think.

Life, stable for ten years, kicks up its heels,
fractious as a bull,
for even a young man's
healthy skull's no guarantee against the
tendency of flesh to bruise and spoil, breeding
uncertainty that what we hold too close our hands
may crush, however green that cup, however full.

Ben's Ennui
January 1994

Tearful at the top of the stairs, you sit
head in hands. "It's just so boring!" is all
you can say when we probe
your woe—one dismal
sea of forgetting. Although you're back in school,
day after active day thins down till
nothing's happened. The teachers agree
you're not yourself. You clown around,
blurt out,
"I want a pizza!" during math, then, "Will

you marry me?" to the drama specialist
and dash about the class. But after school,
the morning's blank, afternoon
shrunk to a dot.
We curse the Phenobarb but that's just part.
Your memory's shot. Hours after an event
the slate's wiped clean, your brain is innocent.

The Concert
April 2, 1994

"Alascom proudly sponsors," and prancing
round the edge, the creatures—lambs, a crow,
a lion, elephant
and donkey—listen
to a boy play violin. Nancy sticks
this poster up with magnets on the fridge
to plug a concert by the Fairbanks Symphony
that features you. Once skinny as
your bow,
you've put on twenty pounds and can't stop eating.

But though your memory leaks data like
a sieve, heart and fingers still remember
music. So in the dark
belly of the hall,
while Nancy and your older brother Jeff
tune with the orchestra, buzz turns to loud
applause as our pudgy boy comes out.

Back Home
"Hey, Dad, it's not like brain surgery!"
June 1997

The river in front of our house is almost dry
as break-up peters out. Gray sky above
gray sandbars. You wear a short goatee
and, back in soccer shape, you have a sure
excuse for everything
that you forget
to do. There is a residue of feeling
in these things
that gnaws my chest and pricks
at the corner of my eyes. Time heals,

they say, but who has wounded time? Thinking of
this I'm moved to grieve but you are not
like me. Your seizures mostly controlled by drugs,
you're full of hope
and horseplay, dig hard rock,
are skilled in math, the violin and soccer,
and your memory will get you round the block.

Speaking of Love/
Reading My Son

Clare Dunsford

The motive for metaphor, shrinking from
The weight of primary noon,
The A B C of being,

The ruddy temper, the hammer
Of red and blue, the hard sound—
Steel against intimation—the sharp flash,
The vital, arrogant, fatal, dominant X.

Wallace Stevens,
"The Motive for Metaphor"

The reading has already started in the mahogany-paneled library of this house on my university's campus, so I slip in quietly and perch on the ledge of the built-in bookcases. I assume my professional listening face—eyes trained on a distant spot, lips pursed, eyebrows slightly lowered, hand to chin. The author, a plump young woman, is reading a short story in a minimalist style, cute and glittering and laconic. This style has the same effect on me as *i*'s dotted with circles or hearts. Shifting on the hard wooden ledge, I can't seem to lose myself in the story.

I'm in a cranky mood. About an hour before, Kathleen, my son's sitter, has called my office.

"I thought you should know," she begins. "J.P. says his mouth hurts."

"Why? What's the matter?" I say, somewhat impatiently, as I am in the middle of a conference with a writing student. "Did he say how he hurt it?"

"Well, no." She hesitates. "I've asked him why and he can't really say. He even got some ice out of the freezer to soothe it, but I can't see any sore or blood in his mouth."

I begin to offer possible scenarios: Could he have bitten his tongue while eating his afterschool snack? Might he have fallen down and bitten his cheek? Could he have a fever blister? Not that she knows of: He seems to be eating, and, aside from being a bit droopy, he is otherwise OK. Feeling nonplussed, I hang up the phone.

The writer is still reading her story at the podium. Her clear, plummy voice carefully enunciates the short, simple sentences *sans* transitions that are apparently a hallmark of her style. Wanting to give her the benefit of the doubt, but irritated by what seems a gratuitous obscurity, I find my mind wandering again to J.P.'s enigmatic pronouncement: "My mouth hurts."

*

Once again I am reading my son. All parents must occasionally read between the lines when their children speak, but my reading skills are more challenged than the average parent's. For me the space between the lines is the difference between, say, a single-spaced manuscript and a triple-spaced one. That's because my son has Fragile X syndrome, a genetic condition that has sent his IQ well into the range of mental retardation, and afflicts him with anxiety, autistic-like behaviors, and the symptom that first caught my attention: a delay in the development of speech.

A passionate talker from an early age myself, I laved my firstborn with words as I changed him and bathed him, as I fed him and held him, as I kept intimate company with him on those endless, lonely days of early motherhood. But the kinds of communication promised in the baby books never arrived.

J.P. never babbled; he simply cried. He cried a lot. During the first two months he cried in pain from colic, and after that he cried at the pain that light, air, noise, and movement could cause his preternaturally alert senses.

And when he cried, I held him and rocked him. Our Victorian house had a curved oak staircase to the second floor that was punctuated by a broad landing, a space so generous that my husband, Harry, and I once had a string quartet play there for a party. But on a daily basis the staircase landing housed our stereo and speakers, and it was here that I set up the rocking chair, backlit by the window, and looking out over the downstairs front hall as from a stage. Harry had an old album of Johnny Mathis songs that I had discovered soothed J.P.'s nerves, and so I sat in the rocking chair, playing Johnny at full volume, crooning over my little boy as he sucked furiously on a pacifier and gazed at me with the blind trust that I could ease his pain. A nimbus of golden oaken light surrounded us, mother and child, as the melodramatic vowels of "Wonderful! Wonderful!" rolled from top to bottom of the house. I have never felt so close to anyone, and I have never felt so all alone.

The months passed, and though his nervous system settled down a bit, J.P. neither babbled nor spoke. It is painful for me to watch the home video Harry shot on J.P.'s first birthday, which we spent in a rented house on Cape Cod along with visiting friends. All I can hear is the shrill voice of a mother who knows something is wrong. It makes me long for the silent home movies of my childhood, like the one in which my five-year-old self chatters away to my little brother in our backyard plastic pool, my monologue as steady as the hose he held, the words now as lost as water down a drain.

As a new mother in 1986 I am all too conscious that Harry and J.P. and I are setting down a piece of family history in this video: I am filling the air with words not for the joy of it, but because my little boy cannot. I am desperately trying to concoct a scenario fit for a photo album, but the starring actor is not ready for his role. While the average one-year-old usually speaks three or four words and can jabber pretty good imitations of sentences, my one-year-old is seen in the video sucking silently on his pacifier or regularly letting out piercing shrieks. As the camera pans over the party, J.P. does not know how to play with the toys I unwrap for him. I hit the keys of a tiny piano, and he cannot imitate me. Although he chortles and smiles in obvious delight, his body is utterly rigid, legs straight out and kicking, arms fluttering constantly, eyes blinking. On the floor toddles the one-year-old son of our friends; calm and centered, he looks the camera in the eye, plays the little piano, and says, "Look a' me."

As time went on, I grew to hate those developmental milestones in the child-raising books. Somewhere between fifteen months ("baby says a two-word sentence") and twenty-four months ("baby says a three-word sentence"), the reassurances of family, friends, and strangers began to stick in my throat, and I made the first appointment with a pediatric neurologist. It would ultimately take four neurologists to change the diagnosis in the chart from the plain and simple description "language delay and attention deficit" to the esoteric designation "Fragile X syndrome."

*

The very fact that J.P. speaks at all is a miracle to me. When he was two and a half, he began to attend an Early Intervention Program for babies and toddlers with developmental delays. He was assigned a speech therapist whom Harry and I began to call Eeyore, after Winnie the Pooh's donkey friend, for her lugubrious ways and pessimistic comments. Utterly lost in this new world of disability, one day I asked Eeyore the kind of direct question that you later learn not to ask: "Will he *ever* talk?"

Without a moment of hesitation, she said bluntly, "We just don't know."

I could hardly believe he would not, for J.P.'s favorite toys from infancy were books; I read to him constantly, and the books he liked I read over and over. J.P. loved the sounds of individual words so much that when one struck his fancy he would laugh out loud and make us repeat it dozens of times. Vocabulary was always his strength, as later we would discover is typical of kids with Fragile X. Words stick out like trapunto in a J.P. sentence: when J.P. was eight or nine his otherwise garbled sentences were studded with knock-'em-dead words—"glamorous" and "sheepish," "nauseous" and "ravishing."

J.P.'s speech, so late in developing, is even today difficult for strangers to understand. It is rapid and has an odd rhythm that is a function of both unusual syntax and intonation. Speech therapists call this "cluttered" speech. It has been a strenuous process to understand his needs these past twenty-one years, to "hear" what he was saying in his shrieks, his abortive word-attempts, his single words, his rapid, cluttered speech. I have to listen carefully, to decipher what I can and infer the rest; I have to catch meaning on the fly, feint and dodge to feel it hit, but when it does ... it hits home.

One morning when he was ten years old, J.P. was eating breakfast and announced, "You're a great cook, Mommy." Since he was eating peach yogurt from a carton and store-bought muffins, this compliment was a stretch. A minute or two later, he stood up, juice glass in hand, and said, "This juice is delicious. It tastes like popcorn-marmalade." He then came over and hugged me with a twinkle in his eye that usually means he's been up to mischief. Suddenly, his meaning dawned. The night before, I had microwaved popcorn and put the uneaten portion in a bag that I left on top of the breadbox.

"Did you eat the popcorn in the bag?" I asked J.P.

"Yes," he answered promptly. Evidently he had found the popcorn before I got up that morning, and, in his own indirect way, wanted to 'fess up to finishing it. Orange juice plus popcorn equals popcorn-marmalade. The metaphor is decoded.

Metaphor is J.P.'s forte. The moon is a cinnamon cookie,

J.P. declared one crisp autumn night at age eight. The summer he attended a special school for children more severely affected by their disabilities than he is, he struggled with his self-image and seemed anguished that his parents thought he belonged there. The other kids, he wailed, were "diaper-wipes!"

When assigned to write poems in elementary school, J.P. often came up with striking images that once earned him the chance to have his poem read at a school assembly. Asked to describe his concept of "wilderness" in terms of the five senses, J.P. began:

> Wilderness feels like
> a rainy day
> soft as a mealworm
> safe from cars.
>
> Wilderness tastes like
> apples and
> cockroaches.

J.P. has a way of capturing the essence of people he knows with the names he devises for them, either compounds of his own invention or the names of characters from fairy tales, Disney, or TV. You could know something quite accurate about each of the female classmates he describes in this excerpt from his eighth-grade classroom journal. Asked to reflect on what distracts him in school, he dictated this to his teacher:

Sometimes I think about girlfriends too much. I think about their pigtails and their loveliness. I daydream about Heather, who looks like a mermaid, and Jessie, who looks like Snow White, Melissa, who looks like Tinker Bell, and Shannon, who reminds me of her beautiness, and Liana, who reminds me of Minnie Mouse, and Danielle, who reminds me of Barbie. All these ladies make my mind run like the Titanic. I need to kick them out of my skull so I can slow down and learn.

Like his hard-won diagnosis, with its oddly metaphorical name, J.P.'s utterances are often elusive and riddling. Some might call them incoherent, but I delight in their Dadaist ingenuity. One night after dinner, when he is fourteen, J.P. is scribbling at the kitchen table. He does not look up, but he knows I'm there. "She always gets my drift of negative boldness," he says, astonishingly. I wait, holding my breath, to see what he'll say next. Still without looking at me, he dashes off another line, announcing with a bouncy lilt, "She had me as a baby. She always gives me lunch of salad and Doritos." A budding Beat poet is writing a tribute to Mom, right here in my own kitchen.

*

The world of those with Fragile X syndrome, as for many cognitively challenged persons, is highly concrete, making abstractions like mathematics almost unconquerable. But this world yields the key to other mysteries. At Mass on Christmas Day, J.P. sees wine and bread carried to the altar in the offertory procession and exclaims, "Yuck! I hate blood!" J.P. made his First Communion, thanks to a loving and patient nun who gave him religious instruction, so he knew the Catholic belief that bread and wine are transformed into the body and blood of Christ in the sacrament of the Mass. No sooner has he said "yuck" on this Christmas morning than he announces, "I'll go to Communion," and rubs his stomach—"yum-yum!" He has an instinctive sacramental understanding of the world, which must be both terrifying and consoling. The Christmas gospel according to John announces, "The Word became flesh and dwelt among us." I know this is true because of my son.

J.P. is utterly literal. When the priest intones the ceremonial command, "Let us stand," my son answers loudly and incredulously, "Why?" After the ritual "Alleluia," he cheers, "That's right, guys!" An old ceremony glints with new shine in my son's ebullient presence.

Our life together has a surreal extravagance. At this same

Christmas Mass, J.P. enters the church, only to rush up to the crèche and dramatically kiss the statue of the infant Jesus in the manger. He then looks up at the candelabrum on the altar and says so all can hear, "There's a menorah!" One moment he is singing with the congregation, making up some of the words of the hymn in a kind of riff on love, and the next he is crying. I cannot predict or control his moods or their expression.

J.P. speaks in shifting registers of diction that mirror the shifting tectonic plates of his emotions. One moment he drawls like a country song, "I've got my mom and that's all I need"; the next he invokes fairy tale, as he trills the *r*: "You look r-r-r-ravishing! You're the princess of my dreams." Sometimes he speaks in what I think of as his "We are the World" mode: "We are a famil-y, living in harmon-y," he croons as I fix our dinner. Occasionally, he lapses into the language of old-fashioned storybooks, as when he intones, "Woe is me," over his cereal bowl.

Then there is the language of romance novels, often heard during middle school as he fell in love with a new classmate every week. "I'm going to make her my wife," he declared at age thirteen of his first love, Shannon, whom he also once called "my little rose blossom." Another morning he stopped eating breakfast dramatically, hand on his heart: "I think I'm in love.... My heart is beating.... She's my heart, my soul, my beloved.... It's my destiny!" Of these love affairs, which come and go in the middle-school classroom with such velocity and publicity, he dreamily remarked one day, after listing all his classmates' crushes, "Love is in the air."

*

To live with a person who does not communicate in the same way you do is to know a terrible loneliness. J.P. thrives on repetition. Some nights, as I sit across from J.P. at the dinner table, and hear the same answers to my questions as the night before, I feel trapped by the tropes of his—of our—narrow life. If I ask about his friend Shannon, I can be sure that "she's showing off *some*where," and about his teacher, that she is still a "hottie"; that Oprah today was about "sex and death," that Ellen was "FUN-NY," and that tomorrow he will say these things again. Every night he says, "Watch the Bear tomorrow?" and as he leaves the house for school, "Watch Raven tonight?"—two television programs that bookend his day. And yet he also says every day, each time with the urgency of a new discovery, "You're the best mom in the world" and "I love you to pieces!"

I wonder sometimes whether J.P. is as lonely as I am. He yearns for connection, but his nervous system chokes his attempts to reach out to his friends. In his social anxiety J.P. is like those living with autism, and in fact, 15 to 33 percent of children with Fragile X meet the full criteria for autism, according to the National Fragile X Foundation. To put it the other way around, several screening studies have found that 2.5 to 6 percent of boys with autism have Fragile X syndrome. The effects of additional background genes may one day explain why some children have these dual diagnoses. In general, J.P. and his fellow "X-men" are gregarious and social creatures: even as they look away, they hang around the action. However, I have seen firsthand that Fragile X and autism can look a lot alike.

J.P. and I are at our local grocery store when I spot Jim, a young man with autism who lives in our town and attends the same school program as J.P.

"Hey, J.P., isn't that Jim?" I ask him, pointing to Jim, who, having just seen us, has turned on his heel and is scurrying down the frozen-foods aisle.

"No," J.P. grunts, without even looking Jim's way.

"JaaayPeeeee! Look *that* way. I know that's Jim, the kid from school."

"Oh, yeaaaah," he draws it out as if he is just realizing, though I know he's simply trying to placate me, and he probably saw Jim before I did.

"That little scoundrel," he says with a grin.

"Why don't you go say hi to him?"

"No, I'll stay here," he says in a fast, choppy monotone.

"Come on, J.P. He's a nice kid. Don't be rude." (Why on earth do I talk like this? Why won't I ever give up?)

"No, I'm fine." At this point, Jim comes down the pasta aisle, shoots a quick glance our way, and darts away faster than a runaway cart. Clearly he is intrigued, but he doesn't want a closer encounter. At some point I see Jim's father and chat with him, laughing about our boys' mutual avoidance. J.P. scoots off to the magazine section. What if he runs into Jim? They can always look at magazines side by side, bodies twitching as their senses zing, all the while carefully ignoring each other.

Some of J.P.'s classmates are, as he reminds me solemnly, "nonverbal," but even those who are "verbal," as he is, do not use words with ease or clarity. When he was in seventh grade I often asked J.P. whether he and his girlfriend du jour, Jessie, ever talked, or if he knew what kinds of things she liked, but he routinely shrugged off my question. I knew that whenever they laid eyes on each other, they made a seal-like bark that sounded like "Ork! Ork!" and I found myself badgering him: "How can you be friends if you don't talk? You say you're in love with her, but you just make sounds at her. You need to talk to her." Suddenly I heard myself and realized how untrue this was, how untrue even to my own experience. Love takes root in what we feel, not what we know; communication can take many forms other than words. What's more, every pair of lovers creates their own love talk. "Ork-ing" is what lovers do.

My mother tells a story of my infancy that has always enchanted me. When my father would walk in the door from work in the evening, I would light up and cry, "Ocky-noony, Daddy-doe," to which my father would never fail to answer, "Noony-noony, Clarey." As my mother saw it, our passionate attachment gave rise to a language of our own, unique and exclusive.

Lately, when I come home from work, J.P. comes to the door between the house and garage and calls out, "Who's there?"

I answer, "Mommy."

"Mommy who?" he replies. "The girl of my dreams? The one I love?" Tired and weighed down by briefcase and purse, I smile and wearily answer, "Yes," and he lets me in.

One night he won't open the door. "What's the password?" he asks.

Without thinking I answer, "Love."

"You're ab-sol-utely right!" he cries.

*

"Wo-o-o-of! Woof! Woof!" J.P. is barking like a dog again, a trick he picked up from an eighth-grade classmate who has Williams syndrome, another genetic condition that confers unusual skills of verbal imitation. The two of them, J.P. and Charles, bark back and forth the livelong day, much to their teachers' consternation. This particular morning, no sooner has J.P. finished barking than he calls out, apropos of what I have no idea, "Mom, that's hooligan-ish!" A minute later, "I'm feeling lemur-ish!" My head spins with his jabberwocky—I'm Alice in my own Wonderland, a place that is alarmingly foreign but somehow as familiar as home.

Around this time, I begin a new romantic relationship. One night I do what I have never done since my divorce: I arrange for J.P., who spends most weekends with his father, to spend an evening with my new boyfriend and me. Not just a quick introduction, but dinner and, of all things, decorating the Christmas tree.

My gamble pays off. The evening has a surreal magic that I've come to know as my version of motherhood, maybe my version of love. The three of us dance and sing and laugh and even have what J.P. calls a group hug. But the real miracle occurs as I am putting J.P. to bed and tell him to call good-night to Stephen, who is in another room. J.P. instead lets out a bark, and, without skipping a beat, from the living room, Stephen barks back. My son's face breaks open in a grin. I know right then that we are understood.

Ordinary Time

Carol Zapata-Whelan

*The Sandos, in their late thirties, have a vitality
and charm that transcend their surprising physical
appearance. Both recline in power wheelchairs.
Andy's body is virtually straight, with his legs
slightly crossed, while Nancy is mildly bent at
the waist. Nancy's jaw is fused, and recently,
Andy's fused as well, a circumstance that forced
him to give up the trumpet...*

Thomas Maeder
"A Few Hundred People Turned to Bone"
The Atlantic Monthly February, 1998

"Why are you so late?" asks Salvador from the curb. A rhetorical question, my son well knows, one with a million reasons for it, one with no real answer at all. Why, indeed? Lateness is a trait, like a thick middle or a round face. I am happy with none of it, but what can I do? God knows; I've tried.

"Sorry" is my answer for today, a day with a sky too blue to ruin with excuses. It is an expansive September afternoon in the San Joaquin Valley. Yesterday's rains have dispelled our haze and thrown open the horizon, revealing the Sierra Nevada Mountains, their dark rock and glamour of snow apparent only every now and then, a reminder of something ancient and planetary, saved from time.

Salvador slides open the minivan, tosses his trumpet case on the floor, backpack on the booster seat, and carries out his loading procedure: spine to the passenger side, backwards flop on the captain's chair, dark hair grazing the arch of door, swivel to the front. Every time, I suppress a wince.

He gives me his quiet smile, dear Sal, sways obligingly, and I kiss the soft stubble on the side of his head. Today we skip "How was school?" His answer is always the same, anyway, always a clipped "fine."

"When do we have to be there tonight?" I ask.

"The real time?" he answers. Salvador, like our other four children, like the rest of the population in town, knows I have no sense of time and must be fitted with a different schedule, one with artificial numbers—a prosthetic schedule. I am the one always just missing bells and buses, entire days of time, in fact, lost like socks in a dryer.

"The real time."

Salvador checks his watch (I don't seem to be wearing one), looks to the sky, and gives me a number I write in red pen across my palm.

"Too bad we don't have a ring," he says, without regret in his voice. Salvador has learned not to regret—or at least to distract it with trigonometry and the trumpet. He is staring out the window at the students waiting for rides, grouped indolently on a wooden platform. Except for their Catholic school uniforms, they remind me of a congregation of birds bobbing lazily on a dock.

"Well, it's too late for that, anyway." *Too late*. "And you know we couldn't afford it." For his sixteenth birthday, it was either the royal blue jacket with a patch of red spelling "BAND," or the class ring.

"I know," he says lightly.

"I wish you'd at least given them a rosary to bless, that wooden one," I say. My son frowns. He'd rather just have one of the roses heaped in a basket at the altar. Most juniors already have their May Shamrock or September Sapphire Class of 2004 rings or holy medals lined up on velvet, ready to bless tonight at the Junior Class Ring Ceremony. I know all this from my friend Carmen, who drills me on dates and deadlines. I have her son, Luke, in a picture with Sal, the photograph where a little boy with dark hair and a little boy with light hair extend their arms wide, wide, wide, like planes, like gulls, gliding and laughing over the blacktop's yellow half-moons and painted boundaries. That was before—a few years before, exactly two years before—Sal started limping. Exactly three years and three months before he stopped raising his right hand in fourth grade. Four years to the October he couldn't raise his left hand—five before the summer his hip... I clear my head of the gliding boys. I clear my head.

"Seatbelt?" I nod to Sal. He is already buckled, no doubt, but I glance over anyway. And then I see something: blue. Heaven's vault blue, rainbow blue, unmarked and unmarred, round as a ring. My son is wearing it.

"*Eso*," I point. Sal raises an eyebrow. He's good at that, the only one in the family who can keep one eyebrow at rest while the other rears up like a question mark. (I know because we have all sat around the table straining foreheads.)

"That's it, *m'hijo*."

Salvador follows my gaze; then, the look of someone who has just heard a good riddle starts in his intelligent brown eyes, moves down his face. My son smiles slightly to himself, turns his neck as far as it will go, and looks right at me. I can see the silver of his retainer.

"Can they bless one more thing?" I wonder.

"Mrs. Jones might still be there. Number 73."

I climb down from the minivan, leave Sal in the car by the platform of students, a group dwindling as parents pull up and pull away; I jog along the adobe mission buildings, the art deco Media Center, past an ivory statue of Our Lady of

Guadalupe and the ice-blue water in tiers of the Spanish fountain. I round a familiar corner and grab the knob on door number 73. Locked. I peek in a little rectangle of window. The room is darkened.

Oh well.

The school bell's brutal buzz, a minute off, startles me. I know I am now late to pick up my girls: the bells from the chapel gong elegantly, three times, over an echo of the alarm that has just blasted my bones.

Why me? Me, in charge. Someone always missing things, never at the right place at the right time, even before the first dark film slapped across a light panel, long before rings started flying off my hands in waiting rooms, before anyone could ever pronounce a one in 2 million genetic curse: fibrodysplasia ossificans progressiva. All this happens on my watch, to someone who tells her children sitting on sofas to fasten their seatbelts when she thinks she is saying, put on your shoes! Salvador no longer can.

On my way back to the car I do not jog. I do not breathe in a medicinal scent of sage and earth released by the rains.

And I do not see the car. Salvador. In a reflex of panic, I scan the school. This is not a good part of town, and I just lost my purse to it, an old Mexican handbag distended by a camera loaded with film, worthless to the man with dirty blond hair who ducked in our garage in the morning and ordered pizza by noon to an address on this very street. He signed my full name on check number 1001: Maria Luz Quilatzli De La Torre, in girlish loops I lost long ago. And he must have managed to look like the picture on my California Driver's License, where I am much better than in real life: a smooth-faced Latina with a vague hairdo and an innocent smile. The only thing I've had time to replace is the camera.

There! There it is, cobalt blue in the emptying senior parking lot across the street; I see Salvador's profile, stiff distinction of a Spanish doubloon or holy medal, framed in the car window.

He is talking to someone, a guy in a leather jacket with a motorcycle helmet under an arm.

As I approach the car, I see that Salvador's attention is on Father Manuel, a bearded bear of a man with eyes the color of eucalyptus, a priest for whom (I've heard) parishes give standing ovations. I know Father Manuel from high school, this high school, when he was Manny, one of those Mickey-Mouse-track kids who lit cigarettes with cigarettes in cars that scraped the road with their bumpers. Now he's chaplain and assistant band director. And he's looking like a Hell's Angel—again.

Father Manuel, Manny, makes a show of creaking a leather sleeve and checking his wrist. "I'm so late *hasta la Señora De La Torre* beat me," he says, with an accomplice's grin. "Hey, girl, I moved you out of the red zone."

Salvador has the same accomplice grin, like he and this priest, together, have just solved a riddle or shared a joke I missed. This annoys me, though I know it shouldn't.

"You have something else to bless," I say evenly.

Father Manuel extends his large paw of a hand, opened toward the sky and the prehistoric palms in their thatched jackets, looming.

*

"Mom! I can't find my other sock!" The refrain starts to filter in, override my online fixation. Even though I sometimes just delete, the same way I hid the first *FOP Guide for Families* in an underwear drawer, its booklet cover a perfect blue butterfly painted by a young man with permanently crossed arms. "Mom, WHERE IS MY—" I block out Sofia for just one more moment. My heart is riding the incandescent letters from a mother in France:

> *Severine was misdiagnosed until the age of 13 years and her first bone formation was at the age of nine years so she was able to go to dancing class, swimming lessons, ski, horse, golf, sailing.*

"Ask Saint Anthony to find it," says Gabriela from very far away, farther than Paris. "Saint Anthony, please find Sofia's sock. Thank you." At five, Gabriela doesn't know yet that in our modest home, where we have tossed salads of shoes and clothes in every room, her sister has as good a chance of digging up a Paleolithic fossil as she does of finding a sock.

"Why do you say 'thank you'?" asks Salvador, carefully handing Gabriela a microwaved quesadilla. "He hasn't found it yet."

She has broken many times arm, foot, tooth because she was very stiff, she had no looseness but we didn't know that she was not supposed to do sports and she liked to be always in movement.

"He's no good! I hate you, Saint Anthony!" Sofia is yelling at the living room ceiling. "He takes too long! He takes two weeks!!" I ought to say something to my ten-year-old for this. Instead, I stir the mouse on the mouse pad.

She didn't like to work at school and to stay quiet . . . now she is 26 and have to stay quiet because her body can't allow her to move like in her youth. When she was 16, she was in art school but she could no longer paint with her arms blocked. Two years ago she want to die because her jaw freeze and it is too hard to live like that; she didn't eat anymore. . . .

"Sofia," Gabriela enunciates. "Saint Anthony doesn't just ring the doorbell and say, 'Here's your sock!'" I check the ink on my palm. It's probably time—exactly now—to leave for the ring ceremony, but I cannot take my eyes off the last words on the screen:

I told her that I was there near her but I couldn't eat in her place, and after a long time she decided to live with the FOP.

"Drive faster, Mom!" In the captain's seat next to me, Salvador is resplendent, if a little pale, in a white shirt and one of his father's ties assembled around his neck with the help of a FAX. My husband, Antonio, is out of town for the packing-house; our eldest, Carlos, drove Rafael to the eighth grade soccer clinic; and my dad left for Mexico, so Father Manuel sent Sal a cheat sheet. And on tiptoe, I used blue Dep hair gel to tamp down the waves on the top of my son's head. He will not use the catalog device that can arc a comb over his crown.

"Mom?" says Sofia, as we accelerate through a yellow light. "When I'm a grown-up, will I have a mustache?"

"Of course not."

"Because Raf said mustaches are hereditary," explains Sofia. "And you have one." I involuntarily check myself in the rearview mirror.

"Slugbug! Green!" shouts Gabriela from her booster, hitting Sofia's arm as we pass a Volkswagen. A no-it's-not yes-it-is no-it's-not exchange follows for longer than most parents will bear, but I'm driving too hard to speak.

"Hummer!" calls Salvador, stopping the fight. His shoulder blades hurt, and he cannot turn back to tag. Everyone knows it's forbidden to hit Sal. But the military jeep falls behind, into the twilight, and there are no cars near us to finish the game, anyway.

"In high school you don't get to color," Gabriela complains, out of the blue. "And you have to divide!" She has a pink tiara in her tea-colored curls, which I will forget to grab before we get inside.

"By then you'll be smarter," remarks Sofia. She launches helpfully into a parable with a door-to-door king distributing jellybeans through his kingdom. I myself am having trouble keeping track of the king's zeros and check the rearview mirror. Gabriela is paying most of her attention to a slatted truck shedding white chicken feathers along the highway.

"I'll write it down for you when we get home," concludes Sofia as we pull into the parking lot. I fish a brush from a tangle of toys and school papers on the floor between seats, reach back and take a few swipes down my daughter's long black hair.

"Me and Gabby missed Celina's party," says Sofia, shrugging away the brush. I notice she is wearing one sock.

Oh no.

"Did you ask her when it was?" I ask lamely. Gabriela is defiantly adjusting her tiara, which doesn't go with a plaid scrunchy or the navy uniform pants she and Sofia are wearing. I use fingers like a comb on my hair. We will just have to move on as we are.

"She stuck her hand in front of my face and said, 'Talk to the hand.'"

Oh.

Sal forges ahead, stronger than his limp. At least we're here, on time—I'm certain of it—at the right spot, a well-lighted hangar of a church with goal post structures on the altar and a crucifix that looks like exploding metal. There are times when I miss the dim Spanish chapels of my childhood with their natural-sized saints, gold leaf and baroque excess. Salvador reaches for a hand from each little sister and guides the girls around the indoor amphitheater to where his class is segregated by RESERVED signs in large bold font at the end of each pew. Sal leaves us to sit by his friend Luke, but is shooed away to an assigned section by an official looking woman in lilac, Mrs. Jones, most likely. I know my son will be uneasy between kids he does not know.

"Wait! Sal!" I call. Salvador stops. I pull the new camera from my purse; he pulls a face. Photography isn't a hobby, it's a compulsion, humored only by our five-year-old. Somewhere in my drawer of film rolls, yellow cylinders confused with old prescriptions and batteries, are the negatives of sullen profiles, crossed eyes, knives stabbing cakes decorated with candles. But a compulsion is a compulsion. I set the flash and get a shot of Sal shaking his head at the goal posts.

*

A trio of sophomores with thin voices sings hymns I no longer recognize, as altar servers and clergy file in. The ceremony's main celebrant is a priest from India, a striking young man with white hair. His tongue moves delicately over the hard consonants of English as he speaks to the meaning of the ring ceremony. I see the light palms of his dark hands opened, his gestures slow, as if pausing, itself, were a sacred act. Behind him is Father Manuel, looking more like a man of the cloth; and a new priest, a former Episcopalian they say is married. This is the first time I have seen one of these clergymen in person and I look for signs of his state, a more anchored body, perhaps, a different virility. I study the ash blond priest, his full frame, and watch his fingers to find out how many rings he has. I can't tell, and remember my own son doesn't have even one, as each teacher and administrator at the lectern speaks to the promise of youth, of eternity spelled in a ring.

The Indian priest starts to look like a saint in one of the holy cards I saved in another life. The girls snort suddenly, and I wedge myself between them. It is getting difficult, tiring, to make out the words of the priest, who keeps saying "our fate," when he means, "our faith."

But then I see Salvador. He has moved directly across us, to the front of the church, and is leaning against a baby grand's inside curve, his weight on the better leg. He stands behind two rigid blond girls with flutes, and they play "Morning Has Broken." My son's breath in the gold notes of the trumpet stings my eyes. Sofia is still. Gabriela leans her warm weight into me as if to sleep.

Father Manuel, Manny, is clearing his throat at the mike. (I still can't believe he's a priest; I can still see his big back blocking the Ramirez brothers, their noses running with blood, his beefy shoulders rounded in Brother Joseph's office. But Sal likes the man, with his bull-in-a-china-shop faith, never too polite, never asking how Sal is feeling.) I scan the pews for my son, who is back to sitting very straight between the two boys I don't recognize.

He breathes with his diaphragm muscles and basically walks with the remaining muscles in the back part of his legs that have not hardened. This on the screen last week: how is it I remember?

I force my attention back on Father Manuel, who is reading:

Thus says the Lord: Say to those whose hearts are frightened: Be strong, fear not! Here is your God, he comes with vindication; with divine recompense he comes to save you. Then will the eyes of the blind be opened, the ears of the deaf be cleared, then will the lame leap like a stag, then the tongue of the mute will sing—

In another life, I've heard this passage, one more Biblical prescription. But tonight the words surprise me like smoke, like incense, filtering in and through me, like a deep breath filling the honeycomb of loss in my soul, settling like a blessing, leaving me with something like peace. I do not really see the juniors called up name by name, parading self-consciously down the aisle, the hunching youths and their convalescent walk, the bounding athletes, the glamorous young women, the unfinished girls ashamed of their skin or dress size. I do not hold my breath or even my camera as Salvador goes up the half moon of gold steps, with the dignified limp that will not show in a photograph. And though I am too far away to see, I know that Salvador's hands open for the silver weave that binds the blue circle, the immaculate face unmarked by numbers and unmarred by lines.

*

The Junior Ring Ceremony is over, and we congregate in the mild autumn evening by a white fountain. Father Manuel is moving toward us, near a table of Gatorade and homemade cakes where Salvador has posed with a group of friends, boys with strong smiles and clear eyes—cameras raised by other mothers, who will, no doubt, hand me photographs next week in the parking lot.

"So, you got your time blessed, *m'hijo*," Father Manuel says.

Salvador smiles quietly, looks directly at me. I press my cheek to his bony shoulder. There is something I need to know: "Manny, your passage—"

Father Manuel is about to put a Dixie cup with Gatorade to his lips. "The prophet Isaiah?"

"Did you pick it for any special reason?" I spot Sofia and Gabriela at another table loading napkins with brownies, and pantomime at them. Gabriela, the tip of her nose brushed with frosting, delicately returns a few of the treats with chocolate-coated fingers.

"I didn't exactly choose it," Father Manuel says, following my eyes. "Mrs. Jones wanted to keep everything close to the 23rd Sunday in Ordinary Time—and that's the first reading scheduled in the Missal."

He gives me a wily look. Manny, Father Manuel, is not used to this type of question from me. He watches Salvador, who arches one eyebrow; and then, like an actor realizing he's missed a cue, the priest announces: "Salvador has something to show you!"

Salvador extends his arms out in front of himself as far as he can raise them, which is just below shoulder height. His white sleeve hitches up from the blessed blue watch, a Fossil, the one Antonio slipped him for his birthday. Except now it's green, prism green; rose stem green; green, the color of hope. I admire it closely. "You switched?" I ask. My husband told us the watch could change its face. "It's beautiful."

Salvador nods absently, as if I'm missing the obvious. He exaggeratedly rotates his other arm. It takes me a moment to register what I see.

"Remember?" Strapped around Salvador's right wrist is a band of cracked leather holding a Mickey Mouse watch, the cartoon in red lederhosen, one white gloved finger pointing straight up, the other signaling East: three o'clock.

I am stunned.

I haven't seen this watch, my watch, my high school watch, in six years. Not since those hours at Children's, with Sal lying still in white MRI tunnels, all my jewelry removed. And those days after, when the rings, my rings, grew too big and rolled across floors as I talked to specialists: silver circles with turquoise, my gold band, the zirconium engagement ring, all returned to me by sympathetic receptionists, all in envelopes with a giraffe mascot on them.

I can formulate no response. "I thought I—"

"Father Manny found it."

"Manny? Today? Where—?" The reception is thinning out, mothers are throwing open their arms at one other and boys are hooking fingers in ties.

Father Manuel looks uncharacteristically sheepish. A group of parents and juniors comes by to greet him, but veers off, shaking hands with the Indian priest and the Episcopalian. I see Sofia and Gabriela balancing on the white perimeter of the fountain.

"I have a confession to make," says Father Manuel. "I've had it for six years."

Exactly six years minus two months. I am starting to feel angry, nauseous.

"It was in the confessional, well, not in—"

"And you just kept it? Isn't that some kind of special sin?" I realize I've raised my voice when boys in a cluster by the Gatorade turn their heads.

"I'm sorry, Luz. It was that day you..." The priest's eyes search the church's abstract stained glass, as if he might find something there for this explanation. But he doesn't have to say anything. I know the day. The day after Sal's diagnosis. The day the tule fog hung on past noon, choking sight, erasing landmarks with air like chalk dust. Saturday, November 9, at 11:55 a.m., when the line at the confessional still snaked past the bank of blue candles, and Sal had been standing for too, too long, and I lost my temper with whichever priest was giving therapy instead of absolution, and banged on the dark door in the middle, and it flew open, and I slammed it when I saw the surprised face, and I grabbed Salvador's still-perfect right arm and left the church.

"I figured I'd give it to you when you came back," said Father Manuel simply.

There is nothing I can say, not in front of my son, not in front of anyone. Sal is strapping the watch on my wrist, and I check it, a reflex lost six years ago. Mickey Mouse's smiling face made a mockery of things the last time I saw it.

"It's stuck on three o'clock," is all I can say, raising Mickey to Father Manuel and Sal, my hand a fist. The piece obviously hasn't ticked for some time.

"The hour of mercy," the priest says quietly.

The hour of mercy. Yes. Yes, I know that, I realize. When Christ was taken down from the cross.

The girls jog up to me, Sofia is barefoot and her uniform pants are rolled to her knees, the cuffs soaked.

"She falled in the fountain!" announces Gabby triumphantly. A few junior girls, young women I barely recognize from the years I taught at the parish school, are looking our way. I can tell they want to say something about Sofia's shoes, but are deciding not to.

"Fell," Sal corrects. He runs a hand through Gabby's brown curls. She moves behind him for protection.

"Tattletale," says Sofia. She thinks I wouldn't have noticed anything, but she is wrong now.

"Father Manuel blessed your watch, too." Sal looks at me hopefully. "We thought it up today."

In response, I consider Mickey Mouse. He has changed in six years; he has certainly changed since high school.

It takes me longer than I would like to find my voice. "Throw in an absolution and some batteries and we're even," I finally say to the priest. Father Manuel puts a hand to his beard, nods soberly, then gives his big bucktoothed laugh.

I scoop up Gabriela, who is charmed by the treasure I wear. She is just learning to tell time and pronounces it as a question. Sofia checks Mickey Mouse's hands and laughs.

In the distance of the parking lot I am surprised to see my husband, Antonio, my sons Carlos and Rafael. Salvador lopes over and the four, all now even in height, all dark haired and handsome, glorious, smile at me and the girls, at Father Manuel looking back, moving off with his arm across the Indian priest's shoulders.

"I know we're too late, but we came anyway," calls Antonio from the curb.

"You made it at exactly the right time," I call back over dispersing little groups, raising a hand, raising my watch like a torch.

Moonrise

Penny Wolfson

1. Moonrise, 1983

At the Center for Creative Photography in Tucson, Arizona, my husband Joe and I are looking at prints of *Moonrise, Hernandez, New Mexico* by Ansel Adams. A slender young man in a suit has brought us, as requested, three versions of this famous photograph; before removing each 18" x 24" enlargement from its glassine sheath, he dons a pair of white gloves, opens the hinged glass viewing case in front of us, and places them carefully, lovingly, on a slanted white board inside. He stands there while we examine the pictures; when we are done, he will repeat the process in reverse.

I don't know exactly where Hernandez, New Mexico, is, but it reminds me a bit of Sacaton, 90 miles north of here, the Pima Indian village where we have lived since July. We have made the trip to Tucson expressly to view the Ansel Adams photos, though we had not imagined that there were so many prints, each somewhat different, of the same negative.

In *Moonrise*, two-thirds of the space is usurped by a rich black sky; a gibbous moon floats, like a hot air balloon in an otherworldly—and yet absolutely Southwestern—landscape. A gauzy strip of low clouds or filtered light drifts along the horizon, distant mountains lit by waning sun or rising moon. Then very low, among scrubby earth and sparsely scattered trees, in the bottom third of the photo, human settlement: a small collection of modest stucco houses and one larger building, of concrete or adobe, perhaps a kiva, or ceremonial building. Around the edge of the village, crosses rise from the ground at many angles, white crosses that at first resemble clotheslines strung with sheets or socks, but on later examination obviously mark graves.

The prints differ greatly in quality from the reproductions one usually sees, and also differ slightly from each other; here, we see a more defined darkness, burnt in by the photographer, there, a variation in exposure, a grainier texture. But that cannot change the essential meaning of the photograph, a meaning one never forgets in the Southwest: Nature dominates. Human life is small, fragile, and finite. And yet, still, beautiful.

2. Falling, 1998

Ansel and I are at the Grand Union. It's raining. He begged to come so I brought him, not really wanting to, because then there's his wheelchair to bring, too: it weighs 200 pounds, and isn't easy to maneuver into the car. Even though a ramp leads into the side door of the minivan I still have to grab and tug the motorized chair till it faces forward and then, bending and squeezing into the narrow confines of the car's interior, I have to belt it down to the floor with several clasping tie-downs. By the time I do all this even once I'm irritable. A trip to the supermarket means doing it four times.

Anyway, we're done with our shopping now and we leave the supermarket. Ansel's in his chair, without his nice yellow raincoat with the hood from L.L.Bean, because he's decided, at the age of thirteen, that a raincoat is babyish, not cool. He's afraid people at school will laugh at him. Maybe this is true, I tell him, but I think it's stupid. Why get wet when you can stay dry? Needless to say, I lose this argument.

While I'm loading the trunk I open the car doors so Ansel can get into the front seat, where he always sits if Joe, his dad, isn't with us. He parks his chair at a distance from the minivan, so that I'll have room for the ramp, and starts to rise. No, "rise" sounds too easy; like smoke going up a flume, airy, like bread from those fine grainy bits of yeast, crumbly, rising in the oven. Ansel does not rise. He shifts sideways in the seat, pulls himself up, heavily, propping his 80 pounds against the armrest of the chair for balance. He leans with his left arm; he twists his right shoulder around to straighten up and brings his hip and buttocks up to a partly standing position. Actually, he's sort of bent in half, with his hands still on the chair's joystick. There is a moment, now, of imbalance. His feet are planted far apart, farther out than his hips, and he needs to bounce back and forth a few times to bring his feet together. Finally, he's up. He begins walking towards the door in his waddling, tiptoed way. His spine is curved, his stomach is forward, his hands are out at his sides chest-high, back, his fingers outstretched.

His balance is so tenuous his five-year-old brother Toby can knock him down. Sometimes Ansel will bellow: "I'm tired of everyone always leaving things all over the floor! Don't they know I'll fall?" It's true we're a little careless about this. But Ansel will trip over anything: an unevenness in the sidewalk, the dog's water dish, some bits of food on the floor, things expected and unexpected—and sometimes over nothing. Sooner or later, he falls. It's part of the routine. And the older he gets, the more he falls.

And now, in the Grand Union parking lot, he falls. He's in the skinny aisle of asphalt between our car and the one parked next to us and who knows why—could be the wet ground, but not necessarily. He falls, and it's pouring, and I'm still loading grocery bags into the back.

"Mom!" he calls at me, half-barking, half-crying. "I fell!" There's such anguish, such anger, in his voice when he falls, and such resignation. He never thinks I hear him.

And why am I so angry, suddenly? Such terrible impatience rises in me now. Am I really such a witch, such a bad mother, that when I'm loading groceries and my son falls, I don't have the time or patience to cope? Why am I so angry?

"Wait a minute," I say. "I'll be there in a minute."

So he sits there on the wet ground between the cars. I know his sweatpants are at this moment soaking through. I can see that the wheelchair, still also waiting to be rolled up the ramp, still needing to be pushed and yanked into position, is also getting wet. Its foamy nylon seat will need drying out later.

A middle-aged blond woman has wheeled her shopping cart into the lot and approaches us. "Can I help?"

No, you definitely cannot help, runs through my head. And this is both true and self-righteous. Physically, the job's not meant for two; it's easier for me to do on my own. How would we two, and Ansel, even fit between the cars?

I grit my teeth and smile and say, "No, no thanks, really. I can do it." People always seem so puzzled and upset when they see him fall. It's so sudden, an instant crumpling, without warning. They can't see the weakness, the steady deterioration of his pelvis. Maybe anyone would fall this way if they'd been hit hard, in the solar plexus; I don't know. But his feet really do give way for no apparent reason, and he's down.

The blond woman has heard me, but keeps standing there, her hands clamped around the handle of her wagon, her eyes moving from Ansel to the grocery bags to me. I know she means to be helpful, and in a way I do want something from her—pity? An acknowledgment that I am more noble than she? But mostly I want her to go away. Don't look at me. Don't watch this.

"Mom! Where *are* you?"

I turn from the blond woman; she fades away. "OK, I'm coming." I try to wedge myself in between the cars so I can retrieve Ansel. There's a special way to pick him up: You have to come from behind and grab him under the arms, raise him a little farther than standing, his toes dangling just above the ground, and then set his feet down precisely the right distance apart.

I'm in pretty good shape, but Ansel is completely dead weight. Another child would help you, put his hands around your neck. His feet would come off the ground when there was even the suggestion of lifting. But Ansel is pulling me down, his limp shoulders, his big, heavy leg braces, his sodden pants, his clumsy sneakers. I can't hold him. My own sneakers slip on the wet ground.

3. Chaos, 1999

The New York Academy of Medicine, on 103rd Street and Fifth Avenue, is not exactly in the slums, but it's not the Upper East Side, either. On a dreary, drizzly morning I park at the Metropolitan Museum garage on 80th Street and walk up Madison, past the Banana Republic and Ann Taylor and the patisseries and the fancy meat purveyors and the little French children's clothing shops with names like Bonpoint that display sashed dresses with hand-embroidered yokes in their windows. Above 96th Street, near the Mount Sinai Hospital complex, the scenery and the people abruptly change; everything's older and more rundown. Street peddlers hawk books, batteries, Yankee caps, cheap scarves, acrylic ski caps, $5 handbags. I see an obese black man leaning on a cane, harried-looking workers with hospital badges, a woman exiting a hospital building through a revolving door with crutches in her hand.

Twelve years ago, when he was three, my son Ansel was diagnosed with a hereditary form of muscular dystrophy called Duchenne, which rapidly destroys muscle tissue, confining affected boys to wheelchairs by adolescence and invariably resulting in early death. Because of its "X-linked" inheritance pattern—like hemophilia, it is almost always transmitted to sons from asymptomatic "carrier" mothers—Duchenne's muscular dystrophy, or DMD, is a disorder seen rarely in girls. In my own extended family, which produced an overwhelming number of daughters and nearly no sons for two generations, the existence of the Duchenne gene—or more correctly, the existence of an altered gene, which doesn't properly code for a particular muscle protein—was a secret even to us, a subterranean truth. My mother and sister and I, all carriers without outward signs, never guessed at this defect in our genetic heritage.

Joe and I had given our son, conceived and born in Arizona, the name of the great photographer we admired who'd died earlier that year. It seemed apt; he was, as people told us often, prettier than a picture, amber-haired and round-eyed, with a perpetually quizzical but serene countenance and the build of a slender but sturdy miniature football player. For two years he'd developed normally, reaching all the typical benchmarks on or close to schedule. An engaging and beautiful boy, special, gifted, one suspected, in some intangible way. When his teacher in nursery school began to point out Ansel's deficits in language, in gross motor skills—he couldn't alternate legs on the stairs, couldn't master rudimentary grammar—we refused to see any problem. It was impossible for us to believe that this perfectly wonderful child, our child, was not perfect at all, that he was handicapped, in fact, and would become progressively more handicapped.

It took a year to accept his differentness, to have him professionally evaluated, to reach a diagnosis. And though we have been to dozens of doctors and dealt with every aspect of his disease, it has taken me twelve years to get up the nerve to come here, to the Academy of Medicine, and look squarely at what will happen to Ansel in the coming years, in a future I have never completely faced.

The library reading room is large and quiet, with a high ceiling and a faded tapestry on the wall behind me. I sit nervously waiting for the books I've requested, at a long oak table beneath a grand chandelier, surrounded by busts of famous scientists, all men, who peer down from atop the bookshelves. It makes sense, I suppose, that Louis Pasteur sits head and shoulders above the lesser knowns.

But even Pasteur, I remind myself, did not cure muscular

dystrophy. Nor did any of the nineteenth-century doctors who described the disease, including the English physicians Sir Charles Bell and Edward Meryon and Sir William Gowers—or even the French neurologist G.B.A. Duchenne, after whom one form of dystrophy is named. And despite hundreds, perhaps thousands, of studies completed, articles written and compiled, perhaps sitting right here in the bound volumes surrounding me in this rarefied room, in the prestigious journals like *Muscle and Nerve* and *Lancet* and *JAMA*, no one, even in this century, has found a way to save my son.

A young woman arrives with my books, a general text on muscular dystrophy from 1993 by a British geneticist named Alan E. H. Emery, as well as two books by Duchenne himself, one from the 1870s and crumbling with age called *A Treatise on Localized Electrization* (in French, *De l'électrisation localisée*), and *The Physiology of Motion*, in a volume translated in the 1950s. But I find the writings of the great doctor inscrutable and bizarre, filled with stuff about electrical impulses and pictures of strange apparatus, like the "dynamometer," or strength gauge, or the harpoon biopsy needle Duchenne invented to study muscles in his patients at different stages in their short lives; before that, muscle tissue was mostly observed at autopsy. The books have nearly no narrative; mostly they consist of pages and pages of minute drawings and observations of every muscle in the human body, with one- and two-page chapters called "Motions of the Thumb" or "Flexion of the Forearm," for example. One forgets that medicine before this century was largely descriptive, and that one of the main issues in understanding muscular dystrophy was figuring out whether it was primarily neurological—affecting the spine and nerves—or truly muscular. Duchenne did show that the disease had no neurogenic basis, through studies whereby he stimulated muscles with electrical current. Nevertheless, there is something obsessive if not downright nutty about him; or maybe my impatient twentieth-century-mother's mind fails to quickly grasp the connections between his writings and his results.

But when I open Emery's book, simply titled *Duchenne Muscular Dystrophy*, everything else vanishes. I read between lines; I am transfixed, by turns elated and restless. For the first time in twelve years I look at pictures of boys in the advanced stages of disease. There are obese retarded boys, and skeletal boys looking like Auschwitz victims, spines twisted, emaciated arms and legs dangling; there is a boy with grotesquely enlarged muscles throughout his body, resembling a deformed child bodybuilder, a waxy musclebound doll, a strange, surprised balloon boy. No attempt has been made to conceal the identities of these boys; their faces are in clear view, and their misshapen bodies are naked, so you can see the deterioration clearly. There is something vulgar and vulnerable about the nakedness of these boys, the genitalia seeming either particularly underdeveloped compared to the other muscles of the body, or else too frankly exposed, a penis hanging between open legs, lewd and useless. At home, I don't see nakedness in my teenaged son as I used to when he was little; I only glimpse the outward signs of deterioration, the thick-veined calves, the legs bruised by falls, and the callused, deformed feet, the increasingly swayed back, the heels that can no longer reach the floor. I focus on the face; despite its fleshy roundness, caused by steroid use, it is still beautiful to me, with its alert, quizzical eyes and arched eyebrows, its stubborn mouth—how easily it registers disgust or frustration or delight!—its little straight, broad nose with a suggestion of freckles, its crown of chestnut hair.

I study an engraving from 1879 of a boy in three positions rising from the floor, in what doctors call a Gower maneuver, named after the physician. In the first scene the boy is on his hands and knees; in the second his rump is raised into the air and his two hands press on the ground for support; in the third he rests one hand at a time on the upper thighs to balance himself. Here I experience the oddest feeling, the thrill of identification—yes! There it is, exactly! My child! So true, so utterly Ansel. But obviously true, too, of other boys, over hundreds, over thousands of years. Less lonely, in a way, but more real. I can't deny what's in the photographs. And there's no denying the statistics in the table, either: over 95 percent of boys with Duchenne die by age twenty. At fifteen, Ansel's age now, half are dead. A nine-year-old we know who has Duchenne can no longer walk. Should I feel happy or sad knowing Ansel is at the far end of the curve?

Some pages I barely glance at; I know the early symptoms and have already witnessed some of the decay. I know that there is a "progressive weakness of movement, first affecting the lower limbs and then later the upper limbs, and a gradual increase in the size of many affected muscles." I have seen that the "lumbar lordosis becomes more exaggerated and the waddling gait increases"; daily I see the shortening of the heel cords.

But as the disease progresses, Emery's book reminds me, the breakdown intensifies: "Muscle weakness becomes more profound, contractures develop, particularly of the elbows, knees, and hips...movements of the shoulders and wrists become limited. The talus bone protrudes prominently under the skin." Finally, as the child becomes confined to a wheelchair, all hell breaks loose: "A severe kyphoscoliosis [curvature of the spine] often develops...and a gradual deterioration in pulmonary function with reduced maximal inspiration and expiratory pressure. Thoracic deformity...restricts adequate pulmonary air flow.... By the later stages there is a significant reduction in total lung capacity." In other words, the spine contorts, compressing the chest cavity, the lung and heart muscles weaken, and finally the child can't breathe. Less commonly, the heart gives out.

In the chapter called "Management," I review the paltry fixes: foot orthoses; braces that extend from ankle to groin;

stretching exercises; steroids (the author, writing in 1993, dismisses their importance); wheelchairs; standing frames; rigid body jackets; surgeries like "spinal stabilization," which involves inserting a rod in the spine, or tenotomy, cutting the Achilles and other tendons; and finally, assisted ventilation and postural drainage. Some sound radical, some gruesome. At any rate, they are only Band-Aids, short-term measures that extend life perhaps one year, perhaps two. Sooner or later, certainly by their mid-twenties, all boys with Duchenne succumb. Of the 144 patients studied by the author, only one made it to his twenty-fifth birthday.

*

Every night, hands in his pockets for balance, tiptoed, his jaw set in a grimace, feet hesitantly reaching and shuffling, leaning longer on the right than the left, Ansel stumbles along the hallway between bedroom and living room, willing himself to walk. It is unheard of, a fifteen-year-old with Duchenne, walking. "Amazing," I tell him, "amazing," as he collapses in his wheelchair. We know it can't last forever, but we keep our fingers crossed.

Sunday morning I wake up, descend the stairs, begin boiling water for coffee. From the stove I get a glimpse of the cabinets Joe fixed yesterday, two low-storage cupboards whose doors had been yanked off repeatedly by the harsh sweep of Ansel's wheelchair. For weeks, the jumble of our kitchen had been exposed, its internal disorder revealed. Saturday Joe had finally mended them, filling in the holes and jimmying the hardware. The doors had hung a bit askew, leaving an empty space like a knocked-out front tooth. Still, for the moment, they had stayed in place.

But now I see one door has pulled off its hinges again; it hangs perilously from a single screw. Inside the darkness, chaos.

4. Moonrise, 2000

Ansel and I are on 165th Street in Washington Heights on our way to the doctor at The Neurological Institute. I picked him up at school and he told me he loved me, as he does at least once a day, and then we drove here and parked in the Kinney Lot, where, because of our handicapped placard, the attendants let us squeeze into a first-level spot that blocked outgoing traffic.

This is the neighborhood where Joe and I lived together first, in medical school housing, in a huge modern building called The Towers, which overlooks the George Washington Bridge. We did not particularly get along with our multiple roommates, and we did not always like each other, but it was our first home, and it holds memories: the "Man in the Pan" early morning lectures where the doctors-in-training studied dissected organs; the late Sunday nights when I searched for Joe and his friend Peter, studying for a Monday exam in the recesses of the vast Health Sciences Library; the white-coated world of the medical complex, with the poor people waiting in line and the marble floor of Presbyterian Hospital, through which I walked when coming home from the subway. I had just read Malcolm X's great book about his life, and I was always aware of our closeness to the Audubon Ballroom, where Malcolm was shot, as well as the darkness and danger of the 168th Street subway station, where several rapes and murders had taken place. In fact, my sister's boyfriend, who worked in a microbiology lab at Presbyterian, had been stabbed in the heart on the A train on his way to work! He recovered, because they made it to the ER fast, but he had a scary, knotty scar in his chest where the mugger's knife had gone in.

There were sweet memories, too, mostly associated with food: the French toast at the Haven coffee shop around the corner, and the farmer cheese from the old Daitch Dairy—a remnant of the now-aging Jewish community—and the old-fashioned luncheonette on 181st and Fort Washington, where a soda jerk whipped up chocolate malteds made with Breyer's ice cream. The apartment in the Towers was where I held a successful surprise party for Joe—I managed to concoct Julia Child's fanciest chocolate cake, the Marquis de Chocolat, without his ever noticing—and where I had to deliver the news to Joe that his adored stepfather had died suddenly, at forty-eight, of a massive heart attack.

*

We are supposed to see Dr. DeVivo at least once a year, but it has been a year and some months since our last visit. When Ansel and I arrive we are told to sit in a secluded, empty waiting room, where he does his math homework and I glance at a magazine called *Healthy Kids.* Joe arrives, in a suit, because now he is an administrator—head of family practice at Catholic Medical Center in Queens—and a receptionist tells him we are in the wrong waiting room. We go and sit, for another twenty minutes, in a much more crowded room. A small boy in a stroller cries; he seems overtired and cranky; his mother, in a foreign language, tries to soothe him. He has tiny white braces on his legs, though I can't make out what his problem is. One never asks, "Why are you here?" though one always wants to know. It sounds too much like "What are you in for?"

When Dr. DeVivo, a white-haired, stocky man with a bulbous nose, enters the room, I am not sure if I recognize him. But he is wearing a white coat, and he seems to be in charge, so we follow him into his large office at the end of the hallway. I am very conscious that at our last visit, Ansel walked from the waiting room to the office, and I remember the look of surprise on the doctor's face: how amazing that a fourteen-year-old with Duchenne's muscular dystrophy could still walk! Now, Ansel wheels his way down the long corridor, and I am the one surprised that he could have walked so far so recently.

Joe, Ansel, and I sit in three upholstered chairs facing Dr. DeVivo, who sits behind a massive desk. I remember suddenly how poorly Joe did in his neurology rotation while in medical school, how he didn't like the neurologists. They were too cerebral and academic, he felt. DeVivo's manner is restrained, and when he speaks he addresses Ansel first. He asks Ansel about school, about the clarinet—the doctor plays trumpet—and gets only the typical teenaged grunts. But now that the pleasantries are aside, he gets to what's important. "Tell me, Ansel, how do you feel, physically, compared with the last time I saw you?"

"Well, I use the wheelchair more," Ansel says. "I get out of the wheelchair three or four times a day and stretch, and then I walk a few steps. That's all. I can't really walk more than that."

He doesn't say it sadly, just as fact, but Joe and I and the doctor know it is sad, and it sits heavily in the air, a presence among us. I think of Ansel, at five, walking into town with me because he suddenly wanted to bake cookies and we had to buy cookie cutters. He walked slowly, but he walked all the way, a quarter of a mile in each direction.

For a moment no one else can speak. There isn't anything else, is there? He gets worse. He will die. Even if it's slow, it will happen. It's a whole life, not a half-life, divided infinitely. Sooner or later it's completely not there.

But there's also a way in which it's not sad. Ansel has spoken, after all, and we all have listened. He is no longer a small child, but the voice of authority. Who can know the answers but Ansel? He has a deep voice, a little trace of a mustache on his upper lip. He and the neurologist discuss the best course of therapy, his medications—would Ansel agree to take three enzyme capsules a day rather than the one he has been taking?—and his adherence to a low-salt, low-fat diet.

Joe, Dr. DeVivo, and Ansel retreat, afterward, to the examining room that adjoins the office—the table, made for small children, is too high for Ansel to mount—but I stay behind, aware that he will not want his mother present when the doctor prods private parts or asks personal questions. I also don't want to see the fat that spills over the elastic of his underpants or the angry calluses on his feet when he removes his splints and shoes and socks. I'd rather look at the stack of magazines on luxury home renovation; at the wall of books at the back of the room; at the color photos of sailboats racing; this must be one of the doctor's hobbies. I look out the dirty window of The Neurological Institute, a half block away from our apartments at the Towers. It is strange to be here, looking out at a past that didn't contain Ansel, not even a flicker of Ansel. Why is it unthinkable looking at a future without him?

*

Joe and I are on the street on a Sunday afternoon, late. The forsythia is in bloom; there is yellow everywhere and a dark sky with just a strip of light over the Palisades. I had not been able to write, and we had tried to talk in our chaotic household, and had immediately been interrupted. Joe wants to know what I am writing, and I talk about this chapter, about Ansel growing up and deteriorating all at once, the "unnaturalness" of a child beginning to die just when he is beginning to flower.

Joe rejects this—is furious, in fact. "What are you saying, because it's not average, not the norm, it's unnatural? That's like saying homosexuality is unnatural," he claims, and I see his eyes flash behind his glasses. "What's unnatural about it?" he reiterates. "It is in fact the natural order of things, that mutations occur. That's who we are, who we have to be, as humans."

"So you have no feelings about Ansel getting worse?" I demand, tearfully. Joe can seem so hard sometimes.

He purses his lips angrily, forces air through them. "Of course I have feelings about it. But why is it necessarily sadder for someone to die young than old? Is it sadder for Ansel to die than a ninety-year-old man who's never done anything, who has nothing to show for his life? Anyway, Ansel's not dead. I can't mourn for him. And I refuse to see my life as a tragedy!"

"Well, that's what I'm writing about. And I'm sorry if you don't think it's sad!" And then I can't speak for ten minutes. I stride along next to Joe, up the hill beside the Food Emporium, and I don't look at him. I am too stubborn, and mad. How can he say a dying child is not heart-rending? How about that boy Zachy, the only child of his colleague, who died at eight or nine of a brain tumor? Wasn't that worse, more tragic, than, say, my father's death at seventy-three? Wasn't my father's life, in concrete and substantial ways, long *enough*, while Zachy's was not?

At the top of the hill, thinking back on Zachy's death and its aftermath—the apartment where his stunned parents sat shiva with its empty, clanging hangers on the coat rack in the hallway and the boy's baseball card collection still in his bedroom—I can no longer hold on to my anger at Joe. I see him simply as a fellow sufferer: trying to construct meaning from ill fate, solace in the destruction of his own firstborn, he is just groping for a spiritual handhold. This is Joe, used to such loss—two fathers and a mother, all young, all loved!—soothing himself, explaining to himself, as a child might, why death comes. And this is just the other half of me.

*

In six months, Ansel will be able to drive. In September he will be sixteen, old enough in New York State to take that step toward adulthood, obtaining a learner's permit. Even though we don't have the details yet, even though his father is not convinced he can, physically, operate a motor vehicle, Ansel and I already talk about driving as reality, how he will take over the wheelchair van and I will buy a tiny red Miata, the car of my dreams. He is not as crazy about cars as some teenaged boys, but one day when he and I see a cab-yellow 1960s-era Camaro idling at the corner of Cedar Street and Broadway in the village where we live, his left eyebrow lifts, he peers at me sideways, and he says, "Wow." He's ready.

*

In the books on dystrophy, one learns there are three stages: onset of disease, date of confinement to a wheelchair, date of death. Ansel is approaching the date of confinement. He will be there, I am sure, by his sixteenth birthday.

*

I have panic attacks nearly every night. Awakened by some minor provocation—my daughter Diana enters the room, for instance, to check the time—I turn over, sit up, and quite suddenly experience dread; there is no other word. I blink my eyes, because I am sure I am going blind, and scratch my middle fingertip with my thumbnail to assure myself I am not paralyzed. I try to take the pulse in my wrist, but I am too scared and can't count right. I am outside my body, physically detached, at the end of a long passageway, drowning—all those melodramatic scenarios of what it's like to die.

Seven years ago, when I was in labor with my third child, the nurse injected me with Stadol, a painkiller, and I became distant and paranoid like this. I held onto Joe's hand, literally, for dear life. "Tell me I am not dying," I said, over and over, to hear my own voice and to hear him respond. What an irony, I thought then, to die giving birth!

Now my heart seems to be racing in my head, but my blood is glacial, cold and slow, like when they put an IV in you and a silver metal fluid trickles through your veins. I have finally gone over the edge! The fear feeds on itself. I get dressed so I can be ready to drive to the emergency room, if need be.

Sitting on the edge of the bed, sure of my own doom, I wonder suddenly: Am I trying to experience my own death in place of Ansel's? Am I the sacrifice?

*

It is the middle of March, and every moment pulls me two ways. In a community church in White Plains that looks like a cross between a pagoda and an airline terminal, I sit with Joe, Diana, and seven-year-old Toby in a fan-shaped room filled with folding chairs. It is a kind of backward room, since one enters via the stage and descends a staircase to the seats. Ansel, who will be performing with an ensemble from his music school, can wheel onto the stage but not into the audience, so after he plays Joe will have to carry him down the steps.

When the woodwinds come on stage and are seated, Ansel seems taller than the others—actually, he's quite short— because for the first time he is playing from his wheelchair. Usually he transfers with difficulty to a regular chair, but it was thought the amount of time before the next group was too brief to allow for that. I can see Ansel now and then through the arms of the conductor. He is puffing out his big cheeks, like Dizzy Gillespie on the horn. He loves the clarinet, the instrument he chose when he began music lessons at school in the fifth grade. Joe was against it. "What's the point," he asked, "when all boys with muscular dystrophy develop breathing difficulties? He won't be able to play for more than a couple of years; it will just be frustrating." As he does with nearly everything, Ansel stood firm, and got his way, and it is good that he did. Clarinet playing is his breathing therapy as well as his joy, and may be the reason his lungs show no deterioration yet.

He progressed slowly when he took lessons at the public school, but as soon as he began at the music school, he flourished. Under the guidance of a gifted teacher, Ansel has become a disciplined music student, who, after many days and nights of mistakes, false starts, and practice, practice, practice, can be depended on to produce a fine sound. So I will enjoy now, when he leaves his door open, the lovely strains of the Weber clarinet concertino or of a Hindemith sonata. He is not a virtuoso; he is more of a plodder, but he plods well. He has learned to respect the difficulty of the task and the beauty of the result.

Sitting at the concert, I feel the pleasure of his playing, but seeing him in the wheelchair, I somehow cannot shake the feeling of loss, a loss that seems sharpest when I love him most. I know that when boys become confined to their wheelchairs, the chest and lungs become constricted. Wind is the first thing to go. Who knows which way the wind blows. Who knows where my love goes, how my love grows, where the time goes? Despite my best efforts, despite my pride in Ansel—that serious, stubborn, laboring face!—a tear wells up in the corner of my eye. I shift my glasses so Diana will not see. She does anyway.

"Mom, why are you crying?" I shake my head.

"Ansel?" She whispers urgently. And I nod, and wordlessly I put my arm around her shoulder—her bare, cool, pubescent shoulder, upon which I perhaps place too great a burden—and hold her close to me. Later, Ansel sits with me, and Diana sits alone all the way in back on a carpet-covered platform. Joe has pulled Toby out, because he is complaining so much about being at a concert. The Festival Orchestra, sounding very professional despite being jerkily led by a very thin, very young conductor, plays Bach. In the midst of the quite proper, cultivated audience, Ansel and I dip and bounce our heads and shoulders to the rhythms. "Have you noticed everybody else here is completely still, no one else but you and me is moving to the music?" Ansel whispers near the end. I have.

*

I keep with me much of the time a letter from a friend of a friend whose boy died of Duchenne's dystrophy at twenty-five. Even though I have never met her, I identify with this mother because her boy did well; he also must have been an outlier, like Ansel, to live to such a ripe old age. My son "was the absolute center of my life," she writes. "Now I feel like the woman in the Hopper painting *Cape Cod Morning*, looking out the bay window, wondering what will come next...."

*

Ansel has been away from the house for almost the entire weekend, attending a Model UN Program at a nearby high school Friday night, all day Saturday, and Sunday morning. We are not used to having him away, and Diana and I both notice his absence. The question doesn't seem to be, "Is this what it will be like when he's away at college?" but rather, "Is this what it will be like when he is dead?"

"Ansel is what makes the house happy," says Diana later that week, and I think back to the moment of his birth, when I'd heard a sound that reminded me of the popping of a champagne cork. I think of his name: a variation of "Anschel," a diminutive of "Asher," which in Hebrew means "happy."

Diana and I try to think about what makes Ansel fun. "He's just a very up person," she says, which is odd, because he is also a big complainer, a class A kvetch. "Puns," I say. "Remember when he wrote that story about the teenage monster who wasn't frightening enough because he didn't have enough 'scaritonin'?" He can't help punning, in fact. The other day, pointing out the car window at a woman passing by, Diana said, "That woman looks like my friend Colette's mother," and Ansel immediately—immediately!—quipped, "1-800-Colette. Hmm. Sounds like a brothel."

"Non sequiturs," Diana offers, and it's true. I used to call Ansel the king of non sequiturs. We all might be having a conversation about, say, the fact that the Lobster Roll is the only restaurant worth going to in the Hamptons. The rest of us might consider the topic exhausted and move rapidly on to two or three other, unrelated topics. We might be talking about the book I am reading for my psychology class, or about how boring Toby finds second grade. And then maybe half an hour later—sometimes a day later—Ansel will pipe up with, "There is that Mexican place in Easthampton," as though there has not been even a tiny break in the conversation. His neuroses are funny, too, I say: like when he worries about global warming every time the temperature in winter is above average. Everyone else is enjoying the sun but Ansel is worried! Then he always worries about being worried: "Should I be worried?" And then he is so much like me, and like my father was, that I can't help laughing at the reflection.

*

I am aware that having a limited future makes Ansel more free. Next year, for example, he plans to attend BOCES, the vocational training program offered by the school system, even though he is a brilliant student. BOCES offers culinary arts, and Ansel knows that is what he wants. Isn't food what he thinks about all the time? The taste of a blood orange or a fresh fig might be the most important, most-commented on part of his day. In English he has chosen "luxury foods" for his special project—he writes of the high cost of hunting for truffles, of the packaging of caviar, of the pleasure of watching the guys behind the appetizing counter at Zabar's slice lox. He faithfully reads the "Dining Out" section of the *Times* and leafs through *Penzy's Spice Catalog*. "Do you know," he will ask dreamily, as I ready my first cup of coffee for breakfast, "that cinnamon stick and ground cinnamon come from different parts of the tree? So you should never grind up cinnamon sticks to use for ground cinnamon."

He doesn't care that taking BOCES each morning at a location in northern Westchester will seriously limit his academic program. He does not want to sit in another year of science, even though it would "look better" on his college applications. He has no time to waste. Ansel calls a meeting with me and his guidance counselor and the director of BOCES, the last of whom he informs: "I can't do something without being serious about it. Otherwise I just don't think it's worth doing." When the BOCES man describes the culinary arts program, which is almost completely hands-on cooking, the corners of Ansel's mouth curve into a little smile, and the counselor, who knows him well, says, "I don't often see that look in Ansel's eyes."

It is apparent cooking is what he must do. BOCES, being a public program, must accommodate him, so he will probably have an aide for such tasks as lifting heavy pots off the stove. It seems exciting, though I am just a bit concerned that Ansel may completely miss out on two years of science, French, and math, which are given during the morning hours, when he will be off school grounds. Afterward I stay behind to speak with the counselor.

"How would it be if he just does BOCES for one year, not two?" I ask. Ansel would like to start BOCES this September, his junior year, but I think it would be better, as far as his admission to college, if he waits till his senior year.

"Yes, I assumed one year," says the counselor. But then she adds, "Preferably his junior year."

I am pleasantly surprised. "Because?"

"Because I know culinary arts will be in the morning next year; I'm not sure of the following year. And that would be better as far as academics go. Because he *has* to take history and English. Also..."

I know the other reason. She lets me say it.

"Because we don't know where he will be, physically, in two years. This may be the only year he *can* do it."

I meet an old friend in the city for lunch. We meet, we walk to the restaurant, and she rattles on about the short story she is writing. I cannot open my mouth; I am sure I will start to cry. For two weeks I have been up every night with shoulder pain: a pinched nerve probably brought on by a slipped disc. The day before my kitchen had been gutted in advance of a major renovation, and there are still bent nails sticking up from the floor every couple of inches.

My friend tells me about her latest challenge. Her therapist has asked her, "What do you want?" Want, as in life, in the large sense want.

"Want," I almost sneer, and as I open my mouth everything spills out, and in the little Vietnamese restaurant on Third Avenue, I start weeping. "Who cares what you want?" I say accusingly, and I am frightened by my own feeling, which comes out so raw and powerful and pitiless. "I want my son to live a long life. So what?" Every word is a choking effort, my tongue swollen and sore, my throat like gravel. Why bother wanting?

*

I have two dreams. In the first, two cars are driving fast in the left lane of the highway, in the wrong direction. Everyone in our car can see as we approach them that this is a very dangerous thing. But it's too late to stop. The cars crash head-on into other cars just in front of us, I can see the drivers thrown aside, into the air, the cars tin-can crushed. But we are saved, only witness the horror, and move on. We don't even stop. What can you do?

In the second dream, Ansel and I come upon a red-rock canyon in the middle of the Southwest desert. We are not really surprised; we have been expecting to find the canyon. The canyon has a lip of rock across its entrance, so that you cannot see beyond. Its contents are secret. But once we get inside we are aware of water and sand, and a very beautiful light glinting off the beach umbrellas. We are at the ocean. Ansel can walk. We stake out our place on the sand. We have brought our lunch and a blanket and we sit together and eat: a crusty French bread, a wedge of Parmigiano Reggiano from Todaro Brothers, slices of ripe mango. We are happy.

*

When Ansel rises from the table today his legs tremble as he transfers to the wheelchair. Our house is in complete disorder: dining table and refrigerator and microwave are all sitting in the living room because we have no kitchen; it is being renovated for Ansel. The half-built living room shelves hold two-by-four's, a sugar bowl, strips of insulation, our good silverware in a blue felt Bloomingdale's bag, a tin candy box filled with paper clips, packing tape, nail clippers, misplaced trinkets and bits of toys, Pokemon cards and Monopoly hotels.

After dinner Ansel is sitting at the table drinking tea and trying to read *Treasure Island*, which he finds difficult because of the antiquated language and because he has been interrupted over and over again by Diana and Toby, who are bored. I am in the next room, also reading, when I hear a commotion: Ansel is screaming and weeping, "Stop! Stop! I can't stand it, stop!" in a weird, high animal-like shriek. When I run in, I see he has taken his empty tea cup and begun to bang it, hard, over and over again, on the table; while I watch, horrified, he puts the cup down and begins to bang his forehead rhythmically.

"What happened?" I demand angrily of Diana. "What *happened*?!" I am stamping my foot, the rage spilling out of me. "What did you do?"

"I didn't do anything!" she retorts. "He was burping again—which he always does!—and I told him he was disgusting and he went crazy! God! You blame me for everything!"

Now Ansel begins to shriek again. "I'm an idiot! I'm an idiot; I did it because I'm an idiot!" His cheeks are big and red, and he can't catch his breath, and he begins to whimper. Embarrassment, comprehension, a normal sibling fight turned abnormal—a fifteen-year-old acting like a three-year-old.

"Pick him up," I say to Joe quietly. "Pick him up and carry him into his room."

Later, I ask Ansel: "What is it like, that anger? Are you on another planet, like I used to be when I had temper tantrums when I was a kid?" Because I know anger is a locked box, but it is also freedom, a soaring, powerful white light.

"I don't know," he says. "I don't know. I just think if I scream and scream and scream maybe I'll stop being angry. Maybe I'll get it all out of me."

"Is there so much anger?" I ask. "What's it about?"

"Please, Mom," he turns his head away. "Please. Let's not talk about it anymore."

*

Another day he comes home from school depressed.

"I'm worried about dying," he says, and I honestly don't know what to say. Since when am I so wise, anyway? I'm tired, and I worry about dying, too. Driving home fast on the Saw Mill Parkway, sometimes I think, *What will happen to my kids if I die? It is always Ansel's face I see; how could he forgive me?*

So I don't respond, not really, and later when he is putting together the pieces of his clarinet, he says—this time he wails melodramatically—"I'm so depressed and no one cares!" Now I feel compelled to react, so I go into his room, and he continues:

"I was depressed in the first place, and then when I got to health class my teacher had written 'The Stages of Grief' up on the blackboard—we're studying death—and it just made me more depressed. . . . And then we saw part of *Schindler's List*, clips of the movie."

"Did you see the part with the little girl in the red coat who is wandering around the ghetto and then gets shot?" I asked, thinking this had upset him.

He looked at me. "She doesn't get shot, Mom. She hides in the building."

"But she does, Ans. Eventually she does get shot."

"Nope," he said. "You're wrong, Mom. You forgot."

I don't want to contradict him again, though I know I'm right. I think of his great capacity for denial. I remember something the physician John Bach wrote in an article about boys with muscular dystrophy: "Successful adaptation does not depend on an accurate perception of reality."

*

This morning I caught sight of Toby's torso while he was dressing. He is seven and a half years old, slender and small, built like a dancer. He has that nice square chest, like a boy is supposed to have, with a line running down the center from breastbone to belly. Ansel would have been beautiful, too, perhaps more. I remember a photo from the summer before Ansel began taking prednisone to slow down the deterioration of his muscles, when he could still walk, ploddingly, up the unrailed front steps. A blue-purple T-shirt, a sun-tinted face: a quite-handsome eleven-year-old. Before the chipmunk cheeks, puffy from steroids. That must have been the summer before the wheelchair. My beautiful son.

*

Ansel's home reading this month: Mark Twain's *Roughing It*; most of Phillip Lopate's *The Art of the Personal Essay*; "The Snows of Kilimanjaro," and other stories by Hemingway; M.F.K. Fisher's memoirs; *The Red Badge of Courage*; *National Geographic*; S.J. Perelman's *The Chicken Inspector*. His election of a project for social studies, any "ism": Dadaism. Favorite music: Louis Armstrong, Thelonious Monk, show tunes, Latin music from the album *Buena Vista Social Club*.

*

Ansel and I are sitting in the living room, late. Everyone else has gone to sleep. He is doing his daily exercises: leaning with his palms against the back of the couch, pushing his heels down toward the floor, one at a time, to lengthen the Achilles tendons, trying to stay mobile for as long as possible. He has had a tough day, and is very tired. Earlier he'd asked Joe to carry him to the bathroom—he usually walks—and when he got there he fell reaching the toilet.

"I don't know why I'm having so much trouble," he says to

me later. "Do you think I'm just tired? Why should I be so tired?"

"I don't know, Ans. It may just be the disease. It's just getting worse, I guess. That's really crummy, isn't it?"

He doesn't say anything. He is cutting his toenails, concentrating on the task of keeping all the parings in one pile on the coffee-table.

"Isn't it?" I repeat.

He looks up. "No. I think everything that happens has a reason."

"I guess that's because you believe in God," I say.

"I used to get depressed thinking about this stuff," he continues, seeming to ignore my remark. "But then I realized it doesn't help. So I don't think about it any more."

"Do you think about the fact that you may not have as many years as other people?" I ask him another time. "No, Mom. I just want to be happy."

*

Ansel says everything that happens has a reason. He uses the toilet in the middle of the night and flushes it, and the flood of water in the pipes wakes up our collie in the basement and she begins barking and I wake up, and it is a quarter to four.

In a way I'm not tired, so I get up and go down to the basement where the dog is kenneled. She is wide awake and on her feet, waiting expectantly, as though we'd planned a rendezvous. She nips my heels and tries to push through my legs as we mount the stairs. Then she shoots outside, and I follow.

It's warm out, very warm for late January, and completely calm; the three-quarter moon is immense and neon yellow, hanging over the Palisades, nearly merging with the horizon. It seems otherworldly, like—and I know this is a ridiculous thought—an object from outer space. In other words, it appears as it is, completely apart from, oblivious to, anything human.

I don't know if it's rising or setting. Joe will be able to tell me in the morning, but right now I don't want to know, not yet. I stand there with the mystery of the moon for some time, with the thrill of knowing its beauty—having it to myself for a few, rare moments—while the dog sniffs under the damp leaves, looking for a place to pee.

When she is done, I take her back to the basement, and bring her a full bowl of water, which she drinks, thirstily. I go to sleep easily, somehow fulfilled. Ansel says everything has a reason. He is fifteen. In two hours it will be daylight.

A Question of Leaves

Carol Schmidt

Years ago, when you were in your teens,
we worked together raking leaves one autumn day.
You were not impressed by the beauty of the sky
or colors that defined the season and the job.
You simply wished the mess would disappear.

We'd rake a giant pile, then help each other
stash them in enormous plastic bags. That sunny,
crackling afternoon you turned to me bewildered
and you asked, *How do the leaves get loose
and back up on the trees in spring?*

It might have been a sudden blast of wind
that made me catch my breath before
explaining to you carefully
that leaves in spring are new,
not the old ones that fell off the trees in fall.
I may have added silently:

*You, too, are anchored here, my son,
as surely as these foolish trees
that grow their leaves and drop them,
then senselessly repeat the process
each and every year.*

It seems so long ago—that autumn of the question
of the leaves—but you are still the boy you were back then.
Time is vague for children who remain,
who calculate their age in numerals, rather than
the joys and sorrows others use to mark the passing of the years.

From *Jewel*

Bret Lott

Brenda Kay stood at the foul line, hands holding the basketball between her legs, knees bent, eyes on the net. Behind her were the rest of the children.

"Let's go, Brenda!" the woman, this Mrs. Klausman, hollered, and it was all I could do not to shout from where I stood with the other mothers, *Brenda Kay, it's Brenda Kay!* But I said nothing, only held my arms tighter across my chest.

Mrs. Klausman blew her whistle, a short bleat of a sound, but loud enough to make it echo off the brick walls of the gymnasium and scare the living daylights out of most every child. Dennis, the boy behind Brenda Kay, had been standing quiet and still behind her, but now quick brought his arms up to his chest, started to twitching his whole head like he does, his thick glasses near falling off with each move. The little girl behind him, Candy was her name, started to twisting back and forth even faster than she'd been doing before. Another boy, Randy, him short as Brenda Kay, his hair near the same color, let out a deep growl, started lifting one foot and then the other, one foot and then the other. The two children who'd already shot, Marcella and Jimmy, sat on the floor behind this Mrs. Klausman, knees tucked up under their chins. Jimmy was already shivering, Marcella swaying back and forth.

Brenda Kay was breathing faster now, her eyes still on the net, her so small there on the floor, that net so far away.

This was the first day to the high school, the children's first gymnasium day. There'd been talk from Mr. White about this eventuality for the last six years, since I'd started in helping at the center and being paid for it. Six years of talk about getting the children across town to West High School to use the gym during the off period, 11:45 to 12:30, so they could get hold of better exercise, better facilities, have more fun.

Until today, exercise time'd been at the old Presbyterian church off Torrance Boulevard. Behind the church was a parking lot painted with stripes for a volleyball court, and we'd all of us march the two blocks up the hill from the Health Center where Mr. White and I held class, the children and the two or three other mothers that showed up each day all holding hands. We'd walk on the sidewalk. Beside us the cars on the street, some of them honking at us now and again, teenagers the same age as Brenda Kay hollering out things these children didn't need to hear, but which most likely meant nothing to them: *morons, retards*. But we'd sing songs or just talk, and then we'd be at the church parking lot, and I'd pull from the duffel bag I carried over my shoulder the ball, and we'd play there on the broken asphalt a game something akin to volleyball.

I myself had only seen it played on the beach whenever Leston used to feel like going to see Wilman and Burton at it, back before they'd gotten married. Now whenever they got to the beach it was with kids in tow, my grandchildren: Burton's girls, Susan, Jeannie, and Jill; Wilman's boys, Brad, Robert, and Timmy. But there'd been a time not too far back, before they'd had to carry playpens and diapers and umbrellas, when the two of them were out on the beach every afternoon, all day Saturday and Sunday, back at Venice Beach and showing off to any girl that'd put eyes on them.

The version we played at the church, though, had no net, no poles, just that painted square on the parking lot. We'd given the ball to one or another of the children, showed them again and again how you held the ball in the palm of one hand, then brought the other up under it, hit it hard so it flew up and into play.

But that didn't happen too often, of course; most of the time the child missed the ball, or only held it in her hand like you showed her, and stared at it or you or the ground. Marcella was the worst about that, her black hair in a ponytail so tight you'd swear she had to work to close her eyes. She'd simply stare at the ball no matter how softly you talked, no matter how calm your hand on her back, no matter how many times you took her hand in yours and swung it up under that ball just to show her. Other children—Dennis in particular—knocked the stuffing out of it, sent the ball flying high and, usually, behind him, to where it'd bounce off the hood of a churchworker's car. One time the pastor himself had been in his old DeSoto, inching out of his slot at the back door to the sanctuary, only to have a ball Dennis had slammed too high and far bounce off his roof. Pastor'd jammed on the brakes and looked everywhere, startled and scared, his old man's face read bleached white with the *whump!* that ball had sounded. All he'd seen, too, was a parking lot full of retarded children and three mothers bent over laughing, hands covering our mouths in some small attempt at hiding. We joked for months after that, about how Mr. McKnight must've thought God was gearing up to speak to him there in his DeSoto, pounding his car roof to get his attention.

The children had fun, even when the ball went too high, or never left a child's hand. We women spoke to them as if they were children, kids out for fun, and that seemed the trick to it all: just to treat them like they were kids themselves, though they ran in age anywhere from fifteen, which was Candy's age, to twenty-four, Dennis's age.

Brenda Kay was one of the younger ones at seventeen. She could get the ball up into the air on occasion, where sometimes it'd make it a couple of times back and forth, one child to the next keeping it in the air. Sometimes it only fell off her hand, rolled a few feet away. But they were playing outside in the open air and moving themselves, their arms and legs.

Then West High School finally caved in to Mr. White, and

of course all we mothers, not to mention Mr. White himself, nearly jumped for joy at the news, at the idea of our children in a real school, if for only an hour or so a day. Mr. White'd had to guarantee in writing the school would have no liabilities for the whole thing, and guarantee the children at the high school would hardly see our children. Even the gym door would be kept locked from the inside, so as not to disturb any of the normal children.

Mrs. Klausman also came with the deal. She was the girls' PE coach, and'd been assigned this duty, her job supposedly to help out the children with organized play time, but, I figured, also to see that they didn't destroy the place, didn't each of them go into mad rages and start to tearing the mats off the walls at either end of the court, didn't throw up and bleed and bash in the wooden bleachers. I'd dealt with people who had no idea what retarded children were about long enough to be able to spot them a mile away. She was one of them; I could see the fear in her by the way she'd tried to smile while telling us at the start of the period what she perceived her role as being: "Coach and friend, friend and coach." Her eyes never landed on the children around her, but always keeping on us, as though we might throw her some lifeline, reel her in from whatever hell she thought she was drowning in.

I wasn't certain how long she'd last: blowing that whistle, hollering out to the children to throw. Marcella'd started swaying so hard she looked near to falling over there on the hardwood floor; when it'd been her turn, she'd merely done what Marcella always did: stared at the ball in her hands for a while. But then maybe because this was a new place, a big building with brick walls and championship flags hanging from the rafters, Marcella'd finally held the basketball just like we'd shown her to hold a volleyball, and for the first time ever she put her other hand beneath the ball, swung it up hard and quick, and gave it a good solid slap. The basketball popped up only a few feet, but it was the action that'd counted to we three mothers over here seated on the bleachers. We'd clapped and cheered, Crystal Holloway—Jimmy's momma—and Terri LaCoste—Dennis's momma—and myself all standing up in our seats.

But Mrs. Klausman had only blown her whistle, shaken her head, and walked to pick up the ball. She held it at her hip, the whistle in her other hand, and stood next to Marcella, bounced the ball a couple times. Then she shot, making that ball go in a perfect arc so that it fell right through the net without even touching the metal hoop. "That's how you do it," she said, and she'd turned, smiling, to where Marcella'd been.

Marcella was already over on the floor, curled up with her knees under her chin like she was right now.

Jimmy had held the ball with two hands like it was a huge rock, his knees buckling a little under him, and he'd pushed it toward the basket, made it bounce twice before it rolled away to the right, where Mrs. Klausman stopped it with her foot. Then she'd done the same thing: stood next to him, shot, turned to him. He'd only looked up at her, his big ears poking out at either side of his head, his hair in that crewcut his momma said made him look at least a little more attentive than he would otherwise. Then he'd turned, gone and sat next to Marcella.

And now it was Brenda Kay's turn. Still she stared at the net, still she held the ball between her knees. She opened and closed her mouth with each breath she took, her eyes, it looked from here, already going red at that whistle.

Mrs. Klausman popped the whistle again, just a short moment's worth of sound, but shrill nonetheless. Randy, at the end of the line, gave a small yelp just as Brenda Kay swung her arms up, let go the ball.

It sailed straight up above her in a perfect line. Brenda Kay looked up at it, watched it a moment before she ducked, turned to get out of the way, bumping hard against Dennis, his hands still at his chest.

The ball came down, bounced on the wood floor, and everyone, even Mrs. Klausman, only watched, let it bounce until it finally stopped, sat right there at the foul line.

Dennis started laughing, his laughter even louder than Brenda Kay's, the sound way up high and cackling like some wild animal's. I wasn't sure what he was laughing at, whether it was Brenda Kay's shot or the ball settling right square back on the line or Brenda Kay ducking and banging into him. But he was laughing.

Brenda Kay turned to him, stared at him a moment, then let out "Huh! Huh! Huh!" almost as loud, and suddenly each of the children was laughing, the gymnasium echoing with laughter so hard and unafraid it was more a haunting sound than anything else, like laughing ghosts in a movie. None of them knew enough to be restrained in how they laughed, that matter of *manners* and *politeness* a notion that only operated in their heads when Momma or Daddy was with them.

Mrs. Klausman hadn't yet picked up the ball, only stood staring at them, the whistle in one hand and close up to her mouth, like she'd been ready to blow it, but couldn't quite get her hand there. Then she shifted her eyes to us, we mothers there on the bleachers.

None of us did anything to help. We only watched, and from the corner of my eyes, I could see in each of us a piece of satisfaction with what was going on, in how the children had set her on edge, let her know they weren't little zombies she could point in the right direction and expect to have operate just fine. We each of us sat there perfectly still, backs straight, chins up high.

*

We'd gotten this far alone, was what I was thinking on the way home from the high school. Mrs. Klausman'd finally given up after she'd been unable to stop the children from laughing. Even Jimmy quit his shivering once he'd started in, his laughter more a silent snickering.

That was when we mothers rounded them up, then went out to the station wagon, herded them in—Dennis and Brenda Kay in the front seat with me, Marcella and Candy and Jimmy in the back seat, Randy all the way in the far back in the foldup seat. Crystal and Terri climbed into Crystal's car, a '57 Chevy she hadn't yet decided to give up to her seventeen-year-old son, Mark, Jimmy's younger brother. And then I set off for the drive back to the health center, Crystal to take Terri home.

*

I pulled the station wagon into the health center parking lot, yet another of these squared-off stucco buildings I'd finally grown used to here. By this time Randy in the far back had started in to his growling and yelping, and no matter how hard I tried to cut that sound out of my head, it was no use. The first gymnasium day was fast on its way from bad to worse: I'd already gotten a headache, and here it was only a little after noon.

There'd be Mr. White to answer to, report on how it'd gone with Mrs. Klausman and basketball. Then arts and crafts this afternoon, all that clay I had to water down and knead up before the children could start with it. We'd roll out the clay into long strings, coil it up on itself into little vases we'd let set in the windows, then paint up, take home sometime next week. It was something we'd done before, but nearly every art project we did we'd done before.

I pulled the keys out of the ignition, turned and opened my door, hollered out to the children to line up on my side of the car, hold hands for the walk back to the classroom, and I wondered exactly how many coil vases and ashtrays and doorstops and unidentifiable other clay whatnots we'd made these years. A hundred at least, I thought, all variations on the same old idea: get them working with their hands, make something they could hold and think *I made it! I made it!* and have it be the truth. For that, I figured as I looked back at them already lined up—Candy and Marcella and Dennis and Brenda Kay and Randy and

Jimmy, him shivering again there at the end of the line—maybe all those red coils of clay were worth it. Dirt well spent.

"Everybody holding hands?" I called out, and turned to the building.

"Ohhhn!" Marcella gave out, and I turned to her, her eyes wide open with the ponytail. Her head was tilted to one side, her mouth open, jaw jutted out. "Ohhn!" she said. "Dennis! Dennis!" she said, and she held up the hand she was supposed to be holding with Dennis, just put it up in the air, empty.

Then Randy gave his yelp, put his hand up the same as Marcella had done. His hand, too, was empty, that hand supposed to be holding on to Brenda Kay's.

I looked at Dennis, at Brenda Kay. They were holding hands, both of them with their heads down, staring at the pavement, mouths closed. Dennis's glasses had slipped down his nose, just barely hanging on at his ears.

I looked at their hands, saw how they were holding on: their fingers were laced together, as soft and gentle as could be, the two of them holding hands like they were courting.

I said, "Now stop that," and a feeling I'd known would come but which I'd refused for so long finally broke in me. It rose in my throat black and hard, and I took two steps to them, reached my hands to theirs, and pulled them apart. I said, "You, Dennis," and took hold of his elbow, pulled him away out of line, "you just stand yourself right on down here next to Randy. You just stand right there," I said, and directed him to the back of the line.

He moved slowly, lifted his free hand and pushed his glasses up. They were heavy horn-rimmed glasses, black, and made his face turn owlish. They made him somehow look intelligent, the thickness of the glass distorting the shape of his eyes so they didn't look so mongoloid, so tapered at the outside edges. When he was at the end of the line, I looked into those eyes, looked into them maybe a moment too long, but a moment I figured needed to be spent this way.

I said, "Now you know we don't hold hands that way. You know that, Dennis," and I tried to hold my eyes firm on him, tried to make myself *authoritative*, a word Mr. White'd stressed for so long, since the first day I'd ever met him.

But he smiled at me, then looked at his hands, stared at them with that smile on his face. He moved his right hand down to Randy's, his eyes on his hand the whole time, and took hold of Randy's hand, held it tight.

He moved his eyes back to the other hand, slowly moved it toward me, and took hold of my hand. Carefully he laced his fingers in mine, held my hand the same as he'd held Brenda Kay's.

He looked up at me. His glasses'd slipped again; my hand in his, he reached up with his middle finger and pushed them back into place. He was still smiling, and looked at me.

"OK lunch OK?" he said and nodded.

I paused and looked at him in that authoritative way I thought I had, eyes boring in on him even through the thick glasses he had on. I hoped he might hear what I was saying, really: *Don't touch my daughter the way you might want to some day.* Then I pulled our hands apart, took hold of his the way I wanted him to: palm to palm, fingers together and holding on.

Still he smiled, and I saw it was lost on him, what I was doing lost on them all; they only started to fidgeting there in line against the station wagon.

I looked away from him and his smile, looked up the line to Brenda Kay. She leaned toward Marcella, said something, a single word. Marcella's eyes were open wide, staring off. Then she got the smallest glint of a smile, her eyes changed somehow, the corners of her mouth just turning up.

Brenda Kay turned, looked at me, said, "Lunch now, Momma!"

"All right," I said, Dennis's hand in mine. I thought to grip it hard, but decided against it. We'd be inside in a minute and now I didn't know if I'd even have to report this incident to Mr.

White, this little holding of hands that might not have been just holding of hands.

"All right," I said again, like I might've been trying to convince myself eating lunch was the only thing needed doing in these children's lives. "Let's go to lunch," I said, and started toward the building.

Doctor in the House

Darshan Perusek

My brother Manu is a dentist, not an M.D., but in the entire neighborhood where he has lived for over thirty years, he is known as "Dr. Sahib." Ask any driver at the taxi stand on the main road, he will tell you where Manu lives, as will the barber or the baker or the fellow who owns the grocery store. "Oh, yes, Dr. Sahib, I know him. Turn left at the next corner, two blocks up the street, that's where he lives. Tell him Jinder sent greetings!" To the families who live on his block, he is not only dentist, psychologist, psychiatrist, pediatrician, gerontologist, but horticulturist, repository of exotic recipes and kitchen god, matchmaker, counselor in family crises, medical referral services, comforting presence by deathbed, and trusted master of funeral rituals and ceremonies. He has helped bring a generation of children into the world and helped send a generation of their grandparents out of it. All this takes a toll on good nature and he sometimes explodes at a little child who has been sent to fetch "Uncle."

"What do you want? My blood? Go find someone else to tell you why Great-Aunt Soma is not breathing. Maybe she's dead, have you thought of that?"

And the child leaves, but comes back and stands timidly across the room from him. "Yes, Great-Aunt Soma is dead. Mummy says, could you send an obituary to the newspaper and also bring the funeral kit for Great-Aunt Soma? Mummy says you know what to get."

Manu is also father to Sonny, twenty-two years old and

mentally retarded, or maybe autistic, nobody knows, just as no-body knows whether he is that way from birth or because of a series of severe illnesses he suffered in infancy. It doesn't matter what or how, anyway, because the blow has been dealt, and nei-ther Sonny's nor Manu's life will ever be like that of other fa-thers and sons who have been spared this particular blow.

Sonny has dark hair that tends to fall over his eyes, a shy smile, and long, loose-hanging arms. He drags his feet when he walks, and his shoulders are slouched. "Lift up your head, hold your shoulders straight," Manu tells Sonny. The shoulders straighten, the head lifts, and for a while there you see Sonny's eyes, which you rarely do because of the hair and because he looks to the side, not at you, when you talk to him. The eyes are timid and anxious. "He can do it when he wants to. You see that, don't you?" Manu wants to know. Then the head slides down again, the shoulders droop, and the eyes retreat.

To find out what Sonny can do when he wants to, Manu has knocked at all the available doors of specialists in the medical services and education and come away empty-handed. There is-n't much medicine can do for Sonny beyond pronouncing the verdict of retardation or autism or whatever, and that verdict Manu doesn't need to be told by professionals; he sees it every day in the eyes of friends and strangers alike, who turn away from Sonny or ask about him in tragic voices: "Was he always like this? What will he do when you are gone?"

It was always a struggle to get Sonny into a kindergarten school, since he didn't look or behave like other children, and when he did get into one, it was another struggle, repeated daily now, to get him to go. God alone knows what internal demons and monsters Sonny fought as he faced the prospect of another day at school, but they were frightening enough to make him cry and throw tantrums, even to become violently sick and throw up. "He can do it if he knows he has to," Manu would say to his wife, teeth gritted as he pulled the book bag over Sonny's shaking shoulders. "Let's go." He stopped trying to send Sonny to school after he went to pick him up one day to find a grim-faced nun standing over a whimpering Sonny: "This boy has no bowel control! Look what he's done!" she shouted. Manu took Sonny by the hand and took him home and cleaned him. The next day he told Sonny, "You don't have to go back there ever again." Sonny was four.

For the next ten years, Manu was Sonny's only teacher, his classroom the home, the streets, the playground. Wherever they were, wherever they went, education went on. Between filling a cavity or crowning a tooth, Manu held Sonny's hand and guided it to form letters on double-lined sheets of paper, the kind he himself had been taught to write on. In the evening, he brought Sonny crayons to color the outlines of elephants and lions, making up stories about each animal to keep Sonny going, and taught Sonny to count with the oranges and guavas they had bought from the fruit vendor in the morning, and instructed Sonny daily as they walked back with their fruit in the basket never to open the door to a stranger but to talk through the iron grill in the door.

He did this for fourteen years because he had no choice, but also because, along the way, he had consulted an astrologer or two recommended by a wise neighbor lady. These "specialists" had declared that when Sonny turned fourteen, the dark planets that had cast their shadow on his life would move on into new and benign configurations and Sonny would be like everybody else. Did he believe it? I don't think so, but what if he did? Hope, even when it comes from dubious quarters, is a good thing to keep you standing on your feet when a hard wind is blowing: "If I keep working with him, by the time he is fourteen Sonny will be ready for school and no one will notice the difference." The astrologers were, of course, wrong. The miracle did not happen. The planets, as we well know, are useless in these matters, as are doctors. "And what do I do now?" Manu asked, searching the skies for a sign he knew he would never see. "*I* can't be his only friend. *He* can't be my only companion."

Sonny did leave home one more time for school, this time at the Okhla School for the Mentally Retarded. Manu's shoulders slumped as he pulled the book bag over Sonny's back, because "retarded" is a word Manu had never let pass his lips, although I am sure it has knocked at his heart long enough these many years. I understand why. It's a word that he fears can change Sonny into an alien being, a thing to be pointed at and put away with other "unfortunates," as he calls them. Without the word, Sonny is still his son. A bit slow, no doubt, and forget college and all that, but who knows, with some training and God willing, a career as an auto mechanic or blue-collar worker in a factory is not beyond the realm of possibility. It's no use arguing that the other "unfortunates" are sons and daughters, too, of parents like himself: "No, he's not like them."

I see no point in telling him about Matthew, our friend Joseph's twenty-year-old brother, who came to visit Joseph. Joseph's respectable neighbors wanted Matthew kept in the apartment, and not allowed to stand on the balcony, because he was one of "them." "Keep your brother inside the house," one concerned father warned, "or I'll give him a beating next time I see him." Joseph, who loves his brother, marched across to the man's apartment, grabbed him by his freshly laundered shirt, pushed him against the wall of his living room, brought his knee up into his respectable groin, and said in a calm voice, "You raise your hand against my brother and I will break every bone in your miserable body." Joseph told us of this incident over dinner one evening, concluding with, "There's nothing more vicious under the sun than the respectable Delhi middle class." Then he gave a fine rendition of Bob Dylan's "Like a Rolling Stone." Joseph loves Dylan as much as he hates the clean-shirted, black-hearted Delhi middle class.

Manu knows all about those black hearts and the poison they beat through the veins of these gentlemen and their decorous wives, but their sons walk confidently with straight shoulders and light feet to a shining future of college degrees and good jobs and pretty brides and laughing children. Thinking of Sonny's future keeps him awake at night and blots the sun out of his days. Money provides a solid foundation for good deeds, and of that, he plans to leave Sonny all that he can within his means. Sonny can also take care of his own personal needs; all those years of teaching have done that. He can even help with some simple chores in the house and do some shopping (provided he wants to, of course!). "He won't be a burden to anyone, I know that," Manu says. But he also knows Sonny needs more than food and shelter; he needs love, he needs respect. "How can I guarantee that?" he asks, his shoulders bent.

Straighten your shoulders, Manu, I want to say. I want to take him by the hand and comfort him with words: "You have done what you could, keep doing what you can," or, "I understand your grief and your fear." I don't take him by the hand because in our family we don't do such embarrassing things, and I don't say what's in my heart. So I have instead sent him a story that I love, Malamud's "Idiots First," in which a dying father, Mendel, forces Death himself to temporarily suspend the "cosmic universal law" to allow him time to put Isaac, his adult retarded son, on the train that will take him across country to his eighty-one-year-old uncle in California. "Be nice to him," Mendel says to the conductor as Isaac boards the train. "Show him where everything is." You will have to trust there will be others along the road who will show Sonny where everything is, I want to say to Manu. But I don't say it; I write it instead. For you, my brother.

Victoria's Wedding

Margaret Mantle

My father is here for the wedding.
He is so frail I hear the bones articulating under his skin.

He asks for a drink and I pour whiskey
into a little flat blue pansy-shaped dish which cannot
    possibly hold it.
He takes it carefully into withered hands with long
    black-painted fingernails.

His cheek is round and pink and smooth.
I kiss it and feel we have completed something.

I know my father is dead and my mother also
who comes barreling across the room angry as a snake
because she has always known that this occasion could
    never happen.

She said when my daughter was born
"She'll have trouble with that baby"
but it was thirty years before my father told me.
And all that time we have labored to make sense of it,
my daughter's child's mind pursuing her adult body
    through the years.
We are not sure how much she knows, or minds.
She worries that she's too old to play with dolls.
We tell her, "Lots of grown-up ladies play with dolls."

Sometimes she says "I'm going to marry Bobby" and we
    ask if he's cute.
She says he is and giggles.

I have seen her first gray hair.
Her eyelids are losing their translucence.
She says "I'm not a baby," and we say "No—you're a
    grown-up woman."

We have always known she could never marry.

Now in these rooms I have dreamed before but never
    inhabited,
I see that I have built a nightmare out of long-discarded
    visions and imaginings.
The mind never lets go of anything entirely.

I have designed the dress,
ordered this monstrosity of a cake topped with its grinning
    plastic couple,
hauled in enough flowers for all our funerals—

Now I must make it all go away before I will be allowed to
    wake up.

Rachel at Work:
Enclosed, a Mother's Report

Jane Bernstein

In the spring of 2002, as the crocuses pushed up and the daffodils blossomed and froze, and I worried about work—not my own, which I love, but what kind of work my developmentally disabled eighteen-year-old daughter, Rachel, might be able to do when she is no longer in the shelter of school.

On one April morning—an average morning, in fact—after quarreling with her because she would not put her dishes in the dishwasher and threatening to take away her Uno cards if she did not brush her teeth, I asked her if she knew what *work* meant. After a few false starts—trying to make a case for computer solitaire as work, for instance—she pretty much nailed it. Work, she said, was "when you have to do stuff they ask you to do."

Did she like to work? I asked.

"Not really."

"How come?"

" 'Cause the way they talk to me is really mean. They talk harsh on me, Ma. Put it this way: when they talk to me, they tell me to be quiet and all that junk."

Outside, a horn honked. I trailed behind Rachel as she reached for the banister and slowly edged her way down the porch steps, then onto the van that takes her to the Children's Institute, where, on a typical day, she will sort and deliver mail, make a bed, and wipe down a table.

After the van pulled away from the sidewalk, I stood for a moment, limp from a combination of exhaustion and relief, since my daughter, with her long list of "special needs" is an exceedingly difficult person, especially in the morning and evening when I ask her to do the routines that most of us do without much thought. Most of us—*us* meaning the population that designates itself "normal"—don't need to be prompted to use the toilet, don't at eighteen insist on wearing a sweatsuit on a day when the temperature might reach eighty. We don't finish breakfast with a ring of food around our mouths—or if we do, are grateful when someone says, "Honey, you've got food on your face." Most of us don't mind touching our own faces to wipe it off. While often I am reminded that Rachel is one of us, deserving of the rights and privileges accorded to her by our constitution, on this morning—during this whole season, while I have been thinking about how to make her into a working girl—I have been reminded instead of all the impediments in her way.

*

I always imagined that Rachel would work. Even after it became obvious that she would never read books or write a single sentence, after I realized that she would never walk on the street alone or live without supervision, I had a vision of her having some sort of job, somewhere. When I saw a janitor or a person busing tables, I would close my eyes and try to picture Rachel doing that job, sure that despite her cognitive deficits, her poor vision and poor fine motor skills, she could be trained for some job, somewhere. I speculated on the challenges of making a worker out of someone like my daughter, who is unable to understand concepts like altruism and loyalty, who doesn't seem to take pleasure from a job well done and would never fear being fired. Still, I went to sleep at night believing that some job would be found and that the structure and routine it provided would be good for her. Unlike many of "us," her capacity for happiness was great, it seemed. All we had to do was help her find a job and a safe place to live, and we would be on our way.

My vague dream was nourished by several factors: First, that Rachel would be in school until she was nearly twenty-two. Second, that she had been given an afterschool job at Café J, a snack bar staffed by people with special needs at the Jewish Community Center (JCC) near our home. Though a trained therapeutic staff-support person (TSS) was always at her side, making sure her behavior was appropriate and keeping her on task, still it was work. Third, I believed in some equally vague way that the law would protect her.

In the back of my mind was the knowledge that if Rachel had been born less than a generation ago, I would have been advised—pressured, perhaps—to put her into an institution. It was where 90 percent of children with developmental disabilities languished until the 1970s. The Education of All Handicapped Children Act of 1975 (Now called Individuals with Disabilities Act, or IDEA) passed only eight years before Rachel's birth. Before Congress enacted this law guaranteeing that children with disabilities had the chance to receive a free, appropriate public education, over a million children were denied the chance to be educated and hundreds of thousands more lacked access to appropriate services. Even if I had ample funds, I would have been hard-pressed to find a nearby school she would have been able to attend. In those days a conversation with the words *school* and *Rachel* in the same sentence would have been problematic. *Work* and *Rachel* in the same sentence wouldn't have been even vaguely feasible.

I was lulled by these laws and by the fact that thus far I had not had to fight for Rachel's right to be educated. In New Jersey, where we had lived until she was eight, she'd had excellent services, starting with an early intervention program she attended as an infant. And when I moved to Pittsburgh, ready to fight if necessary to have her placed in an approved private school of my choosing, the school district looked at her medical and educational documents from New Jersey and cooperated fully with my desires. In 1992 she began attending the Children's Institute, and since then the school has been fulfilling the law by providing her education.

A 1997 revision of IDEA stipulated that the "transition process," the time when we—parents, educators, and Rachel herself—were supposed to begin to prepare her for life beyond school, should begin no later than age sixteen. At Rachel's school, transition began at age fourteen. Each summer since then, I'd filled out long questionnaires with dozens of questions about her likes and dislikes. I listed the agencies that had worked with her, the stores and restaurants she liked. I wrote down her favorite foods and games, her afterschool activities and some activities I wanted to see her try. Could she be trusted with money? I was asked. Did she understand the passage of time? Could she accept responsibility for her actions, make appointments, talk on the phone? I answered these questions carefully, with her best interests in mind. I prided myself on being realistic, believed that I had no illusions about my expectations for my daughter. I could see the big picture, I would have said.

Then in September 2001, I opened a manila envelope from Rachel's school, looked at her curriculum for that academic year, and saw *washing machine, dryer, setting the table*. I didn't think, This is great, or even, This is the law. I thought, full of utter despair, They've given up. Of course I knew that she'd been working at school—she and her class had tried out some lawn-maintenance jobs and had torn paper for the kennels at the Animal Rescue League—but her educational program in past years had included looking at preprimers, sounding out words, learning to develop a sight vocabulary, answering verbal-comprehension questions about a story, counting by rote to thirty-five, identifying seasonal changes, the needs of a plant, the characteristics of lions, tigers, elephants. Though she continued to function well below grade level, the tone in the mostly boilerplate documents had always been full of strategies that would be employed and accommodations that would be made for her, full of hope for what she might yet become.

The language in the document that set out her plan for the 2001–2002 academic year was blunt: "Due to neurological disabilities and extensive need for modification in all areas, Rachel is unable at this time to participate in the general regular education curriculum." She would be in the Life Skills Program instead. Her goals would be to learn the location of classrooms, sort mail by number up to twenty with 60-percent accuracy, count five items without cues, collate four color-coded items with verbal cues. The tasks seemed so meager—so pathetically small. First I bristled. Then I thought, She really *is* retarded, though for eighteen years I had known this, believed I had accepted it fully. But there was something final about it—*is and always will be* "unable to participate." Looking at this document, I was forced to see that progress for this school year was being measured by my eighteen-year-old daughter's ability to deliver mail independently to a two-room route in a building she had known for nine years.

In October at the meeting to discuss her IEP—Individual Educational Program—I said I wanted her teachers to continue working with her on some basic academic skills, since I believed it was important for Rachel to know the difference between Women's Room and Men's Room, between Entrance and Exit, Cheerios and Frosted Flakes. And indeed, with just the spirit of cooperation I'd always felt at these meetings, a few additional goals were drafted: that Rachel would "identify words related to shopping, community signs, menus and recipes," that she would make change up to $1. I thanked her teachers and the representative from the school district for working with Rachel and left the building alone.

I was still reeling, utterly stunned. What about the progress she'd been making at the café? Her TSS had been telling me that lately she had been more cooperative about working, that she was using the cash register and closing up the café without being reminded of the sequence of tasks she had to do. Yes, I understood that Café J was a protected environment and that she had someone at her side prompting and cueing and redirecting. Still, two rooms without distraction—was that the most her teachers at the Children's Institute thought she could achieve?

The only way I would learn whether I was deluded or her teachers underestimated her abilities was to observe her in class. But several months would pass before I stepped into her school. And that, I think, had to do with the fourth reason I had held onto my some-job-somewhere dream and let myself imagine that those 1975 laws would be carried out flawlessly, that along with *some* job for Rachel, there would be *someplace* for her to live, some guaranteed safety net. I was tired. Rachel is a difficult person. She gets funding for mental health services because of her "long history of behavior problems, particularly when she is with her mother." Whatever doesn't require my urgent attention goes into an OK-for-the-present category. Her teachers and staff were there, and so had been her future when she was out of school.

I've tried hard to understand my inscrutable daughter. I listen to her, interact with her, worry about her. I've accommodated her deficits and championed her strengths and thought of myself as her advocate and her interpreter, the one who understood her best. That spring, after visiting Rachel's school, I realized that I had failed to integrate all I knew about Rachel. My view of my daughter was limited. So was my understanding of "work."

Here's what I learned.

1. *Rachel must learn how to make toast.*

She was around five years old when we started working with her to put on her own shoes. An occupational therapist strung elastic laces in her shoes so that tying and untying would be unnecessary. Then we reinforced—and reinforced—the procedure, starting with "off," which was easier. First you sit in a chair. Next you bring one leg up and over the other. Cross that leg. Reach for the heel of the shoe. Pull. It was the first time I considered how complicated, and how frustrating, it might be to take off one's shoe.

I thought about teaching Rachel to put on her shoes when I observed her morning cooking class. The group had been doing a unit on breakfast, and on this particular morning, their teacher, Bob Russell, produced a bag of bread and announced that the topic for the day was toast. Learning to make toast, like putting on one's shoes, is a multistep operation. First you had to wipe down the counter "because you might drop the toast, and germs are *gross!*" Then you had to figure out what you wanted to put on the toast. And then, after the students slowly offered suggestions for what they might put on their bread—butter, peanut butter, margarine, jam—they had to figure out where they might find these things.

For instance, "Where is butter kept?" Bob asked. "What about the jelly?"

So you have this purple jelly. What flavor is purple? What flavor is red?

Sometimes you have to push hard on the handle of the toaster to get the bread to go down. Sometimes you don't.

How do you get the containers open? Sometime you lift the lid. Sometimes you unscrew the jar.

What do you use to get the stuff out—a spoon or a knife? Can you manage a butter knife, or will you need a broad, flexible spreader?

Safety. Germs. Hand-washing. Choice. Spreading what you've chosen to go on the toast as evenly as possible. Trying to cut the toast in half.

That night at dinner, I sat across the table from my daughter and heard myself say, "Don't shove giant chunks into your mouth.... Chew your food—with your mouth closed, please. ... Use a napkin.... Wipe your face and hands."

I thought about work not merely as a specific job or career but as "exertion" and "effort," which also are definitions. I thought of how hard Rachel worked, how for her, getting dressed is work. So is clearing the breakfast table, brushing her teeth, negotiating the front steps on a sunny day. Even eating was full of lessons: You could choke. You'll gross people out. Cleanliness counts. Little is self-evident to my daughter, since she is not attuned to matters of safety or health or other people's judgment of her. And these small, necessary things—cutting her food into smaller pieces, opening the napkin, wiping her fingers—are labor for her.

At the same time, she can be astoundingly lazy, capable of standing for a half-hour in the shower and never once reaching for the soap. She tries to manipulate everyone she meets. The instant a new person is within earshot, my princess of Pittsburgh will get that person to lift, tote, fetch, serve, and attend to her every need.

Rachel must learn to make her own toast. Even if she is blessed with the most accommodating friend or aide, she must learn to choose what she wants to eat and where she wants to go. She must be responsible for basic hygiene and cleanliness. The more independent she becomes, the better chance she has for being out in the world, something my gregarious daughter craves. The domestic skills she learns will carry her beyond the kitchen into the world where things have levers, lids, and screw tops, where things are stored in cabinets behind wooden doors, where there are slots, stairs, escalators that go up and down, revolving doors. Learning to make toast is helping her live with dignity.

Toast is more than toast.

And "life skills" doesn't mean this is the end. They are the necessary skills that will help her be part of a community and part of the working world.

2. Supported employment is not a sure thing.

To most people there's a single face of individuals with mental retardation out there in the workplace: the supermarket bagger. It's the most visible job, the one we see most often. A bagger, like my pal Jimmy, an older man, balding, missing a few teeth, who bags groceries efficiently and carefully at the local supermarket, heavy stuff on the bottom, the eggs in a separate bag. (When Jimmy sees me, he stops, opens his arms wide, grunts with utter glee, and then *pronto*—is back to work.) According to the Arc of the United States, the national organization for people with mental retardation, up to 7.5 million Americans have some degree of mental retardation. About 87 percent are, like Jimmy, mildly affected, a little slower than average in learning new information and skills. In the workplace they have proven to be diligent and loyal; they don't job-hop or pose any additional health or safety issues.

At Rachel's school this kind of "competitive employment" is only one of three categories for students in the transition program and a possibility only for those who can become independent, learn time-management skills, and have ability to use public transportation—all this before mastering the job itself. Other students are learning skills that will enable them to seek "supported employment" in a sheltered environment. In the third group are those with the most extreme health problems and disabilities who will go to respite care or an adult training facility.

In April 2002 I visited a work-production class where students were learning specific skills.

When I visited Bob Russell's class, I learned that making toast was more than figuring out how brown you liked your bread. After I visited Dawn Tomlin's class, I understood that succeeding in work production meant not merely mastering specific job skills, like sorting, counting or tallying, but also improving "time-on-task" skills, such as endurance, work rate, and speed. Good workers must be able to interact properly with each other. They have to learn to ask for supplies when they run short and seek help if there is something they don't understand.

Dawn's room was wonderfully familiar, on its walls a map of the world, a poster of baseball legend Roberto Clemente, a banner that read, UNDERSTAND THE SIMILARITIES. CELEBRATE THE DIFFERENCES.

The day of my visit, seven students sat around a long table. For several class periods they'd been helping refurbish science kits for area schools for the Asset Project. The plastic pieces—thousands of them—for these kits had been separated into storage bins and stacked on the shelves of a cart. That afternoon the first job was sorting two tires into a Ziploc bag.

Two students were in wheelchairs. One had partial use of one hand. The other boy, Robin, writhed continually. On the tray of his wheelchair was a state-of-the-art language board that had been programmed to say at his command the kinds of things any student might need to say, for instance, "I need more supplies." He needed only to touch an icon on the board for it to speak. It was quite forgiving. The board "understood" Robin even when his aim was imperfect.

Five other workers were at the table—two dreamy-looking kids, and three others, including Rachel, on this day wearing her purple shirt and two strands of purple Mardi-Gras beads. A teacher, two aides, and a student teacher were also helping out.

"Everyone will start with a yellow bin," Dawn said in a loud, clear voice. "Everyone will have—what do you have? A tire. You have to put two tires into one bag. This is the first step. OK. Does everybody have a large tire? Everybody should have a large tire. Now, what do you need?

"A bag!" someone eventually offered.

"Set two tires aside. You're going to have to put two—listen, Jake. *Two* tires into *one* bag. OK? This is the first step."

And so they began, each with his or her spectrum of behavioral, cognitive, and physical limitations. Each with issues. In this class, as in cooking, Rachel's were less apparent. My being at her school had put her into a bashful mode.

The boys in the wheelchairs first worked the tires into a plastic container. This made it easier for them to slide the tires into the Ziploc bag. If the sheer effort was obvious, so, too, was the absence of frustration, at least on this day.

The teachers prompted and coached without stop.

"*Two* in a bag."

"Good job, Jake."

"Robin, you are phenomenal!"

"Nice job!"

The language board said in its sci-fi voice, "I need a bag, please."

One boy had a hard time opening the Ziploc bag.

One girl was so slow it was as if she were floating underwater. Beside her a girl filled the bag without prompting or delay, then held up the bag, eyed it, placed it on the table, and very precisely, a fraction of an inch at a time, pressed down on the zip line until the bag was sealed. The whole process took a couple of minutes.

Meanwhile:

"One in each container!"

"You need to *ask* if you need more supplies."

"Dawn! Dawn!" This was my kid's familiar, maddening, attention-getting chime.

Dawn was busy with Jake, asking, "How many are in a bag? How *many*, Jake?"

"Two."

"And how many are in *that* bag?"

Jake looked up, fastened his huge eyes on her.

"I'm running out of bags!" Rachel said. Then, catching my eye, she gestured *come here* with her fingers.

I ignored her, and she went back to her task.

And then—here's the thing—everyone was at work. Except for the teachers' enthusiastic prompts, the room was quiet. There was no sign of discord or unhappiness, no sense that this was drudgery. These students were more focused than the kids in an average public-school class. They were working! They were engaged. And they kept at it for twenty minutes, until the first sorting job was done. The next step would be for them to put smaller tires in the same bags.

But first, break time. A chance to stretch or move about, get a drink of water, chat with their friends. One of the aides put on latex gloves, filled a huge syringe with milky-colored liquid, and squirted it into Robin's mouth. He gurgled and gagged: it was a messy, difficult process.

When Rachel found me, I asked what she was doing. "They have them putting in tires for other people," she said. "They have a lot of stuff for students to sort." Then she whipped out a bottle of purple nail polish from her pocket.

Her classmate, a dark-haired girl, dreamy and angelic-looking, approached, getting right up in my face to sign. I was embarrassed that I did not understand her, reminded that I was a foreigner in this country where my daughter spent most of her time.

At last she formed a word. "Mommy?" she asked.

"Yes, I'm Rachel's mom."

"Boots?" she asked.

I lifted up my pant cuff and showed her. "Yes," I said. "I'm wearing boots."

A boy came over to show me the mean-looking dog on the front of his T-shirt. "Kmart!" he said. I'd already heard him tell the teacher where his mom got the shirt.

When break was over, the students were back in their seats

for a second, shorter session. Dawn reminded them with the same short, crisply delivered sentences that they would be putting two little tires into a bag that already had two bigger tires. And then they were back to work.

When I told Dawn that I was impressed, she agreed that the kids had been working well. "We can't keep them supplied. Their rate and speed has really improved."

I *was* impressed.

I was also stunned—by all the effort it took to put two tires into a plastic bag, by the sight of my daughter with her peers, by the range of ability and disability in that room, the sheer diversity of this population we so blithely lumped together as having "special needs." But mostly what stayed with me was the diligent way the kids worked.

On the way to see Michael Stoehr, who heads the career-education program, I thought how I felt when work goes well, when I have been so absorbed by my tasks, so "in the flow," that time vanishes. I thought about my sense of well-being at the end of a day like that, and how much I wanted that for Rachel, not because work per se would be good for her soul, not because I was pretending her life would resemble mine, but because when she was focused—playing FreeCell or solitaire on the computer, for instance—she was at peace. When we play Uno, one of the few games that fully engages her, she is fun to be with, her constant talking silenced at last.

So I was full of dreamy good cheer when I knocked on Michael Stoehr's door.

We talked about Dawn's class and some of the other work experiences Rachel has had at school—counting, sorting, housekeeping tasks. "One of her biggest difficulties is concentrating—just staying on task," he said. "She's distracted by what's going on around her." Though she was being considered for supported employment, it wasn't a sure thing.

In the world outside school—even in the world of supported employment—she would be expected to be "somewhat independent," he said. The job coaching she would need was "pretty intense, pretty long range. And at this point, the supports just aren't out there."

Supported employment wasn't a sure thing.

Sometimes reality hits like an ax.

3. Sometimes she talks too much; it's hard for either of us to know what she wants.

What did Rachel want? Maybe it was ridiculous the way we were pushing her to do so many things that were so difficult for her, I thought when I left Stoehr's office. Maybe she just didn't want to work. But if she didn't have a job, what would she do all day long when she was no longer in school?

In this era of self-determination and person-centered planning, I was supposed to be asking these kinds of questions. All the literature I got explaining the transition process urged me to view my child as a "total person" and make sure her desires were "at the heart of decision making." The materials prepared by the Allegheny County Department of Human Services, Office of Mental Retardation/Developmental Disabilities reminded me that self determination is "a fundamental human right." People with mental retardation should have "the freedom to choose the services and supports they want, the authority to control limited resources and the responsibility for the decisions they make."

How can I respect Rachel's fundamental human right to choose what she will do after she is out of school without abandoning her to a world she cannot fully understand?

Well, there's conjecture: what I think she wants, based on my observations. And there are the dozens of questions about her likes and dislikes that I attempt to answer for her as honestly as I can when I fill out paperwork. And, I can't deny, there's my own will at work, since left to her own, Rachel would rather sit in front of a trough of potato chips and eat until she falls asleep than go to Special Olympics basketball. But I say, "She likes basketball," because when I spy on her from the doorway, I can see she's enjoying herself. I know I'm cheating, that *I* want her to play basketball and swim because it's good for her. Still, because I really do want to respect her desires, I sometimes set up my little microcassette tape recorder and interview her. I mentioned this to a friend once, and she was somewhat taken aback. "Why don't you just *talk* to her?" she asked.

I interview Rachel so I can hear her. In everyday life, she is so demanding, her nonstop talk so full of what I think of as sheer nothingness—endless questions about each move I make, about future plans, mostly to do with food, which I've answered dozens of times. Yes, I'll make dinner as soon as you hang up your jacket and use the bathroom. Yes (hang up your jacket). Yes (bathroom first.) Yes (did you flush?) yes (did you wash your hands?) yes (with soap?) yes (you didn't flush!) yes. Her conversation is full of things that are real, overheard things that happened to someone else, things that are wrenchingly true.

If Rachel's incessant talking is both her prime means of communication and her strength—she can be funny and charming, full of personality—it is also her most profound, most unmanageable behavioral issue. She is, as one document states, "attention seeking, with a tendency to interrupt and begin talking about a nonrelated topic.... She is difficult to redirect."

Sometimes it is so noisy when I'm with her that I must expend a great amount of energy willing myself not to shriek at her to just shut up.

Sometimes I'm an earthmover, and she is the mountain. I am up there in my little cab, yelling, "Get a move on!" and ramming her.

When I interview her, I wait until she's out of the house before I replay the tape. Sometimes what I hear is how extraordinarily hard it is for her to process more than one or two simple, concrete questions before a tweeting bird or footsteps in another room set her off on a tangent. Sometimes I can sort out someone else's interests from her own. And sometimes in the silence of my room, apart from her, what I hear with great clarity is her heart's desire. Then I am close to all that makes her human. Listening to the tapes, I think about her in bed, lost beneath a huge gorilla and teddy bear and a dozen smaller stuffed animals. I think about her own, very clearly defined sense of "cool"—the hooded sweatshirt and sweatpants her sister chose for her birthday, which she sneaks out of the closet and tries to wear every day, even in summer. I think about the books she cannot read but insists upon getting at the library every Saturday and carrying everywhere, about her purple Mardi Gras beads. I think about her telling a friend that she wants to drink beer when she turns twenty-one.

I recall the day we were preparing for her first-ever sleepover guest and that, when I asked what she wanted to do with Jennie, she said, "Thnuggle." I think about the childish lisp that, given all the crucial therapies, all the urgent tasks she must master, we've never tried to correct, and this most human desire to be close to others, a desire that her incessant talking and her resistance to hygiene threatens to prevent.

I listen to the tapes and hear myself asking and asking what she wants, and I hear her say:

"I want to go on the bus."

"I want to be able to go out with a friend once in a while and do stuff."

"I want to see if I can get a cell phone, Ma."

"I want to look for an apartment."

I ask if she wants to have a job.

"Yes," she says. "Somewhere in this area."

What would she like to do?

"Look for something me and Jennie can do together."

I cue Rachel, try to get her to name some favorite jobs.

"Making dinner," she says. "Computer." "I like to look at the newspaper once in a while."

I back up to try to get her back on track. "What's my job?" I ask.

"Teaching," she says. "Writing."

"What about the JCC?" I ask. "What's your job there?"

"Working at the café."

What does she do there?

"Sell stuff to drink and eat. They have all different ice creams and all that stuff."

"What happens if a person comes and wants something?"

"They don't have any more sandwiches."

"So what happens if—"

"Listen! Listen. Just listen! They don't have any more sandwiches because they sold them all last time, and that's why we're doing this, because we don't have any more. We only have what's on the board."

Again I back up and try to redirect her. What does she do when the customers are gone?

"We clean up. The whole purpose is to clean up after we're done selling candy and selling drinks and locking up machines. And we're doing that because we always have power-walking, but not today. With whatever her name is. She didn't show up, so Jennie left, and then I left."

I remind her that the confusion with power-walking was something that happened a few days ago. Maybe she can tell me about cleaning up.

"There's a big problem with the machines, usually."

What machines?

"The yellow-and-gray machines. The Popsicle machines, Ma. The ice-cream machines. They got locked up wrong yesterday by someone, and what happened was, after the fact that they had them locked up wrong was like a weird compliment, accomplishment, with like after this was going on it was fine, and then after that was—what are you writing down?"

Later I ask if she likes her job at the JCC.

"People talk to me too much, and I just can't stand it. It's hard for me to concentrate. It's better for me to do the dry cleaning, Mom. Better than the café."

Part of that statement is profoundly true. My daughter, with her relentless talking, is so terribly distractible that she cannot concentrate anywhere there is noise or conversation. But the dry cleaning, which she could nicely define ("It's where you take your clothes to the Laundromat, and you have to pay for it") is something she knows only because her friend had some with him one day. Dry cleaning is like drinking beer at twenty-one and going to college—things that others have or discuss, rather than a wish from her own heart.

A few days after my visit to Rachel's work-production class, I asked her what jobs she was doing in school.

"I'm not doing the cups anymore," she said.

"What do you do in the mornings?"

"Only the paper towels."

And what did she do with the paper towels?

"Put them in the holder. In the paper-towel bin."

"And what else do you do?"

"Plates. We fill plates. Although here's the big part, Ma—are you ready for it?—we're selling chips and stuff like that now."

And so we had moved in time and place, from school, perhaps on that day, to her job at Café J on a nameless day in a month that fell as randomly as a snowflake.

4. There is no safety net.

Though Barbara Milch's official title is division director of children, family, and youth, I think of her as the person who has helped make the JCC of Greater Pittsburgh into a near-perfect world, where people with special needs are a visible part of the community. She spearheaded the current programs that make it possible for kids with special needs to be included in afterschool programs and summer camps. Nor have teens and adults been forgotten: most of what Rachel does outside of school—her chance to go to a play, see a ball game, be with friends—originates here at the JCC because of Barbara's efforts.

The café was initially a joint project Barbara initiated with Jewish Residential Services to employ people with chronic mental illness as a primary diagnosis. When funding from a start-up grant ran out, she was able to put anyone in the job. Thus Rachel and her cohort (and their therapeutic staff-support people) were given shifts.

In my some-job-somewhere phase, I took great pleasure in seeing Rachel in her red apron, wearing her staff badge. The JCC is a busy community center with nearly 15,000 members. Lots of people I know who use the athletic facilities or have kids in child care stop at the café and are served by Rachel. It made me feel good to think of my daughter out in the world this way, not merely some mysterious, hidden-away, half-grown child I was rumored to have.

Now that I am looking beyond the gloss made up of relief, gratitude, and fatigue, I am forced to ask: what will happen when Rachel has no TSS?

This is not doomsday thinking. I've already contested the proposed termination of funding for this costly behavior-management therapy, and though I was successful, still I know that these services are designed to "fade," even though her issues may never be completely resolved. Rachel cannot work in the café without this assistance—not for the foreseeable future, at least.

She's learned a lot since she began at the café. She knows the prices of everything and that the customers should check the board to see what is being offered that day. She has memorized the sequence of tasks necessary to close down the café.

Skills are not enough. Before this spring I imagined Rachel's future based merely on her strengths (she's gregarious) and deficits (poor vision, poor fine motor skills). But I had failed to regard the rest of her. It was as if her behavior and attention issues were things that made it hard for *me* to live with her but that they would not impact her ability to work. I had somehow failed to integrate what I had known all along: the greatest obstacle to her working is her distractibility.

At Café J she has "difficulty balancing appropriate socialization with her peers with the need to focus and concentrate on the demands of working in the café," I read. "She continues to ask for assistance with skills she has mastered and can successfully manipulate various JCC staff to engage in 'over-helping.' Often she does not want to follow through with requests to complete her responsibilities for the café."

And didn't she herself manage to tell me exactly why she was struggling? *People talk to me too much, and I just can't stand it. It's hard for me to concentrate.*

Barbara has tried to reassure me. "She will always have a home at the JCC."

But at this time, in the spring of 2002, I am forced to wonder—a home doing what?

Though I cannot underestimate the importance of community, neither can I bear to imagine Rachel wandering the corridors of the JCC, trying to engage unwitting strangers in meaningless talk—unwitting strangers because, if she stays long enough, only strangers will not know to avoid her.

Wandering, following people, trying to engage them—this is what Rachel's day will look like if she cannot be trained for supported employment. It is what she's like at home, that most unstructured place, where everyone else is off doing something—reading, paying bills, talking on the phone, walking up and down the stairs. When we are home for too long together, Rachel's calls for attention, her birdlike *Ma? Mommy? Ma?* is so insistent I choose the most distant part of the house just to escape her.

Michael Stoehr warned me that the supports Rachel gets at school are entitlements mandated by law, that after school these supports are often unavailable. At present they aren't there for millions of individuals in the United States with mild mental retardation. Only 7 to 23 percent of these people are employed full time, in part because of the inadequacy of vocational training. Rachel, with her greater needs, is at far greater jeopardy. At school and at the JCC, she has staff at her side nearly all the time. In the outside world, it's different.

"Some agencies will say they're going to follow her, but the reality is they'll provide support for about a month or two," Stoehr says. "After that they're looking for results and turnaround, ready to pull out.... It's a very unfair system. There are not a lot of easy answers or nice solutions."

I know this is true, just as I understand that distractibility is Rachel's most serious handicap. And yet I have seen her quiet down. I have watched her sit at the computer for long stretches of time. And it makes me wonder. In this era adaptations are made so people can learn and travel and work. There are language boards and gigs and orthotics, bicycles that can be pedaled by hand, computers that speak, lifts to bring wheelchairs onto buses. Must I believe that an adaptation can never be made for Rachel? Must I say that she will never be able to work? If I do that, I am left imagining my daughter wandering aimlessly, trying to engage people, unwittingly pushing them away—a lonely, marginalized person.

5. Take a nap and then wake up.

So you're tired. So what, I need to remind myself. Take a nap, and while you're sleeping, dream some sweet dreams. And then wake up.

You know what she needs. Now search for it. If you can't find it, you'll have to make it happen.

It's exhausting, but what can I say?

She has her work, and I have mine.

What about Meg?

Curtis Smith

True weightlessness. Professor Steven Bridges achieved it last year, a sensation he would later describe to his worrying daughters as skating forward on warm blue ice, frictionless and unworldly beautiful. According to the attending emergency room physician, Steven Bridges was deceased at the time, but no matter. He is, he would honestly tell his younger daughter, Claire, if she had the nerve to ask, looking forward to experiencing it again.

With its new set of plastic valves, Bridges's heart beats stronger than ever and that is fine with him. (Although he can't help thinking of it in odd ways. In the shower he often fingers the scar, smooth and raised from his skin, and envisions his heart as something no longer human, like an old steam boiler locked in a school basement, chugging away through the Pennsylvania winter.)

There are other changes, subtle yet undeniable changes he keeps to himself (Claire thinks he is unsettled enough as it is). He has acquired a taste for Scotch, a glass or two with water and ice being part of his nightly routine. As he sips, he stands on the balcony deck overlooking the backyard, swept up in a tide of smells he has never noticed before, smells of fragrant perfumes and gasoline and wet bark. Below him, a sea of brittle leaves swirls in the drained in-ground pool. And then he gazes upward to the stars, reciting the names of constellations he learned as a boy, wishing he could be sucked up into their vastness.

Tonight it is pleasant, the crisp air creeping down from the mountains and settling in the quiet valley streets. Bridges finishes his drink and steps inside to get the cordless phone Claire bought him for Christmas last year. It's late, but he can't sleep. Too many thoughts swim through his mind. The house is still, the stillness in turn magnifying the fall of his footsteps and the hypnotic chunk-tha-chunk of the ceiling fan. He pauses by the open door of his older daughter's room. Meg, thirty-eight and retarded, sleeps in her canopy bed, snoring unevenly through her gaping mouth. Bridges stops to consider her, stuffed toys bunched by her head, the blue moonlight that bathes her like an oversized angel, and he wonders what her dreams are like, if they are free and uninhibited or if they are dull, full of the syrupy thoughts that permeate the rest of her life.

"Claire?" Bridges says into the receiver. Phone in hand, he has stretched the length of his burly frame across the deck. The wood is cool on his neck. In his hand is the picture of Sarah he keeps in his wallet. She has been dead nearly three years to the day.

"Daddy?" Claire mumbles. "That you?"

"Claire, sweetheart, would you do me a favor?" His words drift as he studies the blinking lights of a passing plane.

"Daddy, are you OK? Do you want me to come over?"

"I'm fine, sweetheart. Just do me a favor and go to your window. The stars are beautiful tonight. I wouldn't want you to miss them."

*

Bridges leans on the banister and yells up the stairs, "Come on, Meg."

"OK."

"Don't want to be late again, do you?"

"I'm coming, I'm coming!"

A door slams. Footsteps scurry overhead. Bridges walks back to the kitchen. The smells of coffee and bacon filter through the house as he makes breakfast. Ever since Sarah's death, he's prepared Meg's meals and made sure she's gotten to work on time.

Meg flops into the kitchen. Awkward and pear-shaped, she carries herself with a choppy walk that borders on being totally out of control. Strands of wet hair are plastered to her cheeks, the rest pulled back in a sloppy ponytail. Her eyes are dull blue and bloodshot red, still circled with sleep lines. With a heavy grunt, she sits at the breakfast table and cradles her ample face between her hands.

"Every day it's the same thing," she says. "Get up and go to work. Come home, watch TV, go to sleep, and go to work again. It's boring!"

Bridges smiles weakly as he turns bacon slices in the skillet. For the last week everything has been "boring." In the past, there have been months full of "crazy," "fascinating," and "ridiculous" things.

"How many eggs do you want, dear?"

Upper lip raised, she scrunches her face in confused wrinkles. "Why eggs all the time? Eggs are so boring."

"So you don't want any?"

"I'll have two." She holds up two fingers and twists her hand back to front.

Bridges sits and sips his coffee as she eats. His head is light from last night's Scotch. He could smell the alcohol creep into his sweat as he completed his morning workout—one hundred push-ups, two hundred sit-ups—the same amount he did in his semi-pro hockey days. He is blessed with the muscular chest and thick arms of a man half his age.

He watches his daughter, her feet widely spaced and planted firmly on the ground, as she concentrates on not letting any food spill on the red-and-white-print shirt and matching red skirt all the female employees at the Pancake House must wear. She has been working the three to eleven shift for thirteen years, longer than any other employee and over twice as long as her current manager. A wood and bronze plaque from the national office of Pancake House Inc. commemorating ten years of service hangs by the refrigerator.

"It's good," she says, looking up to him, her mouth full of food. The thin, powder blue window curtains cast a watery light over her face and the exaggerated motions of her chewing.

"Oh, I almost forgot." She waves her hands as if she has just burnt her fingers. "Nature show is on tonight. Don't forget to tape it, OK?"

"Sure," Bridges says. Penguins, condors, alligators—Meg will watch anything dealing with animals. On Tuesdays, her day off, she sometimes sits mesmerized for hours watching her tapes. In the car, Bridges must be careful to divert her attention whenever they pass a dead animal on the side of the road or else she will burst out in tears.

Meg stares out the window as they drive. Sunlight flickers between the roadside trees, the glare so bright off the hood it nearly shuts Bridges's eyes. He checks his watch and decides to take a shortcut through campus.

"Look, Daddy!" she says. She points with a series of piston thrusts. "It's the stadium!" Lips drawn tight in concentration, she counts silently on her hand. "Only two months to football!"

The stadium rises from a lush summer field, all cement and exposed steel girders and strangely hollow in the July haze. Bridges used to take his daughters to a few games each season. Claire lost interest after junior high, but Meg and Bridges have gone to every home game for the past fifteen years (season tickets—a faculty perk). Dressed in blue and white like a slice of autumn sky, she raises her fists and screams, stomping boldly on the aluminum flooring, holding onto the cheers for a second or two longer than anyone else in their section. And at the start of the second half, when the students sing their version of the alma mater (a repetitive, in-tune chant of "we don't know the god-damn words!"), she covers her mouth with her mittened hands and glances sideways at her father, her blue eyes streaming with tears as she attempts to restrain her laughter.

Bridges pulls alongside the curb beneath the slanted red roof of the Pancake House. "Pick you up at eleven, dear," he says. "Have a good day at work."

"You always say that." She rolls her eyes. "It's so boring to hear that all the time. Now don't forget about the nature show on TV." She slams the door and scurries toward the entrance, nearly bowling over a mother and her stroller.

"Meg!" Bridges calls out, but she has already gone inside. On the seat of the car is a red apron and a red name tag. "Hello," the tag reads, "My name is MEG."

*

Hercules. Lyra. Scorpius. Bridges reclines on the wooden planks of the balcony deck and traces the patched quilt of the sky with his sausage-thick fingers. A six-inch reflector telescope gathers dust in the basement. It is a monstrous thing, undeniably expensive, a birthday present from Claire. He has used it before, to pinpoint comets and photograph lunar eclipses, but for the most part he leaves it alone. The power to focus obliterates the relations between worlds. It is better, he thinks, to view the heavens unbroken to truly appreciate their splendor.

Air conditioners drone through the humid night, and Bridges detects the odor of fresh mulch from a neighbor's garden. A loosely gripped glass of Scotch rests on his scarred chest. The ice cubes swirl with each breath.

He raises his hand and touches the stars. Canis Major. Leo. Hercules.

The cordless phone sits on his stomach, but he has turned the ringer off. He is tired of it. Claire and her thousand well-intentioned but exhausting questions. Meeting dates set with realtors. Confirmation calls to the directors of local and state agencies for retarded citizens. He takes another sip and glances toward the house. Meg's window shines with the pale glow of her Spiderman night-light.

He rises and leans against the railing, surveying the hole in his backyard where most people his age have planted gardens. The pool is empty, a naked belly of cracked concrete still lined by last fall's crinkled leaves. Three years ago, Bridges drained the pool himself, although he can't actually remember doing it. He thinks of the sailors that first crossed the ocean and the astronauts who sat on the launch pad, waiting to be hurled into space. Nothing, he thinks, is certain until it is part of the past.

He upturns his glass and lets the ice cubes tumble to the earth. They clatter like wind chimes in the wet air.

In the kitchen he pours another drink. Ice is piled to the rim, and it numbs his lips. He takes a seat at the kitchen table. Being alone at night does not bother him. There is an embracing coolness to the indigo light, to the shadows of familiar objects. In the three years since Sarah's death, he has made a practice of avoiding his home until evening. Claire invites him over for dinner at least three times a week, and Bridges knows he stays later than he should. He spoils his grandsons with presents and does push-ups with them riding his back. Claire worries about the stress this puts on his heart, but she knows it would do no good to argue with him. She just smiles and sighs, a throw-your-hands-up, "What am I going to do with you?" sigh.

It is only during the day that being alone in the house becomes difficult. Bridges can't stand the way the late afternoon sun slants in through the windows and lights up the place like an unused museum. Tables and vases wade in puddles of white sunshine—all the things Sarah and Claire bought over the years—they might as well belong to strangers. Bridges secretly fears that the soft areas of his heart have been roped off.

He retrieves the spiral notebook he hides in the cabinet above the refrigerator. Inside the notebook is a list he is making, a list of everything he owns. He has decided that when he moves, he will get rid of it all. Claire and Meg can have whatever they want and the rest can go to charity or the dump. Making the list swells his heart with joy. It is like seeing his house new for the first time, each room whitewashed and vacant. He picks up a pen and walks into the living room, and with each page he completes, he is engulfed by a warm, buoyant wave, a wave that carries him so high he must duck his head from hitting the blades of the slowly turning ceiling fan.

*

Bridges stands at the deep end of the pool. There were thunderstorms last night, but today it is beautiful. Long afternoon shadows fall about him in crisp, defined lines. He is bare-chested, clad only in khaki work pants and unbuckled rubber boots. Sweat gleams beneath the tufts of gray hair on his forearms.

Using a spade and a stiff push broom, he lugs bucketfuls of wet leaves from the pool floor. Beetles scurry through the muck. He pauses, runs his fingers over the scar on his chest, and gazes upward. His perspective, hemmed in by the lip of the pool, holds the railing of the balcony deck and an oval of flawless summer sky fringed by the overhanging maples.

It was Bridges himself who fished Sarah out of the pool. Like a grainy nickelodeon short, the scene still plays ceaselessly in his mind. Meg sitting stupefied on the apron, feet dangling in the water, no ripples from her rounded calves. Sarah in the heart of the water, her limbs frozen and outstretched like a four-pointed star. Dripping wet in his street clothes, Bridges attempted mouth to mouth, but Sarah's lips had already turned the color of sick moonlight. Paramedics said it was a massive coronary infarction, that she was most likely dead before she hit the water. Meg was treated for shock and didn't speak a word for the next two weeks.

And Bridges, drunk for only the second time in his life, took it upon himself to drain the pool the night of her funeral. Dressed in his somber blue suit, he fell asleep on the deck to the lullaby of crickets and the hiss of the pump as it bled a gentle flow of water down the driveway and into the street. And although he has never questioned Meg about her silence following Sarah's death, he can't help believing that Meg was somewhat envious when she saw how peacefully her mother floated, no worries, no cares on a still summer day.

"Daddy!"

Bridges looks up and sees Claire standing on the rim of the pool. She is out of breath, and with great difficulty, she lowers her seven-months-pregnant body so that her feet hang over the edge.

"Hello, sweetheart."

"I looked all over the house for you." She draws a deep breath. She does not say, "I was afraid I'd find you sprawled half naked and nearly dead on the kitchen floor, the way I did last year," although he can tell this is what she's thinking.

"Been out here since I dropped Meg off. Realtor said I should have the house in shape before I put it up."

"You shouldn't be working so hard," she says. Her tone is alternately relieved and concerned.

"Haven't you heard?" He taps his chest. "I have modern medicine on my side."

"Honestly, Daddy," she sighs.

He shields his eyes and regards her, her brown hair lit in the afternoon sun. Suddenly, he is taken back by the tiny scraps of his wife that rise to the surface of her face.

"I'll bet Meg is happy you're fixing the pool."

He laughs. "She shrieked all the way to work when I told her. Says she can't wait."

Claire glances toward the house. "That girl is a fish. Remember how she'd stay in the pool until her skin wrinkled? Mom would have to practically drag her out to eat."

Bridges resumes his shoveling. "Your mother and I almost didn't build the pool because of her. We stayed up every night for a week arguing about it. She was convinced Meg was going to drown in it."

"So," Claire says, pausing for a second before continuing, "you're really going to sell the house." She hugs herself as if caught in a fall breeze. "You know it won't seem right driving by and not being able to stop in."

The spade scrapes against the concrete, and with the curved white floor beneath his feet, Bridges thinks of the new baby that floats in the juices of his daughter's stomach. He wishes he could tell her about the list in the spiral notebook. Wishes he could summon the words to explain how, even at this moment with nothing but blue sky above him, he can feel the entire weight of the house—the kitchen tiles, the plumbing, the plaster, everything—pressing down upon him.

"So what are you going to do?" she asks.

"I've been checking into apartments and condos in town. The whole thing is up in the air right now. Maybe I'll travel for a while. I've got three semesters of unused sabbatical."

"What about Meg, Daddy?" Her words ring in the emptiness of the pool.

"I've been making some calls; it's all stuff we've discussed before, sweetheart. Remember last year when we put her name on the county's list for group home assignments?" He looks to her and waits until she nods in agreement. "They called and said there's a placement open for her."

Claire bites her lip. "She won't like it," she says quietly.

"I know." He pats another spadeful into the bucket. "It was easier when your mother was alive. Now it seems I spend half my life dragging her out of bed and driving her to work, patrolling the house to make sure she hasn't left the iron on or the bath water running. I don't think I can do it anymore." He smiles and winks at her. "And she can't come live with you, can she?"

Claire bows her head, trying to conceal her own smile. Just the week before, Meg and Bridges had joined Claire and her family for Fourth of July fireworks down by the lake, and Meg, with her hands clasped over her ears, howled with piercing cries of joy that had scared the wits out of Claire's two sons.

"When are you going to tell her, Daddy?"

Bridges studies a puddle of amber water that has collected by his boots. "Soon," he says. "It'll have to be soon."

*

"Claire's house!" Meg exclaims. Bridges nods as he drives Meg home from work. The night is dry and cool. Meg waves at Claire's house, a brick Tudor two story, even though the windows are dark and there is no one in the yard.

At home, Bridges tries to watch the final ten minutes of a tape he's rented. He has not seen a movie in a theater since Sarah's death. Meg has a tendency to call out to the characters on the screen, to laugh out loud at all the wrong times. Ripples of whispers and giggles flow through the theater.

Bridges sits on the couch. "I'm going to watch the end of my movie," he explains. Meg takes off her apron and plunks herself down on the opposite end of the couch. "I've only got a few minutes left, then you can watch whatever you want."

"What about the nature show?" she asks. "You did remember to tape it, didn't you?"

"Yes," Bridges says. "We'll watch it after this, OK?"

Bridges starts the movie. A love scene plays, two shadowy figures drawing closer. The actress kneels on a mattress, the room clouded with misty blue light, and allows her shirt to slip off her shoulders.

"Oh, Daddy!" Meg screams. The long Indian earrings Claire bought for her in Mexico flap against her neck. She laughs hysterically and covers her eyes. "This is so BORING!"

Bridges stops the tape. Without a word, he leaves the room and walks to the deck. Meg follows. All day long Bridges picked his way around the pool, patching the spider-web cracks in the concrete. In the pool, in the shower, in the car, he has rehearsed at least a hundred times the speech he plans to give her. He puts his arm around her shoulders and breathes deeply. The night is full of cricket calls and the scent of honeysuckle, and he wonders if this is how he will always remember this moment.

Meg looks over the backyard. "How long until we can go swimming?"

"I'll fill it up tomorrow," he says. "But it still won't be ready for a couple of days."

He studies her in the soft light that spills from the house and notices with sudden astonishment that she is middle-aged. Her temples are wrinkled and bordered with gray.

She moves away from him. "I want to go in and watch the nature show."

Bridges nods and lets his opportunity slip away.

The show is about sharks, an hour of water-filtered sunlight and gray streamlined bodies. An English narrator goes on behind the pictures—how sharks are wonders of evolution, how they swim from the moment they are born and when they grow too old to swim, they die.

Bridges turns to say something to Meg, but she is already stretched out and snoring on the couch.

*

It is after midnight, and Bridges sits on the deck. The sky is bruised with strips of deep-blue clouds. Soon it will be autumn. Soon the Saturday football games, the roar of 70,000 foaming over the town. Soon Cygnus, Pegasus, Auriga, and Orion. A full moon steps silver over quiet houses and manicured gardens. A romance of chirping insects rises from the maples, an electric buzz like the tingle of Scotch.

Three weeks have passed. The cracks in the pool have been patched. The pump and catch baskets have been cleaned out. Meg, in her red bathing cap and black one-piece, has spent every morning in the pool. Her skin has tanned, and Claire can't get over how much weight she has lost.

Bridges gazes over the pool and contemplates tomorrow's

deadlines. The realtor wants to start placing ads in the local papers. The director of the group home insists on a definite answer or else Meg will lose her placement. Bridges takes another sip and sighs. A shaft of kitchen light falls in a shimmering rectangle upon the still pool water. The light suffuses into the shadows, and it is from the shadows that he detects a human form.

Bridges draws away from the railing, stares, and slowly shakes his head. Her bare feet tiptoe awkwardly over the concrete apron and the swirling eddies of winged maple fruit. She tucks her hair beneath a red bathing cap and tests the water with a sweep of her foot. Bridges watches her move, her skin enameled in the giving moonlight. She holds her breath, and without thought or hesitation, dives into the water, gliding beneath the surface with a grace she'll never know on land, and Bridges can't get over how similar her silhouette is to the sharks they saw one night on television, never hesitating, never stopping for fear she may never move this way again.

Joyful Noise

Maggie Kast

As a child, you followed the rules—that was your job. It was wrong to hit your little sister, to giggle or tickle or otherwise revel in pleasure, to take—or even want—the biggest piece. It was right to let your friends go first, to think of other people before yourself, to sit up straight and use the proper fork. It was downright dangerous to disagree.

That was fifty years ago. Marriage and motherhood have intervened, but you still try to do what's expected, and anything that makes you stand out is a test. Like right now: you are somewhat uncomfortable as you drive your grown son Allen to Chicago's Field Museum for an outdoor performance of music and sonic sculpture. It's the right thing to do, you think, especially for Allen. In fact, he might enjoy it more than any other person on Earth. Everything about it will delight him: strong rhythms, deep vibrations, large scale, massed movement. Nonetheless, small ripples of apprehension spread outward from a knot in your stomach. He talks in the car as you drive from his group home to a lakefront museum: "He like music. Rock 'n' roll too. He like music, yeah."

Wind from the lake has cleansed the city air, and the sun soaks it with warmth and brilliance. You make your way around the museum, wishing Allen would get the hang of walking next to someone, instead of just in front or far behind. You hate stepping on his heels, and you shrink at the thought of how you look, standing and waiting for him, calling his name and telling him to walk fast. He stops to scratch the sidewalk with his fingertips, tries to lick each lamppost as you pass.

"We're going to hear music," you tell him.

"Good music," he says. "I like church. I gotta fourteen. Neighborhood."

Years of experience have taught you to decipher some of this speech. Church and music are easy. "Neighborhood" sums up your habitual response to his request for Burger King: "We don't have one in our neighborhood." "Fourteen" is a mystery.

"I'm fat," Allen continues. "Daddy's dead."

You are no longer surprised or hurt by the abruptness of this statement. "Yes, Daddy's dead," you say, and immerse yourself in the museum's splendid stone façade rising in front of you, the intricate jumble of red and gray skyscrapers on your left, like a cubist painting, the bright open expanse of lake and sky on your right. You take the city in, fill yourself up with it.

You see and enjoy the world on your own now. When you were married, you shared every sight and sound and taste, transformed them into dialogue, heard and retold. You filled each other up, cast a single shadow, shared an outline. It was easy to stand out when the two of you could do it together, and you learned not to care so much what other people thought. You learned to ignore your father's voice, echoing from childhood: *who do you think you are?* The ragged edge your husband left bled you empty, and you lived for years in a shadow world. The air itself was cruel, and even the space of your room seemed vast and empty.

That was ten years ago. Now the youngest of your four children has just gone off to college, and Allen has been happily settled among his peers for the last five. Sure, you regret your losses: the house alive with talk and music, late-night suppers in bed, the predictable satisfaction of cooking for your husband. You are inescapably single. Sometimes you would like to say, "Look!" But solitary pleasures have begun to percolate through the pain, and you gather the bubbles as they rise.

The city intoxicates you. You float through it, a transparent container for colors and images, your figure blending with the ground behind and around you. Your life sings with little joys: the profusion of produce at a farmer's market; the lapping, cold water of the lake. You cook and eat and drink alone, uncensored. Your appetite, your unseen appetite, has become a way of life.

For a long time you failed to notice that the outline you shared with your husband had disappeared. Or rather, the knowledge gathered under little ledges in your mind, hidden from consciousness, as you followed your old tendency to blend in, to accommodate.

Forget accommodation today; today is for Allen. Anyone can see you, circling the museum, Allen still lagging behind. A huge dinosaur skeleton rises starkly in front of you. Reproduced in black metal, it glints with tiny points of light, stands out against the flat gray of the museum. You hear the seductive call of drums. Allen bolts toward the music, and you put a hand on his shoulder to slow him down. He's attached; you don't have to hang on to him. That's your husband's voice, present in your head. He liked to use the image of a toddler's leash to remind you that children are bound to their parents as tightly as parents to their children. Drop the leash and they'll cling to your side.

You approach the terrace, where people sit on the grass or on stone railings among the musicians, and your eyes dart around. You might run into someone you know, and your desire to hide must also be hidden. You act normal, even friendly. You sink gratefully into the anonymous sea of the crowd, alert to the possible presence of someone you recognize and ready to jump up like a sociable fish if necessary.

Here comes someone you know well: Allen's older brother Seth. He has zoomed down the lakefront on his in-line skates to meet you. He arrives wearing black wrist guards. Allen wonders about this unusual accessory, and Seth undoes the Velcro straps and fastens the wrist guards on Allen. Delighted, Allen pretends to skate, following Seth around the terrace. Allen calls the wrist guards "muscles."

"See my muscles," he says, gliding from foot to foot. Allen and Seth befriend a couple sitting on the grass with a dog, while you seek out the museum's food concession to buy some snacks and drinks. When you come out, Allen is playing with the dog, keeping the wrist guards on.

The performance begins. A man sits on a chair placed on a picnic table and bows an amplified cello. Deep multilayered sounds flood over the beat of the drums. Other strings are attached to a wooden frame on the ground, then stretched over a hundred feet to their mounting on the roof of the museum. Musicians with gloved hands reach overhead to stroke these strings with strong pulls of the whole body, making low vibrations you can feel in your gut. You look to see how Allen is reacting. You expect the excitement will agitate him, making him bite the back of his hand, growling and leaving red welts. You figured it would be all right at an outdoor performance, where extraneous noises are less noticeable. His eyes jump around, and his hands jerk, but he remains engrossed and quiet. You want to give yourself up to the music, to let its deep vibrations shake your roots, its melodies float you up to the treetops, but your eyes and your hand keep shifting toward Allen, checking that he is not about to stand up, dart out, or shout. "He's OK, don't worry about him," says your husband.

A dancer whirls with a huge, red silk, wraparound skirt; she undoes it, and it becomes a cape. She trails it behind her, running between the musicians. An older man spins something that looks like a top and makes tiny, squeaky sounds as he touches it with a stick. An athletic man in blue jeans runs in a big circle and blows on a conch shell. The music pauses, and the runner introduces the stringed instrument, the "earth harp," a piece of sonic sculpture he's built.

You move with Allen around the terrace, making sure he sees each musician. Two dancer-drummers play a complex assemblage of percussion instruments, with two drumheads on each end of a tall structure. One drumhead is horizontal, at waist level, and the other is vertical, at eye level. The dancers play rhythms on both heads at once, spinning and jumping between beats, then change places to play the xylophone and bells which connect the two ends.

Before the music is over, Seth heads for home on his skates. He decides to let Allen keep the wrist guards. "Just until he goes back," you say.

"No, he can keep them," says Seth. "I'll get some more."

After the show, people line up to put on cotton gloves and try out the harp. Allen will not ask to play, will not even know that he could. You should encourage him. You should take him and get in line in that revealing sun, show him how to put on the cotton glove and stroke the string. You know he will hold everybody up. He will say, "Glove?" and laugh and bite his hands, afraid to try. People will wait, indulging him and you, and you will shrink with the knowledge that you are taking two or three times as long as anyone else. If someone coughs in line, you will know they are losing patience. You will put on a glove yourself and show him, sliding your hand on the overhead string and startling him with the sound. You will look only at him and the string, avoiding the eyes of the spectators. Maybe he will try it himself, and maybe he won't. "What are you so worried about?" asks your husband.

Suddenly you wonder why you are often reluctant to meet people's eyes. It's a small and subtle thing, this avoidance, and you hadn't looked straight at it before. If you focus only on Allen, perhaps no one will see you. You flash on the realization: you often think this way, like a child playing peek-a-boo. You are embarrassed to waste people's valuable time, and your eyes keep shifting when someone speaks to you, as though you had a bus to catch.

Individuals in the line become a group, as they join in a common enterprise. You stand, undecided. People look at you and

Allen and then away. You feel your head, your shoulders, your hips and legs standing out against the background of stone, like a figure being outlined in black ink. You wish for predictable sequence, like a meal. This event is bound to boil over.

"Liptauer?" says Allen, and everyone looks. "Liptauer today?" Allen is referring to the cheese spread made with paprika that his father loved. Alone of all your children, he remembers and asks for it. He likes to help you buy the cream cheese, blue cheese, and green onion, and he adds the flavorings himself: a drop of Worcestershire, a dollop of mustard, lots of paprika, hot and sweet.

Let's say your husband stands next to you on the terrace. He wouldn't dream of leaving without Allen playing the earth harp. He didn't care what other people thought. You lay his image on the one of Seth joking and skating with Allen before the show, and you smile at the imperfect but striking fit, the match of color and daring, the three-dimensional gestures standing out like the pillared museum against the transparent sky.

You married your husband largely for his freedom and nerve, for the way he suddenly stopped on the street, took a deep breath, and raised his arms to embrace the world, knowing he deserved its gifts. He reached like a tall stalk to speculate about the world beyond his limits, and he sent down searching roots to probe the muddy depths of behavior, his and yours. You weren't so happy when he barged into restaurants without waiting to be seated, but he balanced you. He was somebody, and he knew exactly who he was.

The two of you worked together to raise Allen. He taught Allen how to light the candles on a birthday cake, and you taught Allen how to blow them out. You tried to teach Allen about red and green lights, and your husband taught him to find his own way to the grocery store, was happy if Allen persuaded a stranger to buy him some candy. You bathed and dressed Allen, and your husband took him for walks, encouraging him to greet strangers on the street. Allen still does this, extending his hand and saying, "How you?" to each person he passes.

When Allen was first born, twenty-eight years ago, you both called him "Zen baby" for his peaceful nature. Later, you shared a gnawing suspicion of his floppiness, his failure to sit up on time. Your husband defended Allen against the experts with their tests, hanging on to his conviction that Allen was set apart, special, even holy.

You were the one who put a name to Allen's condition. Nixon's Watergate cover-up was just being exposed. *Retarded*—no one wanted to say that word. *Developmentally delayed*, said the social worker. Allen was three and couldn't walk, and you thought the name couldn't make the thing any worse than it already was. You wanted to say the word before it was said to you. More than anything you hoped Allen would never hear it, would never know this harsh fact about himself. *Retarded, retarded*, you repeated to yourself, coming down lightly on the *r*'s and the *e*'s and clipping the *t*'s and *d*'s. *Retarded* is a fact about a person, but a *reetarrd* is a discard.

You listened to the news about Nixon on the radio in the stark, night-lit kitchen, while Allen played on the floor, lying on his stomach and propped on his hands. Your new reality stood out from accustomed family life as sharply as the black radiator against the yellow wall. You began to use the unacceptable word with your husband. He shared your embattled joy that Allen would never be able to accomplish any serious evil.

"Liptauer today, right?" repeats Allen. "Not tomorrow. Not tomorrow, I know."

You could leave now and go make Liptauer with Allen. You see yourself balanced on a seesaw with your husband. He jumps off, and you crash down, tumbling backward over and over, until you come to a rest in a dark place you never intended to be. He would not be pleased if he could see you now. You realize how much you need his counterweight. But this is your decision, and you will have to make it on your own. How easy to turn and vanish, to duck out—no repercussions. Seth's gone; Allen can't tell. *Coward*, you say to yourself. If you stay, you'll be pricked by a hundred arrowlike eyes, no place to hide. Your eyes skim stone, water, sky. It's too late to fade back into your concealing world.

"Would he like to play the harp?" asks a woman with long earrings and red hair. She moves toward the line and gestures to a space in front of her. "Go ahead." Her gaze is direct and supportive, and your body slips in front of hers before you notice what you've done.

"Liptauer later," you say firmly to Allen, as you put an arm around his shoulder and guide him into the line.

Just ahead of you, a very old lady takes the glove and holds it, not putting it on. She straightens her bent frame and reaches up as high as she can go to squeeze one brief note out of the string.

Allen moves into place, head wobbling from side to side and hands jerking with excitement. "I'm *telligent*," he says. No one can understand the word, but you see people nodding encouragement. You step forward. Your eyes sweep across the crowd and meet the eyes of the woman behind you before moving to the glove, the earth harp, and Allen. "Put it on," you tell him. "Now reach up."

"Like this?" he asks.

"Go ahead and touch it," you say. He is reaching, but not high enough. "A little bit more," you say. "You can do it."

Allen touches the string and makes a tiny blurt of a sound. He is startled but pleased and touches it again. "Rub it hard," says the woman behind you. Allen laughs and bites his hand, then reaches again to pull with more force. A low vibration starts in the heart of the harp, then swells and rises as Allen strokes again and again, bringing all the harmonics of the long string to life. Now he begins to play a neighboring string, using his whole weight and triggering vibrations that bounce off each other, making huge intersecting waves of sound. He is excited by his success and adds his own exuberant roar to the music. He has no intention of stopping.

You meet the eyes of the woman behind you. Somewhere inside each of you a laugh begins. Your bellies jiggle; you cover your mouths, and the growing mirth becomes a wordless dialogue, as joyful noise erupts and cascades from one to the other. Allen whoops, laughter boils over, and the rich pitches of the harp resound. Your tiny triumph has become a cacophonous celebration. High-spirited sounds reverberate from the earth beneath your feet to the heavens, and your heart lifts. Beyond the babel, you can just discern the gentle pitter-patter of the crowd's applause.

The Heart Speaks

Sheila Kohler

I am sitting talking to my daughter, Cybele, her gaze fixed intently on my face, when she puts her hand on my arm and glances around the room. "Where is Masha?" she asks, referring to her eldest daughter.

"Have you seen Masha?" I ask Charlotte, Cybele's middle daughter, who is playing on her own with the Lego set, but she bites her lip and shakes her head, opening her brown eyes wide.

My daughter has three daughters, like the three princesses in the fairy tales. Masha has been named after one of the three women in Chekov's *The Three Sisters*. We are a literary family, you see. Words have always been important to my husband and me.

Cybele scoops up the baby and strides fast through the rooms of our West Side apartment, calling her child's name. My daughter takes after my husband's side of the family: she has endless legs, a graceful neck. When I see her walk in my door, she looks to me, despite the babies in her arms, like a medieval queen, her light brown hair caught up high in a ponytail.

"Masha, are you hiding somewhere?" I ask, my voice rising with panic, as I go through the rooms, looking under beds, behind armchairs, the standing mirror.

Masha, at four, likes to play hide-and-seek. She likes to dress up. I open closet doors, hunting behind dresses, behind my shoes, behind shower curtains. "I hope to goodness she hasn't gone outside," I say, imagining my grandchild taking the elevator into the lobby and stepping out into the dangerous Manhattan street.

"She wouldn't have done that," my daughter reassures me, as she has so often in my life.

Still, it is not until I open the front door that I find Masha, tears running down her face. She is wearing her yellow fairy costume, though it is long past Halloween, and she has lost her wand. She has locked herself outside and has been standing there while we were hunting for her. I kneel down and gather her up in my arms. "But Masha," I ask, "why on earth didn't you just ring the bell?" She sniffs and gazes at me blankly with her gray-green eyes, almost the same color as mine, as I abruptly understand and hold her to my heart.

"If you ever get shut outside like this again, you must ring the doorbell, and I will hear it ringing, even if Mummy cannot, and I will come," I explain.

*

It was my mother-in-law who discovered the deafness, one holiday at the sea.

It is hard now to believe that Cybele was already one year old and that we had noticed nothing—or not much of anything —before. I remember mentioning to our distinguished elderly family physician that our daughter seemed to have a high-pitched voice. "Is that normal?" I asked him. He looked at me disapprovingly through thick glasses and said solemnly, "What does the word normal mean?" I didn't dare ask anything else.

My husband and I were just twenty years old and did not notice much except ourselves. We had married, for love, while he was still a student at Yale, studying French literature, and had come that summer to visit his mother, who lived on the Italian coast. One hot morning, the three of us sat on the beach in the sun, as one did in those prelapsarian days. I sat across my husband's knees, my arms around his neck, gazing into his eyes.

Draped across a deck chair, my mother-in-law, a long, lean lady from Kentucky, watched Cybele playing with her green bucket near the water. The calm sea glittered. Nothing moved in the still air. My mother-in-law called out to Cybele, who went on playing in the sand; she clapped her hands loudly three times. It was then that my mother-in-law put a hand on my arm and said, in her Southern drawl, "Do you know, I don't believe that child can hear!"

I remember thinking, "That woman, that woman, she is always looking for the fly in the ointment." I picked up my little girl, clutched her to my heart, and carried her down to the edge of the sea. I waded in up to my knees, to her toes. I swung her around and listened to her laugh and watched her bare feet rise and fall, and the drops of water glisten in the bright air, and realized, in spite of myself, that I would never see the world quite like that again.

I have a picture of Cybele that summer: a little girl with light brown hair and dark brown eyes in a blue-and-white-striped romper, crouching down, her knees fat and pink and innocent.

It was August and very hot when we returned to New York, and it seemed the doctors had all left town. I sat on the living room floor and flipped through the yellow pages with my sticky fingers. There was no air-conditioning in the brownstone where we had rented rooms.

When I finally found a specialist, he told us that, had we each married someone else, it would not have happened. We must both carry the same recessive gene. Perhaps we had a common ancestor? Even at that moment, as he did not himself use the word "deafness," I continued to deny the obvious. Much later, when it broke through upon me, and I once found myself weeping, my husband said, "That's not going to help." So I stopped.

What the doctor did tell us was to talk to our daughter, as if she could hear—no, more than we would have if she had been able to. "You can at least teach her to use words," he said encouragingly.

"How can you teach a deaf child to use words?" my husband asked, with his logical mind, honed on French literature. As for me, I did not ask questions of that kind. I did as I was told. It seemed the easiest thing to do, being, as I was, diligent, or perhaps just stubborn.

"You must make her as aware of sound as possible," the doctor had explained. There were few people entirely devoid of hearing. Hearing aids might help at least to modulate the quality of her voice, if they did not make her speech absolutely intelligible. He had fitted Cybele with two heavy rectangular gray boxes, worn about her body, containing microphones, which amplified the sound and sent it by wires to small speakers in her ears. Then he had given her a lollipop, telling me, "Talk to her. Don't give her ice cream until she can say the words 'ice cream.'"

She wore these bulky hearing aids in a cotton bodice under her smocked dresses, her plump body weighed down, so that she tipped forward like a teapot as she tottered along.

Next, I was introduced to a speech therapist, a good lady with orange curls. "Follow me," she said, and I followed her into the freight elevator, with my daughter clutched in my arms. We went down into the bowels of the hospital, down a green corridor with thick pipes along the ceiling, past an open door where vast women in white, who stood ironing sheets, cooed at my child. The therapist ushered me into a small, airless cubicle where we sat together with Cybele on my lap under the soundproofed ceiling, and she demonstrated how to teach my child to speak.

*

This was the sixties, and no one spoke to me about signing. Indeed, I was told not to use my hands to make words. "You must be firm to be kind," the therapist had said. "You must give her a lesson every day."

So, every day, I sat my screaming daughter in her high chair and gave her lessons. She did not want to be confined, to be instructed, to practice anything; she wanted to play in the sand with her bucket and spade. It was a battle of wills. While she kicked her little red lace-up shoes against the steel tray and waved her fists in the air and wailed loudly at me, I held up the animals in the puzzle. "The pig says oink, oink. The duck goes quack, quack. The lamb goes baaahhh," I bleated at her, opening my mouth wide, while she opened hers to yell back at me.

We sweated in the New York summer heat, and we screamed, we hit, we grappled with each other, fighting over the animals as though they were prizes. She grabbed them, put them in her mouth, chewed them, and tried to swallow them. I stuck my fingers into her mouth and down her throat, extracting them, damp and tooth-marked, and put them back in their places, covering the puzzle with my splayed fingers. I would not have skipped an animal if my life depended on it. She would not have stopped screaming to save hers. We were relentless, locked in a battle to the death.

I had no real understanding of what my child must have been feeling at moments like that, her inability to comprehend my words, or the reason I was saying them to her, and she, of course, could not understand my own wounded pride, my determination, but could feel only fury at being forced to do something that gave her no pleasure and whose purpose she could not comprehend.

For what I was determined to do was not merely to teach my deaf child to use words, as the specialist had encouraged me to do; I was determined to teach her to speak just like all the other little girls, whatever the cost. What she wanted was to throw that barking dog on the floor. She was determined to kick a hole in her tray, a hole in my knee, a hole in the dumb and uncomprehending world.

No matter how loudly she screamed, I kept up the whole routine: "The dog says woof, woof." We fought through the summer and into the fall and winter. Every day we did exactly the same thing, as though we were two characters in a fairy story, condemned to repetition. I believed that if I altered one word, all the magic would flee, and Cybele would never become the perfect, fairy-tale princess I needed her to be.

Brought forth by the screams, my husband would wander into the kitchen to suggest I might vary things, change a word here or there, liven it up a bit, could I not? But I, a would-be writer, after all, and blessed with imagination, would not, or perhaps I could not. There was security in the sameness of the words I repeated. Despite my English background, I began, my husband told me with some dismay, to sound like the speech therapist, who hailed from Brooklyn.

Every day the plastic nesting cups, which came in different colors and sizes, had to be fitted into one another and put "up, up, up." How else could one teach a child a preposition? But she was determined they would go "down, down, down," and with a scream, rather than a word, at that. Her mother went down with them, scrambling around on the sticky, black linoleum floor to pick them up and start all over again. The end of the lesson, the final insult, was my showing her the photograph of the perfect pink-and-white baby, while mouthing the words, "Mummy, Mummy, Mummy," as my deaf daughter screamed at me in a paroxysm of rage.

*

My daughter's first word, though, when it came, was, of course, not "Mummy" at all. It was no animal sound, either, no bleat or quack or woof. It was a word that I had never pronounced, and it was not said to her screaming mother or to her logical father.

My daughter's first word was said to a little boy she played with in the sandbox at the park.

It was a cool spring morning when, exhausted from one of our daily battles over the animals, we were staggering to the park. All the trees were in bloom, and the shadows shifted on the pavement. We were crossing a wide, windy avenue when Cybele caught sight of the little boy. He waved from his stroller and called out, "Hi" to her, and she waved back and said quite casually and extraordinarily, "Hi."

This victory was, of course, a pyrrhic one, and not the end of the war. Though the words continued to come, each one was fought over like a piece of terrain in some endless campaign. It seemed, at times, as if the English language were not Cybele's mother tongue, but rather a foreign one, some secret, esoteric, and hermetic tongue, like Sanskrit. Though she learned to speak in complete sentences before she was three, her voice remained that of one who has come to a language from a great distance. The voice was that of a foreigner, I suppose you might say, and her understanding came from that most impossible of arts, which she practiced with great expertise: the reading of lips.

*

Though my daughter continued to learn more words and could understand almost anything I said, what I feared now was that she would have no one with whom she could speak. In my heart of hearts, what I dreaded was her being ostracized, left out, left alone, shut up and shunned in her silent world.

All this, you understand, took place in the days when women still had the time and the inclination to invite one another to tea. I would dress my child up in her elaborate smocked dresses and matching pants and nervously adjust the little Dutch cap I had bought in a vain and absurd effort to cover the ear pieces of her hearing aids, and we would sally forth to visit. I would watch her rush off eagerly with the child of the house, my tea cup

trembling in its saucer on my knees, smiling stiffly, asking polite questions, and pretending to show great interest in my host-
ess' chatter but listening instead for the sounds of disaster.
Often the little friend would come wailing back to report some
crime, a doll whose eyes had been poked out, a smashed toy, a
book shredded, and we would not, of course, be invited again.

Still, I strived to claim a place for my child in the wider
world. I learned to cultivate and flatter, and when that did not
work, I stooped to the basest bribery and corruption: I offered
carousel and carriage rides, elaborate teas at Rumplemeyers,
and extravagant presents to the startled women and children I
was able to cajole into these outings.

Then there loomed the shadow of school. Though not
Catholic ourselves, we thought the nuns might be generously
disposed to a child of this kind. The head of the school told us
she had to consider her teachers, after all, and there was already
a dwarf in the class. The private school that finally accepted Cybele did so with great trepidation. I remember the nursery
school teacher, a frail and elderly lady asking me if I could teach
my daughter the word "gentle," and requiring that I come every
morning to watch her, a remarkably agile and dexterous little
girl, lest she fall as she played on the jungle gym.

I hoped that the privileged children in these places would be
kind. But the world, inevitably, behaved as I had feared. On Cybele's sixth birthday we planned a party. I made the cake and
decorated it with white icing and jelly beans in all the colors of
the rainbow. I think I still have a picture somewhere of the lop-
sided thing. We laid the table with a starched white cloth and
flowers, elaborate party favors, blowers and balloons. There
were multicolored jellies trembling in cups, candies in great
pyramids, cupcakes. There was a new dress for our daughter
with a blue sash and lace around the collar and cuffs. We had invited the entire class for greatest security. We waited eagerly for
their arrival. I kept looking at my watch and trying to think of
how to distract our child. The afternoon wore on, and the tele-

phone instead of the doorbell continued to ring. One by one the mothers declined. Once, someone rang the doorbell, but it was our doorman delivering a present someone had dropped off. We continued to wait and hope until nightfall, but no one came in the end.

The friends Cybele made on her own, eventually, were friends she has kept ever since, all her life. The intense attention that lip-reading demanded helped her develop into a gifted listener—loving, understanding, and loyal. Her friends were often children who had been left out themselves, who knew about being different, about solitude, about scorn. There was Claudia, the little curly-headed girl from Brazil, who could speak only Portuguese; Jess, a child with a Botticelli face who was born paralyzed down one side and still walks with a slight limp; and Jeanne, a tall black student from Haiti who spoke with a French accent.

*

I no longer remember what crime she had committed that day to warrant such a punishment. Perhaps she had torn up some book of mine, or one of hers. I never stopped reading to her, her little hand hovering over the pages to turn to the next picture, or to tear out the incomprehensible words. The place I chose for the punishment was the bathroom. I thought it a safe place: there was nothing anyone could break; it did not matter if something was spilled on the green, tiled floor. Also, there was no window. I put her into the bathroom for a moment to calm her down, or more probably, to calm myself down. What I did not think of was the lock on the inside of the door. But when she turned it and trapped herself in there in a misguided effort to escape, we had no way to explain through the door that she had not been left inside in retribution for an act of consummate wickedness. Until the locksmith finally came, hours later, and broke open the lock, we could do nothing to comfort her, and could only listen to her, wailing and beating with her little fists on the wood.

It was then, when the door was finally open, that she said something that I, with my strict English upbringing, had not taught a daughter to say to her mother, and more importantly, something I had not previously been willing to hear. Her face black with tears, she stamped her little foot and looked up at us, her eyes filled with rage, and said, quite clearly, "I am angry with you." It was then that I realized what a terrible burden I had imposed on her, insisting that she become part of my hearing world.

*

When we have dried Masha's tears and brought her a dish of ice cream, she sits beside her mother and her little sisters, and I tell her a story about how her mother had once locked herself inside a room, as Masha has just locked herself out, and how we could not explain why she was in the room for such a long time, all alone. I tell Masha how we struggled to teach her mother to talk, how she learned despite our lack of understanding of her difficulties. How she went on to the same famous university where her father had gone before her and became the very first deaf student there. I tell Masha how her mother studied art at that university and became an artist, who paints the world for us as she sees it in all its colors, and how she met her husband, Masha's daddy, at the same university and fell in love with him.

One day I will tell Masha that it was her mother's courage and intelligence, her ability to love and to forgive, more than my desperate efforts to instruct her, that helped her to find her way through life. It was not we who taught her to speak, but rather she who taught us to listen.

Contributors' Notes

Rebecca Balcárcel's writings have appeared in *North American Review*, *Concho River Review*, *South Dakota Review*, and elsewhere. She earned her MFA from Bennington College and teaches creative writing at Tarrant County College.

Michele Battiste's work appears in *5 AM*, *The Laurel Review*, *Nimrod*, *DIAGRAM*, and *Rattle*. Her first book, *Ink for an Odd Cartography*, will be published by Black Lawrence Press. She lives in New York City.

Jane Bernstein is a professor of English and creative writing at Carnegie Mellon University. She is the author of five books, among them *Loving Rachel* and *Rachel in the World*.

Michael Bérubé is the Paterno Family Professor in Literature at Penn State University, where he codirects (with his wife, Janet Lyon) Penn State's Disability Studies Program.

Ellen Bihler is a registered nurse, working with severely disabled children. Her poetry has appeared in *Cream City Review*, *Square Lake*, *International Poetry Review*, and elsewhere. She is also the author of the chapbook *An Avalanche of Blue Sky* (Foothills Publishing). She resides in Hackettstown, New Jersey, with her husband.

Catherine Brady is an assistant professor in the MFA in Writing Program at the University of San Francisco. She is the author of two collections of short stories, *The End of the Class War* and *Curled in the Bed of Love* (a winner of the 2002 Flannery O'Connor Award for Short Fiction), and the nonfiction book *Elizabeth Blackburn and the Story of Telomeres: Deciphering the Ends of DNA*.

Barbara Crooker is the mother of a son with autism, who, along with other family members, is often the subject of her poems. *Radiance*, her first full-length book, won the 2005 Word Press First Book competition.

Clare Dunsford is an associate dean in the College of Arts and Sciences at Boston College. "Speaking of Love/Reading My Son" is excerpted from her memoir, *Spelling Love with an X: A Mother, a Son, and the Gene That Binds Them*, published by Beacon Press in the fall of 2007.

Gina Forberg is a physical elementary teacher in Westport, Connecticut. Her work has appeared in *Slant Magazine*, *The New Delta Review*, and numerous other literary journals. She lives in Fairfield, Connecticut, with her son, Griffin, and husband, Jim.

Vicki Forman teaches creative writing at the University of Southern California. Her work has been nominated for a Pushcart Prize and has appeared in *Philosophical Mother*, *The Santa Monica Review*, *Writer to Writer*, and *Faultline*. She lives in Southern California with her husband and two children.

Hannah Holborn lives in British Columbia with her husband, two sons, and a Jack Russell terrier. Her writing draws on her experiences with foster care and social services. "Without

Strings" is part of a collection to be published in Canada by McClelland & Stewart.

Maggie Kast has published stories in *The Sun, Nimrod, Rosebud, Paper Street,* and others. Her essays have appeared in a variety of journals, including *Writer's Chronicle* and *Image.* She has recently completed a memoir, excerpts of which have appeared in *America, Image,* and *ACM* (*Another Chicago Magazine*). The latter received a Pushcart nomination and a Literary Award from the Illinois Arts Council.

Sheila Kohler has published six novels and three collections of short stories. Her latest novel, *Bluebird or the Invention of Happiness,* is based on the life of a French aristocrat who came to America during the French Revolution and became a dairy farmer. She teaches at Bennington College and Princeton University.

Marie Myung-Ok Lee has written about life issues for the *New York Times,* the *Washington Post,* and *Newsweek.* She is the author of *Somebody's Daughter* and is the writer-in-residence at the Center for the Study of Race and Ethnicity at Brown University.

Bret Lott is the author of five novels, including *Jewel* (an Oprah Book Club Selection in 1999), two short story collections, and a memoir. He is a professor of English at Louisiana State University where he is also editor of the *Southern Review.*

Margaret Mantle is the mother of two beautiful daughters, Victoria and Emma Kate, and the author of *Some Just Clap Their Hands: Raising a Handicapped Child* (Adama Books, 1985), which was inspired by Victoria, who has mental retardation.

John Morgan has published three books of poetry (*The Bone-Duster, The Arctic Herd*, and *Walking Past Midnight*), as well as four chapbooks. He has received two writing fellowships from the Alaska State Council on the Arts, a John Atherton Scholarship to Bread Loaf, and a fellowship from the Fine Arts Work Center in Provincetown, Massachusetts.

Darshan Perusek, Ph.D., is editor emeritus of *Kaleidoscope: International Magazine of Literature, Fine Arts, and Disability*, and the mother of a daughter with cerebral palsy. She teaches at the University of Wisconsin–Stout.

Jayne Anne Phillips is the author of two collections of stories, *Fast Lanes* and *Black Tickets*, and three novels: *Motherkind*, which was nominated for the 2001 Orange Prize; *Shelter*; and *Machine Dreams*. "Termite's Birthday, 1959" was named one of the 100 Best American Short Stories of 2004. It is taken from *Termite*, forthcoming from Knopf in February 2009. Phillips is the director of the Rutgers-Newark MFA Program.

Carol Schmidt began writing poetry when she retired from teaching ten years ago. Her work has appeared in *Oberon, Performance Poets Literary Review*, and other magazines. She lives with her husband and son in Setauket, New York.

Evelyn Sharenov is a book reviewer for the *Oregonian* newspaper, a feature writer for *Bitch* magazine, as well as a nonfiction editor for the *Oregon Literary Review*. She is currently nominated for a Pushcart Prize. "Magic Affinities" was a notable in *Best American Short Stories*. She has been awarded an Oregon Literary Arts grant in fiction.

Marcy Sheiner has edited eight anthologies of women's fiction. She has raised a child who was born with hydrocephalus, which she wrote about in her memoir *Perfectly Normal*. She has also written for many print and online publications on the topic of disability. She is currently keeping a daily blog and writing a memoir about mothers and daughters.

Curtis Smith has published a novel, *An Unadorned Life*, and two collections of short-short fiction. His most recent book is *The Species Crown: A Novella and Stories*. His forthcoming novels are *Sound and Noise* (Casperian Books, 2008) and *Truth* (Atomic Quill, 2009). "What about Meg?" was named to the Best American Short Stories Distinguished Stories List. He lives in Pennsylvania.

Carol Zapata-Whelan teaches writing at California State University, Fresno. Her work has appeared in *Newsweek*, *LA Times News Syndicate*, *Rotarian*, and *Under the Fifth Sun: Latino Literature from California* (Heyday Books). Her memoir, *Finding Magic Mountain: Life with Five Glorious Kids and a Rogue Gene Called FOP* (Avalon Publishing Group), is newly out in Mandarin and Korean.

Penny Wolfson's essay "Moonrise" was the basis for a memoir published in 2003, received a National Magazine Award in 2002, and was selected for inclusion in *The Best American Essays* anthology. She and her family live in Dobbs Ferry, New York.

Acknowledgments

The following selections have been previously published, sometimes in slightly different form:

" 'Severe Language Delay': In the Kitchen with My Three-Year-Old" by Rebecca Balcárcel. First published in *Kaleidoscope: Exploring the Experience of Disability through Literature and the Fine Arts*, Winter/Spring 2003. Reprinted by permission of the author.

"Rachel at Work: Enclosed, a Mother's Report," by Jane Bernstein. First published in *Creative Nonfiction* no. 20, 2003. Reprinted by permission of the author.

"The Lives of the Saints," fiction by Catherine Brady. Reprinted from *The End of the Class War* by Catherine Brady, published by CALYX Books, 1999, by permission of the publisher.

"Doing Jigsaw Puzzles," by Barbara Crooker. First published in *Phoebe*, 1997. "Form and Void," by Barbara Crooker. First published in *Poets On*, 1995. Reprinted by permission of the author.

"Coming to Samsara," by Vicki Forman. First published in *Santa Monica Review*, Spring 2004. Reprinted by permission of the author.

"Without Strings," fiction by Hannah Holborn. Copyright 2007 Hannah Holborn.

"Joyful Noise," fiction by Maggie Kast. First published in *The Sun*, February 2001. Reprinted by permission of the author.

"The Heart Speaks," by Sheila Kohler. Copyright 2004 by Sheila Kohler. First published as "Can You Hear Me?" in *O Magazine*, May 2004. Reprinted by permission of the author and her agent, Robin Straus Agency Inc.

Excerpt from *Jewel*, fiction by Bret Lott. Reprinted with the permission of Atria Books, an imprint of Simon & Schuster Adult Publishing Group, from *Jewel: A Novel* by Bret Lott. Copyright 1991 by Bret Lott.

Excerpt from *Spells and Auguries*, by John Morgan. Musk Ox Press, 2000. Reprinted by permission of the author.

"Doctor in the House," by Darshan Perusek. First published in *Kaleidoscope: International Magazine of Literature, Fine Arts, and Disability*, Summer/Fall 1996.

"Termite's Birthday, 1959," fiction by Jayne Anne Phillips. From the forthcoming novel *Termite* by Jayne Anne Phillips, to be published by Alfred A. Knopf, a division of Random House Inc. Used by permission of Alfred A. Knopf. First published in *Granta* no. 82, 2003.

"Magic Affinities," fiction by Evelyn Sharenov. First published in *Glimmer Train*, Summer 1992. Reprinted by permission of the author.

"A Homecoming," fiction by Marcy Sheiner. First published in *Perfectly Normal: A Mother's Memoir*, 2002. Reprinted by permission of the author.

"What about Meg?" fiction by Curtis Smith. First published in *Antietam Review*, 1991. Reprinted by permission of the author.

"Ordinary Time," fiction by Carol Zapata-Whelan. First published in *Dreams and Visions*, Summer 2003, Skysong Press. Reprinted by permission of the author.

"Moonrise," by Penny Wolfson. First published in *The Atlantic Monthly*, December 2001. Reprinted by permission of the author.